THE GEOPOLITICS OF SPECTACLE

THE GEOPOLITICS OF SPECTACLE

Space, Synecdoche, and the New Capitals of Asia

NATALIE KOCH

CORNELL UNIVERSITY PRESS
ITHACA AND LONDON

First published 2018 by Cornell University Press

Printed in the United States of America

Library of Congress Cataloging-in-Publication Data

Names: Koch, Natalie, author.
Title: The geopolitics of spectacle : space, synecdoche, and the new capitals of Asia / Natalie Koch.
Description: Ithaca : Cornell University Press, 2018. | Includes bibliographical references and index.
Identifiers: LCCN 2017060053 (print) | LCCN 2018000740 (ebook) | ISBN 9781501720925 (pdf) | ISBN 9781501720932 (ret) | ISBN 9781501720918 | ISBN 9781501720918 (cloth ; alk. paper)
Subjects: LCSH: Urban renewal x Political aspects—Asia. | City planning—Political aspects—Asia. | New towns—Political aspects—Asia. | Spectacular, The—Political aspects—Asia. | Capitals (Cities)—Asia.
Classification: LCC HT178.A78 (ebook) | LCC HT178.A78 K63 2018 (print) | DDC 307.3/416095—dc23
LC record available at https://lccn.loc.gov/2017060053

For Gulya

Personal violence *shows*. The object of personal violence perceives the violence, usually, and may complain—the object of structural violence may be persuaded not to perceive this at all. Personal violence represents change and dynamism—not only ripples on waves, but waves on otherwise tranquil waters. Structural violence is silent, it does not show—it is essentially static, it *is* the tranquil waters. In a *static* society, personal violence will be registered, whereas structural violence may be seen as about as natural as the air around us.

—Johan Galtung,
"Violence, Peace, and Peace Research" (1969)

Contents

ILLUSTRATIONS

ACKNOWLEDGMENTS

My foray into international research began when I was an undergradu-ate at Dartmouth College, when I traveled to Kazakhstan for my senior honors thesis. My first trip there could not have been possible without the unwavering support of Ambassador Kenneth Yalowitz, who was then heading the college's Dickey Center for International Understanding. This research was generously supported by a grant from the Dickey Center, as well as a Dean of Faculty Waterhouse Research Award and an Andrew W. Mellon Foundation Grant. My Dartmouth professors also gave me tremendous inspiration and guidance as I discovered field research, espe-cially Martin Dimitrov, Coleen Fox, Ben Forest, and Richard Wright. Just as important to my undergraduate research endeavors were (and con-tinue to be) my classmates and friends Ingrid Nelson, Tina Urbano, Liz Harrington, Sasha Prokhorova, Irina Kholkina, Mike Belinskiy, Anton Kunayev, and Shaunak Mewada.

Much of the research for this book was conducted when I was at the University of Colorado, Boulder, where John O'Loughlin provided unwav-ering support throughout my graduate studies. This project owes much to his encouragement and critiques, as well as that of Timothy Oakes, Najeeb Jan, Gearóid Ó Tuathail, and Edward Schatz. I am indebted to Ken Foote for his insights about research design and book projects. At Colorado I benefited (and continue to benefit) from the intellectual stimulation and companionship of Adam Levy, Afton Clarke-Sather, the brilliant Cole Akeson, Ted Holland, Andrew Linke, Magdalena Stawkowski, and Jenn Dinaburg, who passed too early.

I have had the privilege of working with many other colleagues in the United States and abroad who have helped to shape my thinking over the years. Thanks especially to Martin Müller, Anssi Paasi, Beth Mitchnek, Alec Murphy, Mateusz Laszczkowski, Adrien Fauve, Alima Bissenova, Kulshat Medeuova, Kristopher White, Nick Megoran, Marlene Laruelle, Anar Valiyev, David Mould, Kyle Marquardt, Sarah Cameron, Neha Vora, James Sidaway, Robina Mohammad, Khairul Hazmi, Orhon Myadar, Juliet Johnson, Dmitry Gorenburg, Alex Diener, Lauren Martin, Oliver Belcher, Lorraine Dowler, Michael Gentile, Josh Hagen, Sara Moser, Virginie Mamadouh, Sami Moisio, Pauliina Raento, Jason Dittmer, Reece Jones, Marco Antonsich, Lisa Wedeen, Gwenn Okruhlik, Tanya Kane, Jessica Graybill, Kyle Evered, Tamar Mayer, Kris Olds, and Matt Stone. Though I shall not name them here out of concern for their safety, I thank countless colleagues and friends in Kazakhstan. Without their support, and the generosity of research participants willing to share their time, tea, and thoughts, this project would have been impossible. At Syracuse, Margie Johnson has my eternal gratitude for her tireless help and patience. Last, I thank my family for always supporting me and trusting my judgment through the travels, trials, and travails over the ten years of this project.

My graduate and postdoctoral research was generously supported by the National Science Foundation (NSF), including a Graduate Research Fellowship and a Nordic Research Opportunity supplement to the fellowship. This project was also made possible by funding from an NSF Doctoral Dissertation Improvement grant (number 1003836), an IREX Individual Advanced Research Opportunity grant, and a U.S. State Department Title VIII grant for work at the University of Illinois Summer Research Laboratory on Russia, Eastern Europe, and Eurasia. My research has been supported at various stages by a Social Sciences Research Council (SSRC) Postdoctoral Fellowship for Transregional Research with funds provided by the Andrew W. Mellon Foundation; grants from Syracuse University's Office of Sponsored Programs, Geography Department, and the Maxwell School for Citizenship and Public Affairs; and a Central Asia Fellowship from the University of Helsinki's Aleksanteri Institute.

In addition to numerous engaging discussions and exchanges at invited campus visits and conferences, this research benefited from my sponsored participation in several key events: the 2013 SSRC workshop for Inter-Asian postdoctoral fellows; the 2014 Kazakhstan workshop sponsored by George Washington University's Central Asia Program, the Uppsala University Center for Russian and Eurasian Studies, and Riksbankens Jubileumsfond; the 2015 "Authoritarianism in a Global Context" Richard C. Holbrooke Forum for the Study of Diplomacy and Governance Statecraft in the 21st Century at the American Academy in Berlin; the 2015 "Area Studies & Geography" workshop at the National University of Singapore; as well as several PONARS Eurasia workshops in Washington, D.C., and abroad. Any opinions, findings, and conclusions or recommendations expressed in this book are those of the author and do not necessarily reflect the views of the National Science Foundation or any other granting organization. Any errors here are my own.

Parts of this text have been adapted from the previously published articles "Technologizing Complacency: Spectacle, Structural Violence, and 'Living Normally' in a Resource-Rich State," *Political Geography* 37 (2013): A1–A2; "The 'Heart' of Eurasia? Kazakhstan's Centrally Located Capital City," *Central Asian Survey* 32, no. 2 (2013): 134–47; and "Exploring Divergences in Comparative Research: Citizenship Regimes and the Spectacular Cities of Central Asia and the GCC," *Area* 47, no. 4 (2015): 436–42.

THE GEOPOLITICS OF SPECTACLE

INTRODUCTION

Spectacular Urbanism and the New Capitals of Asia

It is easy to conjure images of Asia's spectacular high-rise cities: bustling with life and brimming with gleaming skyscrapers and ultramodern infrastructure. For foreign visitors and ordinary citizens alike, the cities of Asia have become iconic of the region's state-led modernization agendas and increasing integration with the world economy. Asia's impressive urbanization can largely be explained by pro-market globalization processes under way since the end of World War II, but also in the wake of collapsing communist regimes across the region since the early 1990s.[1] There is, however, a subset of cities whose stunning growth stands apart from this general trend: the new or recently transformed capital cities of the region's resource-rich states. Political and economic logics well beyond (but not exclusive of) tighter integration with global market capitalism are at work in these cities, seven of which are the subject of this book. The central case is Kazakhstan's capital, Astana. Other examples in post-Soviet Central Asia include Baku, Azerbaijan, and Ashgabat, Turkmenistan. In the Arabian Peninsula, spectacular capitals can be found in Abu Dhabi in the

United Arab Emirates (UAE) and Doha, Qatar, and, in East Asia, Naypy-idaw, Myanmar, and Bandar Seri Begawan, Brunei.

Seeking to explain the apparent convergence around spectacular urbanism in Asia's new capitals, I ask: What makes a city spectacular and for whom? How do spectacular city projects factor into local and regional politics, and what sets them apart from other cities in the region? And more generally, what can they teach us about place, power, and political geography? Most of these cities' recent building booms have involved transforming the existing urban fabric, while others have entailed developing an entirely new capital (namely, Astana and Naypyidaw). Their differences are important, as we will see. But each is, in one form or another, spectacular. In particular, they have several key commonalities: (1) they are located in nondemocratic and resource-rich states; (2) they have been developed on the basis of strong state planning, quickly, and on an unprecedented scale for their region; (3) they boast lavish built landscapes and celebrations that represent a stark contrast with their surrounding context; and (4) they are designed to display the government's prosperity and ostensible benevolence in a manner that contrasts significantly with other forms of state austerity and violence found elsewhere. While these capitals are not uniformly successful, these elements all suggest that the image and shape of spectacular cities involves a degree of state intervention and guidance that is atypical of urban development in most cities of the world today.

Spectacular Cities and Their Others

Spectacular urban development is not new. Urban landscapes, and those of capital cities in particular, have long been privileged places for political leaders to express the state's power and their nation's unity, promise, and modernity. State planners have put their visions of modernity on display through monumental capital city projects in places as diverse as Ankara, Beijing, Brasília, Islamabad, Paris, Rabat, Riyadh, and St. Petersburg.[2] When they were first developed, each of these cities was, in one way or another, spectacular—an effect largely achieved through autocratic master planning that was unprecedented for their context. Yet that context was always historically and geographically specific; many people would be hard-pressed to characterize any of these cities as spectacular today. Formerly stunning architectural icons and modernist urban order now look outmoded and fail to visually impress. Not only are visual displays of urban modernity historically and geographically contextual, but also fleeting. As such, to understand how spectacular urbanism works in and across time and space, a decidedly *geographic* approach is needed. Developing such an approach is the goal of this book.

Anyone interested in global politics will readily note that leaders in some countries take statist spectacle far more seriously than in others. For reasons discussed in chapter 1, today it is primarily, though not exclusively, used in highly centralized ("nondemocratic," "authoritarian," or "illiberal") states. Orchestrating spectacle requires substantial resources, which may be financial or political, obtained through coercion or persuasion as well as corrupt or legal means. Indeed, we shall see these variations at work in the case countries considered here, all of which have substantial natural resource wealth and governments that depend heavily on revenues from these extractive industries. In addition to requiring a certain amount of resources, statist spectacle is always the product of mixed agendas. The producers and participants of any given spectacle will invariably interpret and appropriate it in contrasting ways, but state-based elites publicly aim to unify the message that a spectacle is meant to send. This message often centers on broader identity narratives about the nation, the state, or the government itself. In Kazakhstan, for example, the government's decision in the 1990s to develop a new capital city, Astana, has been at the center of its political leaders' effort to institutionalize their power and materially inscribe their vision of modernity in the post-Soviet period.

Spectacular cities, like Astana, are an example of statist spectacle *par excellence*. But a central argument of this book is that looking at spectacular cities themselves is insufficient to understand the broader geopolitics of spectacle. As a political tactic, spectacle depends on, and indeed reproduces, deeply political understandings of geography. For something to be deemed spectacular, it must stand apart in space, time, magnitude, perceived experience, or some combination thereof. This also implies that it is only ever spectacular over a defined space, for certain individuals, and in contrast to specific images and experiences of the *unspectacular*. This relationship between the spectacular and the unspectacular is never fixed; it is always contingent on the perspective of any given observer. While these perspectives are also never fixed, geographers seek to discern general patterns in how people make sense of the world and map concepts like spectacular/unspectacular onto certain spaces, places, and experiences. These ways of thinking about space and time are called *spatial imaginaries*, and they are reproduced in both language and practice, rhetorically and materially.[3] Accordingly, to understand the effects of spectacular urbanism as a geopolitical tactic, I examine the spatial imaginaries of individuals who are engaged as spectators, participants, and producers of spectacle.

This approach requires discerning who these people are as political actors, but also raises specifically geographic questions about where they are located and how they interact with one another in and through the material spaces that spectacular urban development conjures—and neglects. While my analysis considers the geopolitical relations and conditions that have given rise to Asia's diverse spectacular capital cities, I am especially concerned with identifying and locating the unspectacular "Others" that make these cities intelligible as a form of spectacle. These are the spaces and social experiences that spectacular urban development neglects, and they take an infinitely varied number of forms and unfold at many different scales and temporalities. To understand the *geopolitics of spectacle*, we must take seriously the diverse and diffuse Others that give it meaning. Of course, I cannot do this comprehensively for each city discussed in this book. Rather, in illustrating what such an approach would look like, I mean to highlight the value of *jointly* analyzing spectacle and its Others.

In Central Asia, where I have been conducting research since 2005, I argue that the spectacular capital city schemes are largely developed on the basis of marking a radical break with the Soviet past. The three cities considered here, Ashgabat in Turkmenistan, Baku in Azerbaijan, and Astana, are all capitals of Caspian littoral states with access to significant oil and gas reserves in and around the sea. Because of this access to resource wealth, they have been able to set themselves apart from other regional neighbors and to do so through the opulent urban development schemes in their capitals. In these cases, the Soviet past, as well as their poor and politically weak regional neighbors, constitute unspectacular Others. The spectacle of the capital cities in Central Asia is also made possible by the significant social inequalities between ordinary citizens and the elites. This is most vividly illustrated in the case of Kazakhstan, where I unite the view *from* Astana with the view *of* Astana from the vantage point of rural residents in the environmentally devastated Aral Sea region.

In the Arabian Peninsula, I focus on recent urban development in Doha, Qatar, and Abu Dhabi, UAE, where I have been conducting research since 2012. Rapid urban development in this region has likewise been made possible by the wealth from local oil and gas extraction for global export. But the UAE and Qatar are quite different from the Central Asian states in that they all have extremely small territories, and an unusually small percentage of their total population has formal citizenship (under 15 percent each). Here I show that a state-centered approach can be a hindrance to locating the social and political Others that make spectacle possible in these two monarchies. Doing so requires a wider understanding of the Arab Gulf capitals' hinterlands as extending well beyond the state boundaries to touch many countries across Asia and Africa where large numbers of migrant workers in the Arabian Peninsula originate. From this perspective, the center-periphery relations that are conjured through the spectacular city schemes in the Arabian Peninsula, including similarly dramatic social inequalities, begin to look more like those considered in Central Asia.

Last, in East Asia, I consider the capitals of Naypyidaw in Myanmar and Bandar Seri Begawan in Brunei, where I conducted fieldwork in 2015. These two cities represent the biggest contrast to the other cases insofar as planners have not oriented recent developments around crafting an iconic image of the capital. That is, while Naypyidaw and Bandar Seri Begawan *are* spectacular capitals, they have not been designed around projecting a coherent image of the city to circulate internationally, or even domestically (as we find with the intense city-branding exercises in places like Astana or Doha). The more decentralized planning of Bandar Seri Begawan, for example, pushes against iconicity, while Naypyidaw has actually been closed to the media and foreigners until very recently. In both cases, however, the cities draw much of their spectacular nature from the visual order of modernist urban planning that works to "other" the past and older urban forms (such as the prevailing water village settlements in Brunei). In Brunei and Myanmar, we also find that the spectacular cities are made possible by the state's monopolization of wealth from the country's rich natural resource reserves—resulting in a grossly unequal distribution of wealth justified through paternalist assertions of benevolent rule and a passively accepting population.

Approaching Spectacle Geographically

Spectacle has long been a subject of academic concern, but scholars have not yet sought to theorize it geographically. A geographic approach is important because spectacle has both spatial and temporal dimensions. Typically defined as a large-scale show or display, it is spatially point-based. This means that, while it unfolds at any scale, it is staged at one particular location, such as a city as a whole or a public square within a city. Spectacle is also temporally exceptional: it happens sporadically, occasionally, or only once. Since time and space are relative, so too is spectacle: what is spectacular in one context may be entirely unspectacular in another. Most academic analyses gloss over the relative nature of spectacle, as they tend to focus inward—that is, considering a spectacle itself rather than its place in a broader context. The failure of scholars to adopt a wider lens, however, may be less a theoretical oversight than an indication of a major analytical challenge in studying spectacles: they do not have an easily measurable set of political outcomes. They are spatially diffuse, are experienced contingently, and extend across uneven temporalities. Focusing on the contextual nature of spectacle thus raises important theoretical questions about how to define its Others—those spaces, activities, temporalities, routines, and affects that inform how people draw borders between the spectacular and the ordinary. The relational approach to spectacle I develop spotlights these questions and works to account for a spectacle's diffuse Others beyond the singular site or event.

As a study in political geography, this book emphasizes the power relations that shape and are shaped by spectacle. While spectacle is certainly not confined to state-led events or projects, my analysis is limited to state-sponsored (or "statist") spectacle.[4] This is because, when employed by government leaders, it takes on special geopolitical significance. At the most general level, statist spectacle has two variations: celebratory and punitive.[5] Whereas punitive spectacle may include public torture or executions, celebratory spectacles include parades, festivals, capital city development schemes, engineering mega-projects, or iconic buildings such as ultra-tall towers or palaces.[6] Both celebratory and punitive variants tend to be at work in any given political system, albeit to varying extents. A handful of studies, in political contexts ranging from the Dominican Republic under Trujillo to the Soviet Union under Stalin, have considered the role of state violence as a sort of spectacle, but few do little more than note the apparent contradictions of regimes that simultaneously engage in spectacular forms of state violence *and* ostentatious celebration culture.[7]

Yet even under the most brutal regimes, leaders will seek to minimize public discussion of the state's most punitive tactics. In such cases, where state violence is truly pervasive and the general population is well aware of it (as with Stalinist and Nazi persecution), open conversation about it is nearly always off limits. Public discussion about state benevolence, by contrast, is usually vigorously promoted. Using the full range of public relations and ideological tools, repressive regimes tend to amplify the significance of celebratory spectacles and their nonpunitive policies. In their efforts to control and guide popular discourse, authoritarian elites are logically concerned with the *spatial manifestation* of state benevolence vis-à-vis state violence. This is not merely about grabbing their subjects' attention and putting celebratory spectacle in their direct line of vision; by making expressions or metaphors of beneficence more visible, a regime can make accusations of violence and austerity appear less credible—sometimes casting them as fictitious or exaggerated claims of its opponents. In both the Dominican and Soviet cases, for example, the state's repressive tactics were felt most intensely in the peripheral reaches of their territory, far from the symbolic centers in their capital cities. And even today, some citizens will question the historical record of those repressive governments' crimes. This is to simplify the matter greatly, but it does point to key questions about the *geography of spectacle* and pushes scholars to ask not only who uses it and with what effect but also *where*.

Given its etymology, *spectacle* raises the question of spectatorship and how to account for its necessarily multiple and ever-changing audiences. I consider the primary case of Astana from several different vantage points, asking how the city's iconic development has been projected across Kazakhstan. Set next to hardship and poverty found elsewhere in the country, spectacular urbanism in Astana is exemplary of how authoritarian governments work to make "inequality enchant" through the use of spectacle of the center.[8] It also illustrates how highly centralized governments are founded on *unspectacular* spaces, temporalities, embodied experiences, and forms of slow or structural violence—the impacts of which are felt most in the territorial peripheries and among marginalized populations. The local context in Kazakhstan, detailed in chapters 2 and 3, is essential to understanding the political geographic implications of the spectacular city project in Astana.

Spectacle is fundamentally *geopolitical*. This is in no small part because it is consistently entangled with normative readings of political regime types and modes of government in the international community. In the Western press, for example, state-promoted spectacle is often caricatured as the staple of megalomaniac autocrats. Its significance is dismissed because of its very theatricality—exemplified in the bemused but disdainful tone of reports on North Korea's Mass Games or Turkmenistan's Novruz celebrations. Such reporting typically implies that participants and audiences do not actually believe in the message on display, but are forced to participate against their will. They are painted as mere pawns following the orders of a megalomaniac autocrat. These simplistic accounts of state-led spectacle stem from, at best, a misunderstanding and, at worst, a deliberate stigmatization of authoritarian states. Ultimately, though, they are rooted in the false assumption that authoritarian states are largely devoid of competitive politics. While autocratic leaders do not stake their legitimacy in competitive elections, their polities have just as many spaces for political contest as in liberal democracies—albeit differently configured.

Through the case of spectacular capital city schemes in Asia, I show that the city is one such site of contestation. Taking these cities seriously means taking authoritarian states seriously.[9] It also requires accounting for the agency of ordinary people in authoritarian contexts. In the West, prevailing stereotypes about nondemocratic states frame these countries as consisting of victimizers and victims, conjuring the image of a thoroughly repressive state apparatus quashing passive citizens. As scholars of authoritarianism have long argued, however, and as I show in this book, a clear-cut division between victimizers and victims is more myth than reality.[10] Furthermore, in writing on spectacle in classical Bali, the anthropologist Clifford Geertz has stressed, "Whatever intelligence it may have to offer us about the nature of politics, it can hardly be that big fish eat little fish, or that the rags of virtue mask the engines of privilege."[11] Although he was writing almost forty years ago, his point about common interpretations of spectacle remains apt: discussions still rapidly descend into mere assertions that the rich and powerful take advantage of the poor and misguided. The result is that observers end up floundering over questions about whether citizens *either* are dissimulating *or* are "true believers." Finding an either-or approach untenable, social scientists informed by poststructuralist theory examine the role of spectacle in shaping certain subjectivities and regimes of governmentality rather than lingering on the question of belief.

In addition to dismissing statist spectacle as a form of fictional theater, Western accounts frequently discount it as something of the *past*. These observers frame it as outdated and irrelevant for "our" modern, reason-based times, or, in other cases, as an overwrought effort to claim modernity while masking a certain backwardness. This is particularly evident in mainstream press accounts of Asia's spectacular cities. In writing about Astana, for example, Western journalists have given the city a wide range of labels that point to its allegedly false claims to modernity, such as "the Jetsons' hometown," "Disneyland of the steppe," "Nowheresville," and "Tomorrowland."[12] Or in the words of one writer: "To look at, Astana is so strange that it has one grasping for images. It's a space station, marooned in an ungraspable expanse of level steppe, its name (to English speakers) having the invented sound of a science fiction writer's creation."[13] Mike Davis's description of Dubai is similarly Orientalizing: "The result is not a hybrid but an eerie chimera: a promiscuous coupling of all the cyclopean fantasies of Barnum, Eiffel, Disney, Spielberg, Jon Jerde, Steve Wynn and Skidmore, Owings & Merrill. Although compared variously to Las Vegas, Manhattan, Orlando, Monaco and Singapore, the sheikhdom is more like their collective summation and mythologization: a hallucinatory pastiche of the big, the bad and the ugly."[14]

This Orientalist rhetoric is of course problematic in itself, but it also grossly oversimplifies the complexity of spectacular urbanism. In addition, these accounts normatively demarcate illiberal states as bizarre and essentially foreign. They position statist spectacle as an index of backwardness—something characterizing only fundamentally *unmodern* people and places. Dubious as they may be, caricatures of spectacle in authoritarian

states are not just clichéd journalism in poor taste. They run deep in political and academic imaginations about global political geographies. For
example, the French theorist Michel Foucault even suggests that spectacle
is a thing of the past ("Antiquity had been a civilization of spectacle"),
which he contrasts with more recent techniques of discipline and biopolitics. These, he claims, extinguish the relevance of spectacle in modern
polities: "The pomp of sovereignty, the necessarily spectacular manifes-
tations of power, were extinguished one by one in the daily exercise of
surveillance, in a panopticism in which the vigilance of intersecting gazes
was soon to render useless both the eagle and the sun."[15]

The irony of this quotation cannot be lost on anyone familiar with the
state flag of Kazakhstan, which depicts a steppe eagle soaring underneath
a large golden sun (see figure I.1). Indeed, through a focus on Kazakhstan,
this book shows that the eagle and the sun are not at all useless, but that
the "pomp of sovereignty" still matters today. Contra Foucault, whose
work otherwise deeply informs my approach in this book, I argue that
as new governmentalities have arisen, spectacle has certainly not faded
in relevance. Spectacle continues to sit squarely at the center of normative mappings of "proper" political configurations that define geopolitical
imaginaries and foreign policies the world over. Critical scholars would be
mistaken to confine it to the past or to approach it as a mere aberration

Figure I.1 The flag of Kazakhstan.
Source: Wikipedia Commons.

characteristic of allegedly backward governments. Understanding contemporary uses of spectacle is essential to understanding power, politics, and space—not only in authoritarian settings but also in ostensibly liberal or democratic settings. It is especially important to examine the overlaps between liberal and illiberal forms of government if we are to resist simplistic accounts of authoritarianism as something bizarre and foreign, and to open up larger questions about how geopolitical maps of liberalism and illiberalism are written and contested, by whom, and with what effects.

Illiberal Government and Practice-Centered Analysis

Spectacle appears to be perennially salient in the full range of polities—from empires, monarchies, fascist dictatorships, and sheikhdoms to authoritarian regimes and democracies.[16] Yet certain governments have historically exhibited a particular penchant for spectacle. Writing on post-Soviet Uzbekistan, Laura Adams has termed such cases *spectacular states*—that is, states where, "more than in most countries, politics is conducted on a symbolic level," and where "spectacle is a technique of mobilization."[17] Geertz describes a similar dynamic in his classic work on Bali. The early Balinese state, he argues, was not organized around a rationalist form of government but pointed instead "toward spectacle, toward ceremony, toward the public dramatization of the ruling obsessions of Balinese culture: social inequality and status pride."[18] In Geertz's reading of precolonial Bali, lavish and costly ceremonies were not a means toward political ends, but "ends themselves, they were what the state was for. Court ceremonialism was the driving force of court politics; and mass ritual was not a device to shore up the state, but rather the state, even in its final gasp, was a device for the enactment of mass ritual. Power served pomp, not pomp power."[19]

The "spectacular state" and "theater-state" concepts offer a useful entry point to examine the specific political dynamics in post-Soviet Uzbekistan and nineteenth-century Bali. But it is hard to generalize from these cases, as the French historian Paul Veyne argues, "unless we allow specifications, historical accidents, and ideological influences to proliferate, at the price of endless verbiage."[20] That is, by putting the state at the center of the analysis, such taxonomies invariably fail in the face of the inexhaustible variations that the state takes and in the way it morphs over time. State-centered approaches also threaten to undercut efforts to explore the *relationship* between spectacle and state-making by taking both concepts for granted. Accordingly, this book adopts a practice-based approach, which treats political tactics, or *technologies of government*, as the primary site of analysis. This means that, rather than seeking to classify (and thus reify) states of a particular sort, I ask: What political *practices* are common to dramatically different contexts like post-Soviet Uzbekistan and classical Bali? And what can this tell us about the very notion of the state and the people who are complicit in conjuring it as an imagined, but not imaginary, *effect*?

Technologies of government are political tactics, methods, or strategies, which may be used to different ends by different actors. Any technology, such as a car, microscope, telephone, or computer, is little more than a potentiality; people who use it need not be accorded a predetermined intentionality. Sometimes we use a computer for work, sometimes for entertainment. Some people may use it for making the world a more just place, others for furthering global inequality. In both cases, they may or may not consciously intend for their use of that particular technology to have such an effect. Technologies are, in short, always subject to multiple uses. Sometimes we use them unthinkingly, other times with strategy. In approaching spectacle as a political technology, we can simultaneously see it as a broader, macro-political practice, stretching across the world and throughout history, but also consisting of more specific micro-political practices arising out of specific geographic contexts. Practice-centered analysis seeks to avoid reification while simultaneously preserving the relativity of any particular technology by embedding it in a particular time and place.

Many social scientists have adopted practice-centered analytics, though my own approach is most directly informed by Foucault's analysis of governmentality.[21] For him, political technologies are the window onto power relations at the state and sub-state levels, as they are "born precisely from the interplay of relations of power and everything which constantly eludes them, at the interface, so to speak, of governors and governed."[22] This approach pushes us away from focusing exclusively on the inner workings of particular political tactics. It instead draws our attention to the concrete practices that lead to their invention, use, metamorphosis, and, at times, disposal. In this book, for example, I am less concerned with the internal logic of spectacle and more with the geopolitics of how it has been adopted in certain parts of the world and with what effects. By placing practices at the center of our analysis, we can cast a new light on the interplay between "governors" and "the governed" and, indeed, on the way these very categories are imagined and constituted in both time and space.[23] Applied to spectacle, this method suggests that we need not (and in fact *should not*) look for a particular essence of spectacle, but ought instead to consider how it works to constitute a particular relationship between those who seek to govern and those whom they seek to govern. Treating spectacle as a political technology affords a more open perspective on how it can be shifted and reworked by multiply positioned actors for different purposes.

The idea of spectacle as a political technology is best suited to keeping the relational nature of spectacle in focus. The openness of this approach is also important in developing a critical stance that does not simply dismiss statist spectacle as a symptom of political backwardness or a form of propaganda. The pejorative tones common in the West are not just unhelpful, but they imply an understanding of spectacle that is too narrow insofar as it assumes a static and geographically disembedded relationship between actors and audiences.[24] When spectacle is seen as a political technology, by contrast, it cannot be endowed with an inherent functionality. Like the car, microscope, or telephone as technologies, spectacle can be used by different people with various intentions and even wider-ranging outcomes. This is true of both producers and consumers of a given spectacle. Considering spectacle as a geographically specific political technology, I suggest, pushes toward a simple set of questions: Who uses it, for whom, and when and where? Or, as applied to the questions raised in this book about capital city development schemes: Who fashions these cities as spectacular, for whom, when, and where?

While my analytical focus is on spectacle as a political technology, my examples are all drawn from authoritarian states—a designation that needs further definition. Nondemocratic governments have fallen under many labels in the West, with popular and academic understandings of world political geography typically revolving around a deeply entrenched set of binaries: countries are either authoritarian or democratic, illiberal or liberal. I use these terms throughout this book, primarily out of necessity. I recognize, however, that this choice is far more than a simple question of terminology but is one of great theoretical importance. In approaching the definitional divide between liberalism and illiberalism, I draw on

Foucault's conceptualization of "regimes of governmentality." These represent a loose confluence of various political tactics that may target individuals, spaces, materials, ideas, or some combination thereof, as well as the broader structures of thought about how to define the relationship between governors and the governed. When saturated in time and space, particular configurations of these tactics can ossify into broader structures or regimes, such that we may identify some regimes of governmentality as "illiberal" or "liberal" in particular places at particular moments in history. But the looseness of these technologies—and their propensity for going out of date and being replaced by new political inventions—implies that they are always in flux. This is evident, for example, in the way that an authoritarian regime shifts its tactics over time, perhaps softening or perhaps hardening, depending on circumstances. Likewise, some democratic governments may use ever-increasing illiberal tactics, such that they tip toward autocracy, as in the case of Germany during Adolf Hitler's ascent to power. Equally unstable, the concept of *subjectivity* works in tandem with regimes of governmentality: particular technologies demand (and produce) particular subjects. This again varies in space and time: just as citizens of North Korea today understand their relationship to the state apparatus in a markedly different fashion from citizens of the United States, so too did Soviet citizens understand their relationship to the state differently under Stalin than under Gorbachev.

In adopting this approach, I treat authoritarianism as a form of illiberal governmentality, in which states govern—and subjects are taught to govern themselves—not through *freedom* but on the basis of *spectacle* and *discipline.* Mapping onto Foucault's conceptualizations of sovereignty (spectacle), discipline (grids), and liberalism (freedom/biopolitics), these tactics constantly overlap through time and space.[25] For example, while the overarching logic of liberal governmentality is to govern through freedom, it never entirely disposes of spectacle and discipline. Similarly, authoritarian regimes of governmentality may be predominantly characterized by anti-liberal tactics, but they nonetheless use many kinds of freedoms and liberal technologies. The most significant implication of this argument is that illiberalism and liberalism are not spatial phenomena. By focusing on political logics and tactics, it becomes readily apparent that actors in authoritarian and democratic states use many of the same tools. And by attending to the *range* of political tactics (from spectacle to discipline to freedom) at work in any given political system, we can avoid reducing authoritarianism to a caricature of totalitarian despotism and democracy to a caricature of liberty and justice for all. Yet we cannot stop there because these caricatures are deeply significant.

The democratic/authoritarian, or liberal/illiberal, divide is one of the most significant discursive binaries characterizing contemporary geopolitics. Freedom being the primary technology that motivates liberal democratic governmentalities, authoritarian circumscription of certain freedoms (primarily free elections and free press) positions authoritarianism as liberalism's demonized Other.[26] In the past several decades, critical scholars have made major strides in destabilizing and rejecting such binaries as specious. Yet feminist scholars also stress the need to hold them in sight, lest we fail to understand the political work they do.[27] The liberal/ illiberal divide is crucial because of how it gets mapped onto the normative discussions about democratization that have animated international relations since World War II. This binary not only shapes popular geopolitical imaginations but also sits at the center of political decision making about foreign policies and, consequently, carries real material effects. Approached academically, however, normative readings of liberalism and illiberalism should not color our analysis. As Michael Mann argues, scholars need to take autocrats and the political and ideological systems they advance very seriously: "They must not be dismissed as crazy, contradictory, or vague."[28] How else can we understand their appeal? How else can we explain their pervasiveness, historically and geographically? And how else can we come to terms with the prolific overlaps between liberal and illiberal tactics of governing and mobilizing populations?

The difference between liberal and illiberal regimes, as I approach it here, is not a normative question. Rather, I consider governmental regimes as an issue of political geography, asking after the geopolitical saturation of political tactics that govern through freedom, spectacle, or discipline. Treating the difference between liberal and illiberal regimes as one of saturation implies a spatial and temporal bounding. Some political systems become more liberal with time, as in the case of postwar Germany, while others become more illiberal over time, as with the end of ancient Roman democracy. Spatially, we are accustomed to thinking of the world as divided between authoritarian and democratic states, but individual states also have internal differentiation. For example, free trade zones or university campuses might be exceptional sites of liberalism within otherwise illiberal contexts. Similarly, some people and places are subject to more illiberal tactics of rule, as in the experience of Indigenous communities or African Americans in the United States, or in the case of breakaway states or territories subject to military rule. In these cases, individuals and places subjected to more punitive tactics are often already marginalized, socially and spatially peripheral. The forms of violence to which they are subjected also tend to work through a different temporality: their struggles are creeping, hard to visualize, and entail topics unpleasant for popular discussion, if not completely off limits. There is, in short, a differential geography to where liberal and illiberal tactics are used and among whom, globally and within states.

For these reasons, it is essential to avoid fixing authoritarianism in one place. Yet a practice-based approach presents a significant methodological challenge for critical scholars of authoritarianism: How is it possible to study illiberal governmentality without exceptionalizing it and spatially fixing it? This difficulty, I argue, is why analyzing technologies of government requires a profoundly geographic approach that looks for insight across regionally grounded cases. For this book, I have chosen to examine spectacular cities; another scholar might have chosen a different tactic entirely. In focusing on spectacular capital city development, I aim to destabilize certain normative categories that prevail in thinking and writing about authoritarian states—among academics and non-academics alike. It is essential to consider these more positive and inclusionary dimensions of authoritarian state-making. While all the states I consider *do* use repressive tactics of governing, these tactics tend to get a disproportionate amount of scholarly and media attention, such that outside observers cannot fathom a world in which authoritarian regimes might be perceived positively by their citizens.[29] When both the media and scholars focus narrowly on those more negative elements of authoritarian rule, or those issues that speak to our own liberal anxieties about free speech and elections, we miss the bigger picture of how power—and pleasure—works in such settings. But by contrast, if too much attention is given to the positive image-making projects of these countries, we can miss the structural violence and other forms of unspectacular injustice upon which they are built.

Thus, in interrogating spectacular urbanism in the authoritarian states of Asia, I focus on how state-based actors (elites acting in the name of the state) use urban development schemes to craft a particular image of the state and themselves as modern or beneficent. Yet it is important to emphasize that a city can never be the top-down imposition of an autocrat. Even the most centralized political system requires a tremendous network of individuals to come together to produce any idea as a material reality. Furthermore, actors with the desire (and means) to transform their ideas into reality always have multiple audiences in mind: sometimes these audiences are primarily domestic, and other times they have a stronger international orientation. These actors and their constituencies are also always in flux; certain individuals move in and out of positions of power, while local, regional, and global realities change both temporally and spatially. In short, there is always a multiplicity and dynamism to the audiences and the cast of actors seeking to narrate a particular identity or set of priorities for the state. This book accordingly advances a relative understanding of spectacle that can account for subjectivity and subject-*making* practices in large state-led urban development schemes. From a geographic standpoint, this actor-focused approach opens up important questions about the spatial imaginaries that spectacle both builds and builds upon.

Spectacular Cities and the Role of Resource Wealth

While spectacle may be favored in autocratic systems, not every country's leadership has the material resources to undertake its most expensive variants—let alone develop a spectacular capital city. Kazakhstan, Azerbaijan, Turkmenistan, Qatar, the UAE, Myanmar, and Brunei are all resource-rich states. They are also characterized by some form of authoritarian rule. Yet my central argument is that authoritarianism and natural resource wealth are insufficient for explaining why local elites choose to undertake grandiose urban development schemes. There are countless cases of illiberal regimes with substantial resources, across history and the world, which have *not* done so. This notwithstanding, one of the most common interpretations of spectacular city projects is that they are symptoms of two related concepts: "rentier states" and the "resource curse." So-called rentier states are said to become dependent on revenues, or "rents," from natural resource extraction, which skews local economies toward exports while undercutting domestic industry.[30] Furthermore, some scholars argue that because countries with large revenues from resource sales often do not need to tax their citizens, this promotes authoritarian political configurations. In the Gulf, for example, a common cliché suggests that the monarchies are defined by a "ruling bargain" whereby citizens are said to exchange political rights for extensive state-provided welfare goods.

The literature on rentier states offers some insight into the economic quandaries of resource-rich countries, but it generally works to reproduce the same stereotypes about authoritarian states just mentioned: citizens are treated as the passive victims of these arrangements, while the political and economic elites in control of resource rents are the conniving victimizers. To be sure, victims and victimizers abound, but the boundaries between those categories are rarely clear—especially when ordinary citizens support their leaders' use of resource rents and the nondemocratic arrangements on offer. Scholarship on rentier states typically dismisses such popular support as somehow fictive, treating it as a government's success in "buying off" its citizens, who kowtow lest they lose their financial benefits. Providing social welfare goods is undoubtedly an effective strategy for deterring political opposition in resource-rich states, but the same could be said of essentially any kind of political system. Moreover, the top-down approach to rentier states obscures the fact that citizens are not merely passive recipients but active promoters of the prevailing system, as we shall see in the coming chapters.

None of this is to say that extractive economies are not relevant to the story of spectacular urbanism. Many resource-rich states emphasize large infrastructure projects, which are funded with resource rents or, perhaps just as often, the mere promise of future revenues and a range of side deals with local and international economic elites. Take the case of Astana. The entire project has been possible only because of Kazakhstan's large natural resource reserves. The country's economy is heavily dependent on extractive industry: oil and oil products constitute 59 percent of its foreign exports, while ferrous metals (predominantly uranium) make up an additional 19 percent. As a result of the recent collapse in oil prices, the petroleum sector now makes up a relatively small percentage of the country's GDP (gross domestic product), but from 2000 until 2014, oil rents contributed between 12 and 20 percent of Kazakhstan's GDP.[31] Astana's history has been tied to this situation from the very beginning of its development as Kazakhstan's capital in the 1990s, intertwined with a set of extralegal economic patronage practices linked to oil, gas, uranium, and metals extraction.

Most of Astana's iconic new structures and infrastructures have been officially sponsored by the government, but it is widely understood to be a normal business practice in Kazakhstan for private companies to develop local infrastructure, on their own initiative or at the request of government officials.[32] In one of his books, President Nursultan Nazarbayev even thanks the governments of friendly countries and CEOs of foreign and domestic companies for contributing grants (at his personal request) to a fund for the new capital—through which he claims to have raised $400 million.[33] Much of Astana's earliest phase of construction was sponsored by similar "contributions" that were solicited from energy companies, or in some cases "volunteered" by them, as a potential deal-sweetener to win favorable terms in oil contracts.[34] As the country has grown wealthier, the stakes have been raised, and the financial acrobatics have become more sophisticated.[35] After being forced into exile, Nazarbayev's former son-in-law Rakhat Aliyev denounced the regime's practice of laundering money from the extractive industries through Astana construction projects, claiming that the city's development has been financed by millions of dollars stolen from the people: "Instead of grandeur, I saw only billions of [dollars] stolen from the people and buried in this ungrateful land."[36]

The story of elite corruption and money laundering is real, but unfortunately it is beyond the scope of this book. Tempting as it may be to trace the sensational side of these schemes, knowing all their obscure intricacies is actually not essential for understanding the political geographies that arise from spectacular city projects like Astana. This is because extractive economies alone cannot explain such urban development schemes. As noted already, countless governments possessing substantial resource wealth have chosen *not* to undertake such projects. Rather, to understand spectacular urbanism in Asia today, spectacular cities cannot be reduced to simple questions of political economy, as rentier state frameworks tend to do. These cities are just as much about competing identity narratives and ideological agendas as they are about elites funneling resource rents offshore and stripping ordinary citizens of their benefits.

Similarly, these capitals cannot be reduced to the top-down vision of autocratic rulers. We must also examine their role in sustaining particular political relations, which requires investigating how ordinary people buy into the ideological visions they purport to represent. Rather than allowing us to arrive with preformed assumptions about power and politics in resource-rich states, a nuanced geographic approach to spectacle pushes us to ask instead: What sort of state-society power relations are enabled, entrenched, and operationalized in the effort to build a spectacular city? And what can such a project tell us about space, spatial imaginaries, and subjectivity more generally? As this book demonstrates, spectacular city projects are both representative and constitutive of the political order in highly centralized states. This is because spectacular urbanism is shaped by the competing and complementary interests and agendas of elite and ordinary citizens, foreigners, and international actors and institutions. But nowhere are the relationships between these actors linear or hierarchical. And they are certainly not straightforward.

Symbolic Landscapes and Representational Economies

"Spectacle and text, image and word, have always been dialectically related, not least in theatre itself, and this unity has been the site of an intense struggle for meaning," write the geographers Stephen Daniels and Denis Cosgrove.[37] Their concern with analyzing these struggles for meaning as a sort of "text" that is written into symbolic landscapes has guided many cultural and urban geographers since the late 1980s.[38] Significant as this work has been, the literature tends to reduce built landscapes to a sign of some deeper social reality, which is imagined to lie beneath the surface. Critical scholars have more recently challenged this idea, arguing that human practices construct, deconstruct, and respond to various material things, but that there can be no ostensibly social realm separate from or layered on top of these materialities.

In his influential critique of the mind-body or social-material divides that arise from many textual analyses, Timothy Mitchell argues that they can be problematic when they are predicated on the "very distinction between what we see as a realm of signs or representations, and an outside or an underneath."[39] Instead, he suggests that scholars are better advised to examine specific embodied and rhetorical practices as the site of analysis. It is futile to search for some "reality" hiding underneath a symbol or exterior of any sort. This is because symbols are never fixed;

their meanings shift in time, space, and the eye of the beholder. Symbols and symbolic landscapes are correlatives of practices, which are *drawn into being* by situated actors. As material sites imbued with meaning, symbolic landscapes can also become a tool of those seeking to govern (though not always). In approaching spectacular capital city projects as jointly symbolic and material sites, therefore, I show how differently positioned actors make sense of the very same sites and symbols and, in turn, how this does or does not enable elites to cultivate legitimacy and inscribe their political authority.

Practice-based methods are particularly valuable for this study because of the way that spectacular cities are portrayed as being somehow false, fictional, or fantasy. Precisely because of their spectacular nature, commentators often question their legitimacy and ask, Are they real or merely theater? When the question is framed in this manner, Western observers seem to already know the answer. If large urban development agendas in Asia are described from the start as farcical or as inorganic impositions of statist planning (rather than more "organic," bottom-up forms of urbanization), the conclusion is more formulaic than analytical: as noted earlier, they are readily reduced to symptoms of megalomania, an inferiority complex, or mere cronyism. There are, of course, many troubling power dynamics and injustices that come together to materialize the spectacular cities considered in this book. Yet these Orientalist interpretations of Asian cities are not just politically and socially suspect; they are intellectually lazy. If we are to understand spectacular urbanism in Asia today, these cities need to be taken seriously as sites where people with contrasting resources come together to promote their competing interests, agendas, and geopolitical affinities. A practice-based analytic aims to account for these multifarious narratives and situated performances, as Paul Veyne indicates, *without presupposing anything else at all.*[40]

I consider the perspective of non-elites and their experiences with spectacular urbanism, as well as the contrasting ways that elites craft their capital cities, both as places and as symbols. For example, the planners promoting spectacular urban development schemes are generally quite skilled at projecting the idea that "the whole world" is looking on in awe at their newly transformed cities. In producing the image of a highly attentive global community, political leaders are also positioning their cities within—and constituting—a spatial hierarchy that valorizes a certain form of urban development. As Aihwa Ong claims, "inter-Asia inter-referencing practices are thus inseparable from and in fact constitutive of an emerging system for the judgment of urban value. Through the favorable mention, allusion, and even endorsement of another city, actors and institutions position their own projects in a language of explicit comparison and ranking, thus vicariously participating in the symbolic values of particular cities."[41] The power of these narratives about cities and their place in a global hierarchy stems, in large part, from the way "urban" tends to be equated with "modern."

Claims to be modern are political. So too are judgments of modernity: when observers accept or reject an individual's or a group's effort to be seen as modern, their evaluations are political pronouncements. As a subjective concept, modernity has no essence hiding underneath the prolific representations.[42] Rather, in ascribing an attribute like modernity to something or someone, people participate in what Timothy Mitchell terms a "representational economy."[43] In these semiotic economies, people wrestle with identity narratives, symbols, and claims to status through rhetorical and material spaces alike. Claims and assessments about modernity reflect on the positionality of the speaker. Who and what do they consider authentically modern? What are the legitimate markers of being modern, and how are they divided from supposedly inauthentic pretensions to modernity? Outside of the academy we are rarely pushed to reflect deeply on such questions, but they pervade everyday understandings of people and places, dividing the real from the false.

A city is a prime site for seeing representational economies in action, given the tremendous range of people and surfaces coming together in time and space. Buildings, streetscapes, skylines, and urban infrastructures are just as important in today's cities for their symbolic meanings as for their functional utility. The idea that built landscapes can be fashioned and interpreted symbolically hinges on a commonplace assumption that the urban form's exterior actually reflects some interior social reality. That is, many buildings, monuments, and even public infrastructures come to be seen as having a symbolic value that extends well beyond their functional purpose. This is most visible with iconic buildings, such as the world's tallest tower, the Burj Khalifa in Dubai. The Burj is a key referent for abstract understandings of Dubai's rapid modernization, but its materiality also factors into concrete political, economic, and quotidian practices.

The Emirati government may describe it as a symbol, the Western media may read and write it as a different symbol, and citizens may see it as yet another symbol. Equally, hundreds of millions of dollars changed hands to bring it to fruition, real people labored to build it, and thousands have experienced its various spaces and services.

Urban icons such as the Burj Khalifa are often the object of tremendous pride for locals when positive identity narratives like modernity are mapped onto their image. Outside observers may dismiss them as monuments to megalomania, but their dismissal is part of the jockeying among differently positioned actors in the representational economy of the city. Competing narratives about the meaning of urban sites are found all around the world. Yet in some places, like the countries I explore in this book, government leaders work especially hard to ensure that their narrative wins. Sometimes they are more successful than other times, and with some audiences rather than others. As we will see in the case of Kazakhstan, the central leadership has been able to mobilize significant domestic support for its gleaming new capital, despite the extreme skepticism of foreign observers. This is largely true of most of the other countries I discuss, where residents speak of their capitals with great pride, even if they find the traffic or social inequalities distasteful. Just as their leaders do, citizens want to feel modern and be taken seriously on the world stage, as "a recognized and respected somebody in the world who counts and is attended to."[44] In the resource-rich states of Asia, iconic capital city projects seem to be offering just that.

While there are indeed large proportions of residents in places like Kazakhstan, Qatar, or Brunei who look favorably on the image of modernity put on display in their capital cities, this should not deflect critical attention from the fact that these positive perceptions rely on a contrast with the unspectacular Others on which spectacle is founded. That is, the representational economies of these cities are not self-contained; they are intelligible only within the context of broader identity narratives and spatial imaginaries. A nuanced geography of spectacular cities thus demands a broader lens, one that might take into account singular events and sites within their less immediate conditions of possibility. All spectacles have effects, symbolic and material, which ripple out from them. Yet the power of spectacle to seduce our attention means that they are systematically overlooked or forgotten. Attending to the diverse and diffuse effects and relations rippling out from spectacular capital cities lies at the heart of my theoretical agenda. In tracing the practices, narratives, and imaginaries that circulate at many different scales and among uniquely situated actors, I aim to develop a nuanced and grounded *geopolitics* of spectacle and spectacular urbanism.

By advancing a critical framework that accounts for the deeply geographic nature of spectacle, I also ask what spectacle might tell us in turn about geography. I suggest that by exploring spectacle's unique reliance on spatial metaphors, we can discern broader patterns of geopolitical thinking across multiple contexts. In some ways, the center-periphery relationships and spatial imaginaries that define and are defined by the Astana project are unique. But in others, they are not. To better understand these relations and the workings of spectacle more generally, the comparative perspective I develop in chapter 4 sheds light on why numerous authoritarian states across Asia have been promoting spectacular capital city development schemes in recent years. This book offers no simple or easy explanation. While it is tempting to return to one of the most obvious truths of geography—*that place matters*—my geographic approach illustrates one way to account for spectacle's diverse and multiply scaled Others. A rich understanding of political and regional geography can begin to illuminate some commonalities uniting spectacular capital cities in Asia, but this must ultimately be rooted in a relational understanding of spectacle that accounts for the unspectacular processes, relations, and experiences that make the spectacle intelligible and, more often than not, possible.

1

APPROACHING SPECTACLE
GEOGRAPHICALLY

"The modern Astana is Kazakhstan in miniature," asserted President Nursultan Nazarbayev in 2010. "Different cultures and traditions meet here. East, West, North and South have found their embodiment in glass and concrete here."[1] The city represents many things for Kazakhstan's longtime president: it is a cultural crossroads, a symbol of future prosperity, and a sign of the independent state's strength in the post-Soviet era. But in this discussion of the country's modernization efforts, Nazarbayev's language is pervaded by the basic image of developments in the *city* as representative of those in the *whole country*: "Astana is Kazakhstan in miniature." The idea of a capital city standing for its country is an old idea, which diplomats and international travelers from across the world understand well. On deeper reflection, most people would readily acknowledge that one city is rarely representative of an entire country's diversity, but rarely do we dwell on the politics of this synecdoche. In some cases, the idea is relatively banal: asserting that Paris *is* France or that Washington, D.C., *is* the United States may gloss over significant regional disparities, but the claim itself would not seem to actively reinforce those disparities. France and the United States both have policies and governance structures that do not unduly prioritize the capital's development over the state's other regions.

But in Kazakhstan, the claim that Astana *is* Kazakhstan has much more political significance. This is especially apparent when viewed from the territorial hinterlands, which have a more antagonistic relationship with the capital because of the intense concentration of federal funds in promoting the city's development. Take, for example, the North Aral Sea region, which we will encounter in chapter 3. This region is a state-designated "ecological disaster zone." The sea's evaporation during Soviet times has resulted in decades of acute environmental problems, accompanied by severe health complications and grinding poverty for the locals. Villages in the region lack the most basic infrastructure, such as adequate medical facilities, roads, waste disposal, and access to clean water (let alone indoor water connections). Kazakhstan's larger cities have their own infrastructural challenges, as does Astana, but the blatant neglect of the Aral Sea region and other peripheral areas like it suggests a stark imbalance in the state's developmental policies. For rural residents who have not been able or willing to migrate to the country's cities, the claim that Astana *is* Kazakhstan can sometimes be perceived as an affront—so false that it feels like a slap in the face. This is not always the case, though. Many people, if not the majority, choose not to pay attention to the injustice of regional disparities exacerbated by the government's focus on building up its spectacular capital city. Regardless of whether residents are resigned to the persistence of these inequalities, the situation in the North Aral Sea suggests that Nazarbayev's seemingly innocuous claim that "Astana is Kazakhstan in miniature" is far more political than it may at first appear.

Nazarbayev is not alone in thinking about the capital city as a miniature model of the country's development plans. He is one of many in a long line of planners from Ankara to St. Petersburg who have sought to put modernity on display in their capitals. The specific urban forms that have resulted from these development projects are just as diverse as the contexts and people that give them life. But why is the city so frequently privileged in these imaging agendas? The city as a site, scale, and space is attractive for many reasons, but foremost among them is the utility of *miniaturization*. In places where leaders want to effect rapid and far-reaching social and political transformation, microcosms can be appealing. Utopians of all sorts find miniatures politically useful, but state-based actors often revel in the limited scale of the city because its unique degree of closure facilitates the implementation of projects that would be far too costly if attempted at the larger scale of a country's entire territory.[2] A microcosm offers the unique benefit of excluding complexity in a way that allows a visionary to achieve his or her lofty ideals, usually at a rapid pace that can satisfy short-term demands for action. When their projects are then realized on a diminished scale, the microcosm becomes a convenient icon of success. It can be put on a pedestal and treated as representative of a leader's vision for a new order, like when Nazarbayev claims that modern Astana is Kazakhstan in miniature. Everywhere but in city-states, the image of the city as a miniature of the state is obviously a fiction. But Nazarbayev here taps into a common trope in which cities, and capitals in particular, are used as a rhetorical device to assert equivalency.[3]

Political actors also find cities to be useful metaphors because of the advantages of *focalization* that come with miniaturization. Singular sites or events, like a parade or a monument or a capital city, can substantiate an abstraction. They lend material form to an ideological narrative that is rather more diffuse, tenuous, or perhaps even illusory. Paul Veyne calls this a "focalization effect." He suggests that the propensity of political leaders to use such a tactic to substantiate their ideology is heightened when they lack the resources to do so in a more spatially, socially, and temporally extensive manner.[4] Building a monument to Lenin or Lincoln, for instance, can be quick, easy, and relatively cheap in comparison to the task of developing entire political systems that actually reflect the values of Soviet communism or American liberalism. Fusing ideological narratives (such as democracy or communism) with a material object or site allows people to interact with them more concretely in everyday life. When mapped onto a material site, such as a monument, a building, or even a city, abstract narratives become tangible and are thus easier to visualize. This in turn endows abstract concepts with more symbolic power than if they were to remain at the level of abstraction as people learn to treat the material referent as evidence of its truth or reality.[5]

The tautological reasoning of focalization is not always as convincing as the architects of such projects may like, nor does it always effectively buttress the desired ideological narrative. For example, under communist rule, citizens of Eastern European countries might have seen Soviet-inspired monuments to Lenin as signs of oppression, rather than as reflections of their commitment to the international brotherhood of socialist states. Regardless of whether it is convincing, focalization works as a *rhetorical device* to promote certain narratives by mapping them onto newly constructed or already existing sites. Because it is so rooted in material sites, focalization also works to shape particular *spatial imaginaries.*

As noted in the introduction, the term *spatial imaginaries* refers to how people think about space to make sense of the social and physical world. Spatial imaginaries are not fixed, since every person has unique ways of thinking about and experiencing space. Specific tropes and metaphors, however, can come to define spatial thought, locally and globally. Focalization, or the idea that a material site *represents* some abstract concept, is one such case. When applied to cities, focalization works through the metaphor of synecdoche, in which the *part* is imagined to stand for the *whole.*[6] This is the trope that Nazarbayev is using when he claims that Astana *is* Kazakhstan. As a metaphorical mode of thinking, synecdoche in this case pushes people to imagine that the capital city of a country is representative of the entire country, that the modernity expressed there is found everywhere, and that the government's largesse is indicative of its beneficence across its lands and toward all its residents.

Synecdoche cannot be judged on the basis of its validity. Like all metaphors, it is a kind of fiction. Simply unmasking its falseness does not help us grasp its role in allowing people to advance and make sense of the political claims of spectacular urban development. Instead we must ask: How does it operate and what work does it do? Synecdoche is key to understanding how people think about cities and their relationship to the territorial state, what values decision makers accord to the symbolic and built form of urban spaces, and why developing a spectacular capital city becomes popular among certain state planners. Social scientists have never systematically considered synecdoche as it relates to cities and states, or even more generally to centers and peripheries.[7] Although offhand references to metonymy or miniaturization are common in urban studies, these tropes do not capture the nuance of synecdoche.[8] Nor do they shed light on the enormous amount of mental contortion needed to imagine a city standing for an entire country. Accordingly, this chapter traces the role of synecdoche in ways of thinking about space and time, and begins to unravel some of the implications of synecdochic thinking for the geopolitics of spectacle.

Spatial Imaginaries and Synecdoche

Geographers have explored the geographic imagination from many angles, but relatively few have given explicit attention to metaphor.[9] The literature on critical geopolitics, however, offers some useful insights into how certain metaphors and tropes come to dominate particular spatial imaginaries, as well as how they are perpetuated. Critical geopolitics is a subfield of political geography that examines the intersection between geopolitics, identity narratives, and geographic imaginations. One of the main tenets of critical geopolitics is that *geography is a field of power/knowledge.* This means that apprehending and knowing the world is inherently political because all actors are embedded in particular contexts and filter the world through specific interpretive lenses. As a result, geopolitical thinkers can never be neutral observers, and the field of geopolitics can never innocently describe the world.[10] Critical geopolitics eschews depoliticized accounts of global affairs by seeking to ground practitioners and their theories in a political geographic context. Geopolitics in this critical framework is approached as a *discourse.* An ensemble of rules by which speech acts and material performances are made meaningful, discourses are both shaped by and shape physical objects, individual capabilities, sociocultural resources, and geographic modes of thinking.[11] As initially conceptualized by Gearóid Ó Tuathail, critical geopolitics was designed to interrogate these discourses, positing that "how people know, categorize and make sense of the world is an interpretive cultural practice."[12]

Political geographers working in this field have also illustrated how certain places are discursively "reduced to security commodities, to geographical abstractions which need to be 'domesticated,' controlled, invaded or bombed rather than understood in their complex reality."[13] Such reductionism frequently unfolds through the use of foreign policy metaphors, like those describing a region or place as a "wild zone," "shatterbelt," "chessboard," "satellite," "quagmire," or a "den" or "lair" harboring suspicious individuals. Albeit sensational, metaphors like this circulate widely in policy communities, news media, and everyday conversations.

These metaphors simultaneously encapsulate and entrench a particular zeitgeist. This is exemplified in the evolution of geopolitical fear-mongering about communism in the United States, from describing the communist threat as an internal "fungus" to the later metaphor "domino theory," which construed Soviet expansion as a more distant but looming threat of geopolitical balancing. Metaphors can be self-fulfilling prophecies, and those characterizing Cold War thinking did in fact influence foreign policy doctrines and strategic decisions, both in the United States and globally.[14] In studying geopolitical imaginaries, however, critical geopolitics scholars have focused almost exclusively on specific metaphorical tropes, like those of fungal infection or dominoes, rather than *root metaphors* such as metonymy, synecdoche, or personification.

Root metaphors are inextricably tied to spatial imaginaries because, as the linguistic scholars George Lakoff and Mark Johnson famously argue, they "govern our everyday functioning, down to the most mundane details. Our concepts structure what we perceive, how we get around in the world, and how we relate to other people." Because metaphors structure our perception of the world, they "create realities for us, especially social realities." The example that Lakoff and Johnson use most frequently is the cliché that "time is money." Time is *not* money, of course, but if we "act as if time is a valuable commodity—a limited resource, even money—we conceive of time that way. Thus we understand and experience time as the kind of thing that can be spent, wasted, budgeted, invested wisely or poorly, saved, or squandered."[15] Metaphor not only structures how we think about the world but also shapes how we behave as we interact and move about the world. In effect, metaphors create the reality they allegedly describe.[16]

Working through the same thought processes, spatial imaginaries consist of various metaphors that structure how people think about the world and define possible courses of action. This structuring effect is central to how scholars now approach the geographic concepts of "territory" and the "state." Territory, writes the political geographer John Agnew, "is not a simple block of space but a complex set of relationships between local, regional, and national levels of social practice and geographic imagination."[17] The idea of territory as a "simple block of space" is nonetheless how it is most commonly viewed. When people today look at a map, they can usually understand that territorial boundaries are politically constructed. It is much harder to grasp the fact that simply viewing and apprehending the world as an abstract representation via the map or the globe is also socially constructed. The bird's-eye view of the world is now so pervasive that most people take it for granted. Yet the ability to imagine space in this manner is relatively new, rooted in Renaissance conceptions of *perspective,* in which an abstract observer is visually and conceptually detached from the world, imagined to have an "objective" view of space.

The contemporary geopolitical imagination hinges on the idea of perspective that allows people to imagine the world as an abstraction—or, rather, to abstract ourselves from the world as separate. Seeing the world in this manner, "as an ordered, structured whole, separates the self who is viewing the world itself. The observer stands outside of terrestrial space, so to speak, and frames the world as apart from and prior to the places and people it contains."[18] The act of dividing the social/mental realm from the material world "out there" is also the foundation of the modernist state system.[19] This system simultaneously divides the earth's surface into individual territories and divides the social stuff from those territorial containers. The resulting "floating-eye" vision of the earth's surface transforms it into a depopulated vision of what Doreen Massey refers to as "smooth space" and Robert Sack calls "abstract space."[20] Sack elaborates:

> [Modernist] territoriality in fact helps create the idea of a socially *emptiable space.* Take the parcel of vacant land in the city. It is describable as an empty lot, though it is not physically empty for there may be grass and soil on it. It is emptiable because it is devoid of socially or economically valuable artifacts or things that were intended to be controlled. In this respect, territoriality conceptually separates place from things and then recombines them as an assignment of things to place and places to things. . . . This tendency can be combined with others to form an extremely important component of modernity—that of emptiable space.[21]

Thinking abstractly about space as emptiable—being able to detach the mind's eye from one's grounded reality—is not at all natural. Demonstrating that space can be, and historically has been, imagined in any range of ways, Sack argues that people must learn to think in this fashion.[22] For this reason, we should not take modernist understandings of emptiable space for granted. Nor should we assume that a socially empty understanding of space is analytically more accurate. Abstract spatial thinking is sustained not "because of its intellectual sophistication," Sack underscores, "but because a particular type of society finds it a useful or significant conception for social action."[23] European colonialists, for example, found it to be especially useful. With its abundant maps and censuses, colonialism was thoroughly dependent on this vision of the world as empty—and emptiable—space. And as colonial powers applied these modes of thinking wherever they sought to rule, they overran other more socially imbued understandings of space and began the process of institutionalizing the global dominance of modernist visions of space.[24]

In addition to disciplining and structuring space, abstract or modernist spatial thinking requires conceptually separating people and place. This process is central to Foucault's discussion of *discipline*, which includes a wide range of practices involving spatial partitioning, as in Bentham's famous Panopticon prison design, plague-struck towns, or the ideal placement of a capital city within a territory.[25] In all these projects, social elements are conceptually detached from the material. Disciplinary arts of government are not just based on the idea that the social is separate from the material but actively *create* this division. Discipline effects social control through spatial partitioning, and it does so effectively because the division of space structures people's available choices for action. Understood in this way, the act of abstracting space from social processes, of imagining it as separate from the human subjects populating it, is intensely political. This is not only because people who make decisions to structure space in one way or another are necessarily political actors, but also because they are often in competition with one another about how to do so. In the examples just given, questions arise such as: Should prisoners live communally or in separate cells? Should a plague epidemic be stopped by confining the ill to their homes or by evacuating an entire town's population? Should a capital city be located in the geometric center of a state's territory, or should it be on the border? In each of these cases, the answers given will reflect certain visions about how to define the "proper" relationship between the social and material elements that one seeks to control or govern.

Abstract visions of space are also fundamental to how ideological claims about a city can be applied to a broader state or territory, which the city is said to represent. When President Nazarbayev claims that "the modern Astana is Kazakhstan in miniature," he is drawing on a common geopolitical imaginary, which synecdochically positions capital cities as representative of the whole country. The convention stems from an old tradition of the modernist statist system, in which capital cities are framed as shop windows for the rest of the world.[26] Today it is reinforced by certain linguistic conventions, especially prominent in the news media, such as using the name of a capital city in lieu of the country's name or that of the ruling regime (e.g., "Moscow maintains high prices in energy talks with Beijing").[27] In the same fashion, reporters commonly use "the White House" or "the Kremlin" to stand in for the United States or Russian government, respectively. This might appear to be an odd, but largely banal, journalistic convention. Nevertheless, it ultimately reinforces a global norm whereby capital cities are understood to represent an entire country. These linguistic norms in turn bolster and lend credibility to claims, such as another one Nazarbayev makes when arguing that it is necessary to develop Astana as the "face of the country [*litso strany*], figuratively speaking, its business card [*vizitnaya kartochka*]."[28] Thus applied, the journalistic cliché is perhaps more political than banal.

To imagine the city as representative of a broader political space or the state's modernization campaign, people must be accustomed to abstract spatial thinking. They must be able to perform what might be called a *synecdochic scale-jump*—the mental trick of synecdoche, whereby the part is imagined to represent the whole. This is an exercise in abstract spatial thinking because it hinges on a depopulated vision of space—one that deliberately overrides attention to the social diversity of a territory that would negate the metaphor. Yet this is precisely the job of an effective metaphor: to "highlight some features of reality and hide others."[29] Not all metaphors resonate with their audiences, and as I discuss later, sometimes the synecdoche fails. Regardless, the very act of using this rhetorical device is a geopolitical claim: the synecdochic scale-jump builds on and from particular spatial imaginaries that highlight the city's reality and hide those of the broader state.

Iconic architecture works through the same synecdochic logic as the capital city cliché. Urban boosters often frame iconic buildings as an opportunity to put their country or city on the map by drawing on the reputation of world-renowned architects enticed through high-profile competitions. The urban icon is then transformed into a key referent in planners' efforts to project a positive image of the city internationally.[30]

According to the logic of iconic architecture, the better it photographs and travels globally, the more important it is. Embedded in a global context in which the symbolic significance of iconic architecture is truly pervasive, state planners commonly prioritize large-scale projects to keep up—or in many cases, catch up—with other cities and states. The synecdochic significance of urban icons is now largely common sense. People all over the world are accustomed to regularly performing the synecdochic scale-jump with respect to urban icons, and so much so that the act of imagining them as symbols of something larger often goes unnoticed.

Synecdoche does its rhetorical work in many domains, and its scale-jumping is not limited to space alone. Consider the case of representative democracy. The literary theorist Kenneth Burke explains that synecdoche is the basis of "all theories of political representation, where some part of the social body (either traditionally established, or elected, or coming into authority by revolution) is held to be 'representative' of the society as a whole."[31] Through one centralized image, the concept of the representative (e.g., a president like Nursultan Nazarbayev), the node (e.g., a city like Astana), an event (e.g., a holiday like Astana Day), or a thing (e.g., a stadium like Astana Arena) obscures all the practices that go into making it possible. These imaginaries are more or less necessary because encounters with things or events are unavoidably ephemeral. No more than a set of practices brought together in time and space, they can never be fixed. They always fade away or come to a close (spatially, temporally, or both). The synecdochic scale-jump offers a way to get beyond the trouble of transience in that it helps to establish certain cognitive frames that guide daily experiences and imaginaries, helping people to remember the *whole* that the part (or partial experience) is imagined to represent.

This process is also visible in the case of nationalism, of imagining oneself to belong to an "imagined community."[32] Synecdoche lies at the heart of Benedict Anderson's famous argument about nationalist thinking: an individual must *imagine* his or her singular experiences as part of a coherent whole, that is, a national community. Nationalism on display at sporting events and spectacles is exemplary of how this works. These events make the imagined community seem more tangible to spectators and participants: one can see, hear, and interact with this community for a short time.[33] Yet that sense of patriotic fervor and unity is always short-lived, since people must disperse and return to their daily routines. While many observers have asked why this unity must be so fleeting, a more incisive question is whether there was ever unity at all. Operating on the basis of a synecdochic imaginary, the impression of unity can only ever be a visual and emotional effect. A nationalist spectacle is successful, however, when people come to extrapolate that effect to their daily existence. When they do, they metaphorically imagine themselves as perpetually embedded in a unified national community, even after the event comes to a close.

Spectacle can thus make visible effects and forces that are otherwise difficult to see. Events such as national festivals, places such as capital cities, or objects such as iconic buildings can give substance to an abstraction, to lend a political order or experience "a clarity it might otherwise lack."[34] This is the focalization effect described earlier. Synecdochic thinking allows people to give concrete form to ideological narratives, often because they can be materialized relatively quickly and with fewer resources than other reforms: "It is much less costly to build . . . a high culture, rich in monuments, than to feed a population more or less adequately."[35] When cities are used in this fashion—that is, to manifest a new ideological system or assert narrowly enacted political agendas as unfolding over an entire territory—this is synecdoche at work. Of course, the more symbolic and centralized the project is, the more one needs to stretch one's imagination to believe that the singularity represents the whole, or that the benefits of one project extend to the periphery. When stretched too far, the metaphor can fail. Effective or not, though, synecdoche plays an important role in spatializing power relations, or at least promoting an ideal vision of how to define the relationship between the social and the material world. It is, in short, a *geopolitical* imaginary. Viewing it thus, we can begin to sketch the contours of a geographic approach to spectacle that attends to root metaphors and the geopolitical imaginaries they advance.

Approaching Spectacle Geographically

To understand the geopolitics of spectacle, it is necessary to foreground place, scale, and time. Like any form of theatrics, spectacles vary widely in their content, scope, frequency, directors, and intended audiences. As a political tactic, spectacle has a *temporality* and *spatiality*. In both respects, it is point-based: it is generally staged at one particular location, and it happens sporadically, occasionally, or only once. But time and space being relative, we must ask: What makes any given spectacle spectacular? Answering this question is fundamentally tied to *scale*—the perception of hierarchies of size, level, and intensity. Scale is not an ontologically given category but must be socially constructed.[36] Our perceptions of scale are learned in and through various life experiences, hinging on various ways of imagining ourselves in time and space. For example, cities are usually seen as representing a lesser or lower scale relative to states. This idea is embedded in how most states administer their territories in a descending fashion: from the federal to regional to urban jurisdictions. When scale is understood with reference to population size, however, some cities are clearly positioned well above certain states. The world's largest metropolitan area, Tokyo, for instance, has 37.6 million residents, which is over twice the population of Kazakhstan and seventeen times that of Qatar.

Perceptions of scale are also constantly in flux. When applied to the time-space of spectacle, the social construction of scale means that the same set of practices, or the same place, may be deemed spectacular in one milieu but definitively unspectacular in another. For example, to someone who has lived his or her entire life in rural Nebraska, New York City is likely to appear quite spectacular. A visitor from Tokyo, by contrast, may not find the city to be particularly so. What makes spectacle spectacular is always relative and rooted in the specific interpretations of individuals. Furthermore, what these examples suggest is that spectacle is considered spectacular in contrast with specific understandings of the *unspectacular*: mundane, everyday experiences as well as slower or spatially diffuse realties. To capture the relative nature of spectacle, it is best understood as a political technology that actors use and relate to in contrasting ways. As noted in the introduction, this approach raises several basic questions: Who uses spectacle, for whom, and when and where?

Who Uses It?

Statist spectacle has been used far more in some political systems than in others. While it has been a staple of highly centralized political systems for centuries, spectacle is certainly not confined to authoritarian polities. For various historical reasons, statist spectacle is largely treated with suspicion in the liberal West today. Yet public ceremony has historically served an important role in institutionalizing state power in more democratic settings as well.[37] As the liberal democracies of our day have come to govern more intensively through neoliberal logics, spectacle has increasingly been pushed to market-defined spaces. This is readily apparent in the United States, where large-scale spectacles are mostly found in special events such as the Macy's Thanksgiving Day parade, or in the multibillion-dollar private sporting franchises of the National Football League and the National Basketball Association. Because of the neoliberal governing rationale, spectacle is largely deemed inappropriate for direct state investment and has been accordingly displaced from the realm of government activity. Of course, this narrative belies the fact that state- and market-based elites in more liberal settings have in fact worked together to resuscitate state funding for spectacle in various forms, such as hosting sporting mega-events like the Olympic Games or the FIFA World Cup.

State spending for these spectacles is justified in democratic states mostly through invoking the idea of "public-private partnership." Despite implying that government money is only a top-off for otherwise private sector spectacles, these spending practices have increasingly come under fire for being a misappropriation of taxpayer funds.[38] Normative judgments aside, the overarching effect of such criticisms is to reaffirm the idea that producing mass spectacles is *not* the rightful domain of state control in liberal polities, that it should be confined to market spaces alone. In illiberal settings, elites share many of the same boosterist aims as their counterparts in liberal democracies. Yet they are generally able to tap into state funds more openly. In producing their spectacles, they too will turn to the private sector for support, as seen in Russia's 2014 Olympic Games in Sochi, in which the government routinely pressed private firms for contributions of funds and services.[39] These commonalities notwithstanding, liberal commentators tend to read spectacles in authoritarian settings as symptomatic of an unhealthy and overly centralized political system.

Liberal critiques of statist spectacle, which often caricature it as the top-down imposition of an autocrat, also erase the fact that spectacles can never be the product of one individual's will; producing a spectacle demands tremendous material resources, bureaucratic capacity, and political momentum.[40] State-based actors must reach far and wide to mobilize both people and the state's resources to produce spectacles, regardless of how entrenched their authority may be. Nor can a spectacle be produced at the drop of a hat. Notably, this applies equally to celebratory *and* punitive spectacle. On both ends of the spectrum, material resources and political hierarchies combine to condition the desired effect of joyful celebration of the state (political-cultural elites able to mobilize and choreograph citizens, musicians, banners, and so on, as in mass parades) or the awed fear of the state (political-military elites able to mobilize and choreograph troops and artillery, as in armed squads ordered to fire on protesters). It can be easier to mobilize the social and political resources needed to give life to any particular spectacle in authoritarian states because leaders have fewer checks on their authority. That said, many authoritarian governments lack the required financial resources to host a sporting mega-event or build a spectacular capital city, which partly explains why we do not see such spectacles used pervasively across all nondemocratic contexts. (Of course, there is a wide range of other reasons, including lack of interest.) But if statist spectacle is not used exclusively in authoritarian states, this raises the question of why political leaders in illiberal settings appear to use it more frequently than their more liberal counterparts. Here it is necessary to return to the idea that spectacle is a political technology.

Like all technologies, spectacle will be used by individuals according to the extent to which it helps them achieve a desired political effect. This effectiveness of a political technology depends on what Foucault refers to as prevailing "economies of power."[41] That is, some political tactics will be preferred to others on the basis of a confluence of political, social, and economic factors, as well as the specific resources that are available to a situated political actor. Take the example of public punishment through torture or execution, which was quite common in Western societies into the eighteenth and nineteenth centuries. Until then, a central government or ruler lacked the political, technical, and financial resources to punish every minor transgression. Thus, it was politically expedient—or *economical*—to punish individuals through public displays of state violence. The larger and more spectacular the display, the more widely the message would spread about the consequences of transgression. But in the case of France by the eighteenth century, Foucault shows how public executions became more and more susceptible to social disturbances, including rioting and ever-increasing attacks on authorities. Instead of serving the purpose of instilling fear and obedience among the masses, they became spectacles of insubordination. Slowly, elites came to fear the effects of public torture and eventually abandoned it entirely. This was not a decision made because of a new sensibility about public cruelty as immoral; rather, it was simply that this kind of punishment no longer supported the state's agenda. Abandoning punitive spectacle was also made possible because more economical forms of punishment had begun to develop, including a range of new technologies of surveillance, police, and managing criminals that allowed authorities to punish individual transgressions in a systematic and, ultimately, less public manner.[42]

Shifting economies of power related to punishment meant that punitive spectacles became obsolete in France, as they did in much of the rest of the world with time, and were replaced by new political technologies for punishing individuals. This example shows how thinking about spectacle is not static, and how spectacle can undergo a significant shift in its political utility. Under one set of conditions, authorities found substantial benefits to using spectacle as a mode of asserting control and communicating with their subjects. Changing geopolitical circumstances then precipitated a warping of the prevailing economy of power, which forced leaders to reconfigure their tactics and eliminate punitive spectacle as a political technology in order to retain their hegemony.

Paul Veyne similarly traces the shifting role of celebratory spectacle in ancient Greece and Rome in his monumental work *Bread and Circuses*. He shows how competing groups of elites in both places actively leveraged festivities, games, and other *largesses* to maintain political dominance, curry favor, or lend splendor to their cities.[43] Over long periods of time, the practice and forms of their spectacles changed, but they also faded away entirely when elites no longer found them useful or could not afford their ruinous costs. Such transitions can be subtle or dramatic, but by searching out moments of rupture, we can begin to understand how "a set of practices, which were accepted without question, which were familiar and 'silent,' out of discussion, becomes a problem, raises discussion and debate, incites new reactions, and induces a crisis in the previously silent behavior, habits, practices, and institutions."[44] In investigating the question of *who* uses spectacle, therefore, spatial and temporal contexts matter greatly.

For Whom?

Equally contextual is the issue of the intended audience of spectacle. Broadly speaking, there are three main categories of audiences that we might identify: (1) the general public of a given polity, (2) local elites, and (3) the international community. Any form of spectacle may emphasize one of these audiences, but with statist spectacle, all three are typically included to some degree. With regard to the general public, the question of popular reception of spectacle has been interpreted differently in liberal and illiberal settings. In the early scholarship on statist spectacle, Western researchers tended to hold a liberal democratic bias about political subjectivity. This bias is rooted in a simplistic conception of resistance, which hinges on a one-dimensional understanding of power. Conceptualizing power as oppressive and imposed top-down on individuals, a one-dimensional approach tends to fetishize overt opposition to the powers that be as the only agent of change or mode of subverting unjust relations.[45] Applied to spectacle, this liberalist bias is manifested in the way that early scholarship tended to search for antiestablishment or contrarian forms of public engagement, which were read as a kind of veiled protest.[46]

Critical scholars of authoritarianism have shown, by contrast, that opposition to political authorities or oppressive conditions in nondemocratic settings usually does not look like resistance as it is understood in liberal democratic terms (e.g., public demonstrations or critical journalism). Nor does it always unfold in the same spaces and through the same vocabularies.[47] More recent work on spectacle captures this nuance by reading oppositional narratives of or during spectacles not as a sign of resistance but as a particular kind of subjectivity, which is facilitated by and enacted through mass events. For example, Karen Petrone shows in her study of Stalinist celebrations that publicly performing the identity of a "loyal Soviet citizen" was "a fluid and rather elastic identity that could be used by workers and peasants to forward their own interests as well as by the state to force compliance with its policies."[48] Her account of how people learned to "speak Bolshevik" is similar to that of Lisa Wedeen's analysis of language in Syria under Hafez al-Assad, where citizens also used regime-sanctioned rhetoric when it was beneficial to them.[49] This fluidity reflects the fact that spectacles are never a unitary experience; they always rely on mixed and overlapping motives to entice spectators and participants alike. When power is understood not as a repressive imposition from above, but as something more nuanced and "capillary," we can begin to understand its seductive and productive nature.[50] By tapping into a wide range of motives, elites orchestrating spectacles enlist participants through their pleasure, aspirations, and ideals, just as much as through their outright complacency or boredom.[51] Viewed from this perspective, authoritarian states look far less exceptional; the same opportunism can be found in any form of political mobilization, in liberal and illiberal states alike.

The "masses" are not always the target demographic of spectacles, however. In fact, elites themselves are often the primary audience for those tasked with putting on a spectacle. In highly centralized regimes, the production of state-sponsored spectacle can be an important disciplining exercise, which works to school cultural elites in the official state line, as well as to secure or distribute patronage.[52] In these settings, spectacles can become important forums for lower-level officials, bureaucrats, and others seeking both symbolic and financial rewards. Often they are in competition with one another, as they seek to curry favor and advance their position by impressing their higher-ups with a job well done. This "rivalry of prestige," which Geertz considered to be a significant driver of Balinese politics, is also described by Laura Adams, who traces the political posturing of cultural elites producing mass spectacles in Uzbekistan.[53] As in other centralized systems, where a circle of cronies surrounding a leader engages in a politics of one-upmanship, she shows how the constant speculation about how best to please the leader ("this is how Karimov would want it") was a fixture of elites' appeals to legitimacy in their decision making. Indeed, doing so was essential to success in their careers.

Adams's work also points to a third audience, which has been made possible through the globalization of media—the global community of spectators. She argues that this was more imagined than real in Uzbekistan, but illustrates how simply invoking a global audience is a key way to mobilize elites, participants, and spectators: "For example, in 1996 the holiday spectacle's directors would regularly admonish performers to work harder since the whole world would be watching them (though, in reality the broadcast probably reached few households outside of Uzbekistan's borders)."[54] The narrative of a watchful world is especially common in the production of global mega-events like the Olympics, the World Cup, or a World's Fair (EXPO). The nationalist call to make the country proud has been invoked around the world to garner support for massive investments in such one-time events. In this narrative, national pride is imagined to emanate outward to all citizens if their country is deemed a successful host. The costs associated with producing these extravagant displays are thus justified with reference to the importance of presenting a positive image to the on-looking world. Using (or abusing) the trickle-down metaphor, advocates of international spectacles also argue that, in addition to the intangible benefits of pride, their financial benefits will in fact percolate out to the masses and to peripheral areas, as if autonomously. More often, however, the economic benefits of mega-events and other singular spectacles are generally quite concentrated and can even be downright ruinous for some cities or countries.[55] Notwithstanding this reality, politicians make frequent use of the idealistic claim that a spectacle's local effects can—*and will*—jump scales, diffuse, or trickle down to benefit the entire country or population. But if all else fails, the people will have a little extra pride in their homeland because "the whole world" was watching.

Spectacular urbanism operates on a similar logic. As we shall see, the government of Kazakhstan has spent extraordinary sums of state funds to develop Astana as a spectacle rising from the Central Asian steppe. Ostensibly impressing a watchful world and giving citizens a renewed sense of pride in their homeland, official narratives suggest that the project's benefits diffuse well beyond the urban elites to the wider population in the farthest reaches of the country. Diffusion metaphors like this are underpinned by the metaphor of synecdoche, which also helps to depoliticize the question of *whose* interests are served by a spectacle. The question of a spectacle's audience can begin to offer some clues. More broadly, though, the question of *for whom* spectacles are performed is deeply geographic: differing scales, political subjectivities, and spatial imaginaries are all implicated in how any audience is conceived.

When and Where?

As a political technology, spectacle has even further geographic significance addressed in the joint questions of *when and where*. The existing literature on spectacle has almost exclusively taken a simple then-and-there perspective. That is, most research has tended to focus on a spectacle's immediate features, such as participant experiences during an event *(but not before and after)*, parade routes *(but not those city spaces excluded)*, or a new capital city project *(but not the impact on its hinterlands)*. Useful as this work has been, it does not suffice for developing a truly relational approach that is premised on seeing the spectacular and the unspectacular as inextricably linked. New lines of inquiry are therefore needed to account for spectacle's unspectacular Others, which "overspill clear boundaries in time and space" and lead to what Rob Nixon describes as a series of "temporal, geographical, rhetorical, and technological displacements."[56] Spectacles are inherently seductive; they harness the power of focalization to draw us in and captivate our attention. But they always have effects that go well beyond their immediate instantiation—and this is why the issue of displacement is so important.

When the wider effects of spectacle are dispersed, temporally and spatially, they become far less visible: not only out of sight and out of mind, but ungraspable. The spatial and temporal nature of spectacle is such that it can "smooth the way for amnesia" about its wider effects, an amnesia that entails very "consequential forgettings."[57] In his analysis of spectacle-centered reporting on environmental problems, Rob Nixon shows how it overwrites the experiences of poor people who are subject to slow, and decidedly unsensational, forms of environmental injustice. In this case, the spectacle facilitates the perpetuation of what he calls "slow violence." The temporally elongated and unspectacular nature of slow violence is similar to what other scholars have variously described as "structural violence" and "silent violence."[58] These concepts all highlight the important point that, in its comparative intensity, spectacle can divert attention from unspectacular forms of violence and social injustice. Nixon further shows that the dispersal of a spectacle's effects can be a significant factor in demobilizing opposition, since critics do not have a tangible target to attack. They become nebulous, indistinct, and difficult to attribute.

How, then, are scholars to account for these effects, or even conceptualize them? Doing so requires a great deal of humility about the limits of social science research and the human imagination. But more immediately, it demands that we broaden questions about when and where spectacle unfolds to incorporate its unspectacular Others. Coming in many forms and manifested across multiple temporal and spatial scales, these effects cannot be understood as a mere "byproduct" or "externality" of spectacle. This would imply that they are separate phenomena. Rather, the two produce each other: the unspectacular is the condition of possibility for the spectacular. The spatiotemporal exceptionalism of spectacle can be exceptional only when put in contrast to something else. This theme is vividly illustrated by Geertz's discussion of nineteenth-century Bali's political order, which was structured around an exemplary center—the *negara*. In this system, Geertz argues, "The state drew its force, which was real enough, from its imaginative energies, its semiotic capacity to make inequality enchant."[59] Spectacle was the primary means of doing so, but Geertz shows that this was always relative to the unspectacular spaces and experiences *beyond* the *negara*. The idea of the spectacular center required that exceptional displays be staged there, but centrality ultimately had to be *imagined* by the state and its subjects: "A structure of action, now bloody, now ceremonious, the *negara* was also, and as such, a structure of thought. To describe it is to describe a constellation of enshrined ideas."[60]

To understand the significance of spectacle, Geertz's writing on the *negara* as an exemplary center directs us to look at these structures of thought that extend well beyond the center. If a state draws its force from making inequality enchant, and if spectacle can only ever be intelligible when contrasted with something markedly different outside its immediate manifestation, those inequalities and alternative experiences beyond spectacle's ritual time-space matter deeply. Just as the "center" is a political production, so too is the "periphery" relative and variably defined. Spectacle's unspectacular Others could thus take the shape of slow environmental violence as in Nixon's study, state terror or outright neglect in a country's rural hinterlands, gross socioeconomic inequality, or even the cultural-aesthetic order of a previous political system. In their infinite variations, spectacle's Others are ultimately about how people imagine space and their place in it. Approaching spectacle geographically therefore raises important questions about the spatial imaginaries that spectacle builds and is built upon.

The spatial imaginary common to nearly all forms of spectacle is synecdoche. Commonsensical as it may now be, the synecdochic imaginary is far from neutral. Spectacular cities can be especially appealing for actors seeking to focalize and materially inscribe their political and ideological claims. Not only does the narrow spatial extent of a city offer a unique degree of closure in which to do this, but also cities' semiotic landscapes create many opportunities for political leaders to concretely narrate certain ideological claims in a way that would be prohibitive at the larger scale of a country's entire territory. Yet these practices of rhetorical and material focalization can make sense only to people who are accustomed to abstract spatial thinking, who are able to perform the synecdochic scale-jump of imagining the part as representing the whole. Through strategically directing the gaze toward the spectacular center, synecdochic thinking allows people to imagine its singularity as having much broader social and spatial reach, while diverting attention from the prevailing realities beyond the center.

As the following chapters illustrate, synecdoche is a powerful geopolitical metaphor, which is frequently put to work in legitimating elitist projects. It is the necessary mental trick through which spectacle conveys meaning. For example, when leaders narrate their cities as spectacular sites of progress and state benevolence, they encourage their audiences to imagine the city metaphorically as representative of progress and benevolence across the *entire* territory. This is evident in the case of Kazakhstan's Astana project, which the government of President Nazarbayev consistently frames as a symbol of the country's progress although it disproportionately benefits the elite. Officials nonetheless point to Astana's dazzling new urban landscape to assert that it reflects development and advances made throughout the country and that the city's benefits are accessible to all. As we shall see, this is a guided metaphor—more fiction than fact.

Seemingly singular sites or events are rarely singularities. They constantly overspill temporal and spatial boundaries, as becomes vividly clear when Astana is viewed from the country's neglected peripheries. A spectacle like developing a grand new capital in the middle of Kazakhstan's arid steppe is, as Nixon puts it, rife with "consequential forgettings."[61] The city's development, like all spectacles and the other cases of spectacular urbanism considered in this book, has depended on specific social and material conditions to make it possible, and its countless effects extend, unevenly, across time and space. If synecdoche works to obscure these connections, it is therefore essential to interrogate the geopolitical implications of thinking through synecdoche. Truth, Lakoff and Johnson note, "is always relative to a conceptual system that is defined in large part by metaphor."[62] This is an old argument, also made by Friedrich Nietzsche, but one with great political significance because "the people who get to impose their metaphors on the culture get to define what we consider to be truth."[63] As a metaphor, the synecdochic imaginary may be fictitious, but it has the power to establish certain regimes of truth. And while it is easy to unmask the *fiction* of synecdoche, to understand *the political work it does*, a close study of political geography is needed. We must ask: Who is in the position to impose his or her metaphors? When, where, and for whom?

2

From Almaty to Astana

Capitalizing the Territory in Kazakhstan

In an interview published in 2010, President Nursultan Nazarbayev declared:

> The transfer of the capital to Astana is a landmark event in the history of a new Kazakhstan. For us, the construction of Astana has become a national idea which has unified society and strengthened our young and independent state. This has become the stimulus for our people and it helped them believe in their strength. Today, Astana is the symbol of our high aspirations, our competiveness and unity. . . . The most important thing is that Astana, throughout its development, has indeed become the major city of Kazakhstan. In their hearts, our people have truly nurtured sincere love for our capital. Every year, thousands of people in Kazakhstan seek to come here just to see this majestic symbol of our state. Foreign guests admire Astana, and this suggests that we have done everything well.[1]

Astana, which means "capital" in Kazakh, became Kazakhstan's capital city in 1997, not long after the breakup of the Soviet Union in 1991.

Figure 2.1 Astana's new administrative center skyline.
Source: Natalie Koch, 2011.

President Nazarbayev conceived of the plan shortly after Kazakhstan gained independence, moving it from Almaty, which was the capital of the Kazakh Soviet Socialist Republic (SSR). Nazarbayev frequently describes the city in the same lofty manner—as a symbol of national unity, the strength of the independent state, a gesture of hope for future prosperity, and a shining beacon of modernity for foreign guests to admire, all embodied in the carefully choreographed architecture of the city's new administrative center (see figure 2.1). Yet Nazarbayev has also emphasized the appeal of moving the capital to a more central place within the state's territory. Drawing on this geometric image of centrality, descriptions of Astana's location consistently refer to it as the "heart" of Kazakhstan, and often of the entire continent of Eurasia. Nazarbayev's book about Astana is tellingly titled *In the Heart of Eurasia*.[2]

Although Nazarbayev might be considered the initiator of this discourse, the symbolism of Astana has come to resonate with Kazakhstan's general population and is reproduced through a dense semiotic web, including everyday conversations. For example, at a conference in Astana in July 2011, I introduced myself to a Kazakh historian before the event started. As I was then a graduate student, he asked me about my dissertation research. As usual, I gave the easiest answer: *"perenos stolitsy"* (the capital change). As with many people I met in Kazakhstan, he was delighted that I was researching what he considered to be such an important issue. He then launched into an explanation of why the government moved the capital in 1997. But unlike most people, who generally drew me a mental map with their words, he, completely unprompted and with great excitement, found a blank piece of paper and drew me an actual map, with a big dot in the middle surrounded by a squiggly oval representing Kazakhstan's territory. "Do you know why they moved the capital? Here is Almaty [pointing to a place in the bottom right], and here is Astana [the dot in the middle]. From there [Astana], it is possible to control here [he drew an arrow up], to control here [he drew an arrow to the right], to control here [he drew an arrow down], and to control here [he drew an arrow to the left]!" He spoke briefly about the demographic constitution of the country, but his narrative about the capital change primarily articulated a depopulated space, bounded by geometric lines and controlled by some abstract authority emanating from the central urban node.

What made this interaction possible? What is the origin of this geometric imaginary of Kazakhstan's territory? What can it tell us about the nature of political sovereignty and how capital cities are imagined in relation to the rest of their territories? And what does it say about how citizens understand themselves vis-à-vis the territorial state and their government? By looking closely at the case of Astana and how it is narrated and imagined by multiple actors, we can begin to answer these questions. In Kazakhstan, as elsewhere in the world, geopolitical imaginaries of the state, territory, and political control are not just symbolically enshrined in the capital city but are actively constructed through everyday conversations and interactions. That is, by rhetorically engaging the concept of a capital city, people actively build these abstractions and naturalize the state-based power relations that come with governing a territorial state— an ostensibly discrete, sovereign unit called Kazakhstan.

Territory and Urbanism in Soviet Central Asia

Imagining the territorial state as a discrete and coherent object is rooted in the abstract understandings of space discussed in the previous chapter. Natural and free-floating as it may appear on a map, the territorial state is ultimately an *effect* of political practices coalescing in time and space. The image of a coherent state is socially produced through a wide range of social practices, materialities, and historically and geographically contingent arts of governing. Critical state theorists advancing this approach to the state have largely been influenced by Michel Foucault's writing on governmentality, as well as the large body of literature to which it has given rise.[3] One question, however, continues to challenge these thinkers: If the social world is nothing more than a dense and chaotic network of materialities and relations, how do concepts such as the state calcify and come to acquire this (analytically undue) image of coherence?

This question consistently animated the structure-agency debates of the late 1970s and early 1980s, in which scholars argued about the relative importance of individual agency (and micro-political analysis) versus social structures (and macro-political approaches) for explaining social phenomena. Eventually, most recognized the imprudence of setting up structure and agency as opponents and started to develop various middle-ground concepts and unified frameworks, such as Anthony Giddens's well-known structuration theory.[4] The more nuanced view that emerged from the heated debate was that scholars need to describe and explain the structure-like character resulting from, and often shaping, the tangled mess of discrete practices undertaken by individual actors. In fact, critics of the Foucauldian approach to governmentality fault him and those working in his intellectual tradition for still fixating excessively on agency. They fail to see a mediating framework that joins structure and agency in research on the "state effect."

Foucault understood this problem quite well, however. Though few scholars have given it due consideration, he did develop his own mediating framework: the notion of "transactional realities" (*réalités de transaction*). A transactional reality is Foucault's term for social constructs such as "madness" or "civil society" that are not timeless, "primary or immediate" realities. But they are "real" insofar as they have real effects in the world. They are also historically dated and transactional, since they are "born precisely from the interplay of relations of power and everything which constantly eludes them, at the interface, so to speak, of governors and governed."[5] Transactional realities, in short, are the cumulative effect of governmental practices. This is Foucault's mediating framework between structures and practices. It encapsulates the process whereby various practices and materialities are channeled and woven into a myth of coherence. The state is one such transactional reality.

Considering the state as a transactional reality pushes us to ask precisely how the state is reified, how it is materially and rhetorically reproduced, and with what effects.[6] It also forces us to grapple with the specific practices that both shape and are shaped by its place in the modern geographic imagination. Like all metaphors we live by, the territorial state system helps to organize experience and "establish certain cognitive frames that guide daily experiences and imaginaries."[7] Most people live and think in a world of discrete units of territory, imagined as neat blocs of depopulated space—just like the map drawn for me by the Kazakh historian. While the territorial state remains the most salient political unit in world affairs today, this abstract spatial imaginary must be learned. But how does that happen? The answers are far less obvious, but some insights can be gleaned from the case of Kazakhstan.

Since Astana took over the capital city role, it has been the centerpiece of the government's state- and nation-building agenda. Official accounts suggest that the site of the capital was chosen for a variety of reasons, but elite and popular narratives repeatedly stress its *central location* within Kazakhstan's territory. The image of territorial centrality must be underpinned by abstract spatial thinking, however; the country has to be visualized as a geometrically defined unit of space in order for this claim to make sense. But once it is imagined as an abstraction, political power is layered on top, as if it could be diffused over the territory with the quick stroke of a pen drawing arrows in every cardinal direction. This geopolitical imaginary, illustrated by the map my colleague in Kazakhstan drew, is actually quite an old one. In Alexandre Le Maître's 1682 text on an ideal capital city, *La Métropolitée*, the author connects the effectiveness of sovereignty to the even circulation of power over space:

> It must be a geometrical relationship in the sense that a good country is one that, in short, must have the form of a circle, and the capital must be right at the center of the circle. A capital at the end of an elongated and irregular territory would not be able to exercise all its necessary functions. In fact, this is where the second, aesthetic and symbolic, relationship between the capital and territory appears. The capital must be the ornament of the territory. But this must also be a political relationship in that the decrees and laws must be implanted in the territory [in such a way] that no tiny corner of the realm escapes this general network of the sovereign's orders and laws.[8]

Upon deeper reflection, the idea that political effectiveness can be *spatially* located and diffused might seem dubious. It is nonetheless a common trope in geopolitical thinking. But of all political sites, it is most often articulated with reference to a city. This raises the question: Why the city? Why not conceive of a diffuse spatiality of power decentralized across the territory? What makes the central, point-based nature of a capital so powerful? Answering these questions with respect to contemporary Kazakhstan demands that we trace the historical role of urbanism locally and regionally.

Urban planning in the Soviet Union is one of the best historical examples of how state-scale actors seek to inscribe their authority and their ideological visions in the built landscape and, in so doing, shape their political subjects.[9] In Soviet planning, cities were deemed ideal venues for promoting a uniquely Soviet way of life. Beginning in the 1930s, Communist Party rhetoric drew extensively on urban development and architectural tropes to define the state's mass social transformation agenda.[10] Urbanism was a key element of their "civilizing mission" across the newly Soviet lands of Eurasia. Marx and Engels had, after all, written of the city in *The Communist Manifesto* as "rescuing the people from the idiocy of rural life."[11] With the Bolshevik rise to power, planners positioned cities as bastions of progress and modernity, and they were tasked with spreading new communist ideals to the rest of the state's territory.[12] In his foundational work on Magnitogorsk, the historian Stephen Kotkin vividly illustrates the central role of city-building in Soviet efforts to consolidate state power, with planners envisioning an ambitious, if metaphorical, army of model cities to advance the state's "internal territorial colonization."[13]

Urbanism in Central Asia was especially symbolic because these territories had only somewhat recently been incorporated into the Russian Empire on the eve of the October Revolution. This meant that the Bolsheviks did not inherit firm bureaucratic networks of territorial administration in the region. Central Asia was also characterized by extremely low levels of urbanization, with the exception of communities in the narrow Fergana Valley and a handful of ancient cities such as Samarkand and Bukhara. Prior to Russian colonialism, the region was elsewhere dominated by nomadic herders moving seasonally across the expansive steppe lands. Despite the limited development of city life at that time, the steppe was never barren or depopulated, as Russian imperial narratives typically suggested. But as with so many other colonial encounters around the world, nomadic populations were not seen as having legitimate claims to the land. Furthermore, their mobile lifestyle was considered a threat and a sign of cultural backwardness. Imperial authorities therefore deemed settlement of these groups imperative for "the advancement of enlightened rule."[14] Colonial efforts to "civilize" space in Central Asia (that is, to fix people in place) had their roots in the Russian imperial era. Nonetheless, many locals were still nomadic when the transition to Bolshevik rule began in the 1920s. The new authorities embarked on relentless sedentarization and collectivization campaigns in the 1920s and 1930s. As wide-reaching as they were brutal, these policies resulted in mass famine and millions of deaths across the region.[15] Local opposition to Soviet rule and the horrific consequences of these campaigns notwithstanding, the Bolsheviks seamlessly adopted Russian colonial narratives about being the bearers of civilization. It was in this context that urban development came to be seen as one of the primary tools of the Soviet civilizing mission in Central Asia.

Where cities were already developed, urban planners sought to reconfigure them around modernist ideals of order and straight lines, already advocated under the Russian Empire. Cities like Tashkent, for example, were imagined by early Russian settlers as dangerous and unhealthy because of their labyrinthine nature, allegedly fostering "fanaticism, disease, and rebellion."[16] Soviet planners likewise dwelled on the primitive, unhealthy, and uncomfortable nature of Central Asian towns. They often spoke derogatorily about the non-gridded urban patterns, which were cast as a symbol of an outdated social order. Prevailing urban structures were also a barrier to their calculation projects, effectively concealing spaces and individuals from the view of police, census takers, and others. Thus, across Central Asia, urban interventions (framed as improvement or renewal campaigns) centered on breaking down "traditional" social relations and fostering new, modern Soviet identities. Through these narratives, the people of Central Asia were cast as cultural Others, or "younger brothers" in Soviet parlance, in stark contrast to their allegedly more civilized Russian counterparts. This civilizational discourse also advanced a hierarchical view that cast Russian cities and territories as naturally superior to their Central Asian counterparts.

Within this geopolitical ordering of Soviet space, Moscow was to become an exemplar for officials seeking to affirm the new state's power. Following the Russian Revolution, Lenin transferred the capital from

St. Petersburg to Moscow in 1918. As the definitively *Bolshevik* capital, Moscow was to be revamped around communist ideological principles and to serve as the USSR's prime model of urban development and morphology. It was not merely the seat of the government; its entire built form was framed as the source of enlightenment for citizens in the farthest reaches of Soviet territory. Moscow was supposed to inspire the vast country's new citizens and serve as a propagandistic shop window at the center of the worldwide communist movement. Josef Stalin was especially vocal about the need for the capital's built environment to reflect the Soviet Union's superpower status. From his skyscrapers to the Moscow Metro, Stalin's mega-projects projected this image with the intent to instill pride in the Soviet masses, strike fear in the Soviet Union's rivals, and—just maybe!—win over new political allies to the communist cause.[17] As with other world capitals, Moscow's symbolism was projected both inward to the imagined national community and outward to the international community, inextricably linking the city to the multifarious processes of state-building. The symbolic importance of the capital was not lost on Communist Party officials, who were quick to advocate ambitious plans for Moscow and, in so doing, claim sovereign authority and international legitimacy for the Soviet state. Visions and visualizations of Moscow were indeed instrumental to achieving their geopolitical aims.

Part of institutionalizing the Soviet Union's nested territorial structure involved assigning each unit a capital, the status of which mirrored the specific territory's place in the state's administrative hierarchy (union-level republics, autonomous republics, regions, and so on). With Moscow at the apex of the country's urban hierarchy, the capitals of the other fourteen union-level republics were the next step down. Republic capitals served a secondary purpose and did not receive the same lavish attention as Moscow, but they were nonetheless adorned according to their status in the urban hierarchy. Other cities around the country took on a unique significance in the USSR's early state-making efforts, such as Stalin's spectacular greenfield development of Magnitogorsk, which Kotkin chronicles, and Tashkent as the privileged showpiece of the Soviet Union's modernizing capabilities in Central Asia.

As a union-level republic, the Kazakh SSR (and today's Kazakhstan) did not have its borders finalized until some years into the development of

the Soviet Union as a territorial state. The republic's first territorial itera-
tion was as the Kyrgyz Autonomous Soviet Socialist Republic in August
1920, and Orenburg, in present-day Russia, was designated as the capital. In April 1925 the territory was renamed the Kazakh Autonomous
Soviet Socialist Republic, with Kyzylorda designated as the new capital.
The capital moved once more, in 1929, to Alma-Ata (originally founded
in 1854 as Vernyi, a military township).[18] Finally, in 1936, the territory
was accorded union-level republic status, officially becoming the Kazakh
Soviet Socialist Republic. The nested territorial hierarchy of the Soviet
Union meant that union-level republics had all the trappings of an independent state already in place, so with the collapse of the USSR in 1991,
the state disintegrated along republican lines. What Russian president
Vladimir Putin later famously called "the greatest geopolitical tragedy of
the twentieth century," the event was fundamentally a transformation of
the representational organization of space: what was once imagined as
one territorial state became a set of fifteen sovereign territorial units, each
with its own predetermined capital.

Alma-Ata, renamed Almaty shortly after Kazakhstan's independence,
was the new state's capital city by default. But not for long. Nursultan
Nazarbayev, who was the Communist Party chair of the Kazakh SSR,
became the country's first president, and in 1994 he announced his inten-
tion to move the capital to Astana. The city officially acquired that status
in 1997, and with it, a new name. Prior to Russian colonization it was
known as Aqmola and was later renamed Tselinograd by Soviet leaders.
To mark its status as the capital of independent Kazakhstan, it became
Astana, which simply means "capital" in Kazakh. Perhaps not ending
there, some presidential cronies have been discussing the possibility of
changing the name once more to Nursultan when the leader eventually
passes. As these various name changes suggest, people during the Soviet
era and still today invest place-names with a great deal of symbolic value.
This is especially true of capitals, largely due to the fact that Soviet citizens,
like so many others around the world, understood them to be principal
sites of encounter with the outside world. As synecdoche, capital cities are
where many foreigners first come to know a polity, place, region, or territory. Whether expressed in the name of a capital or its built environment,
the desire to organize urban space in a particular manner thus stems from

specific, and specifically geopolitical, representational concerns about outside perceptions and projections.

Representational Concerns in Independent Kazakhstan

When Kazakhstan became independent in 1991, its new leaders were keen to craft an image of the country not only as a legitimate sovereign state but also as market-oriented and ready to engage internationally. Authorities wanted (or at least felt compelled) to throw off their former communist identity. Seeing it as their best hope for escaping the economic turmoil that would prevail in the 1990s, they worked strenuously to portray Kazakhstan as a modern polity and an exciting emerging market, ideal for investment. Unfortunately for them, the British comedian Sacha Baron Cohen interfered. Certainly not out of any malice toward Kazakhstan in particular, Cohen was looking for a country that most Western TV viewers would deem obscure for his fictional television character Borat. Said to hail from Kazakhstan, Borat portrayed the country as a backward and intolerant place. When Cohen transformed the short sketches from *Da Ali G Show* into a highly successful feature film in 2006, *Borat: Cultural Learnings of America for Make Benefit Glorious Nation of Kazakhstan*, the country's leadership was sent into a frenzy.[19] To be sure, they were previously preoccupied with Kazakhstan's international image, especially after losing the alleged "great power status" that came with being part of the USSR and which was so fundamental to Soviet nationalism. But Borat's farcical backwardness hit a nerve because it was precisely the image that leaders were trying to efface. In the years since the film's release, the government has relentlessly pursued a strategy of putting Kazakhstan "on the map" in a more positive light, amounting to what is referred to as the state's "image project" (*imidzh proyekt*). They have poured millions of dollars into a multimedia public relations campaign, launched countless internationally oriented projects, and spent lavishly on lobbying in the United States and elsewhere (including hiring think tanks to produce positive reports about the country).[20]

Within this context, Astana took on a special role in the effort to reshape Kazakhstan's image in the mind's eye of both foreigners and citizens. The international image project thus became a nation-building project simultaneously broadcast *inward* to domestic audiences and *outward* for foreign consumption.[21] The dominant themes in Western writing and public discourse about the country do not readily conform to the regime's message of being a young, modern country overseen by President Nazarbayev's "enlightened" leadership, however. Western commentators have instead consistently read and represented the government's various development projects as symptomatic of Nazarbayev's megalomania and false pretensions to modernity. This is exemplified in media coverage of Astana that portrays it as a utopian fantasyland, as described in the previous chapter. This notwithstanding, the Borat scandal lent further credibility and a sense of urgency to the government's imaging campaign—as well as its capital city development scheme in Astana, which had in fact been quite contentious previously.

In his book *Kazakhstan's Way* (*Kazakhstanskii Put'*), President Nazarbayev offers various reasons for his decision to move the capital. The move was initially unpopular because the city was to be developed in the middle of the country's barren steppe, consuming and extending Tselinograd, which was a run-down provincial town in the 1990s. Nazarbayev envisioned a gleaming new city rising both from this steppe and from the hardship of the post-Soviet transition. This spectacular vision was hard for most people to imagine at the time, but it was precisely this impression of spectacle that Nazarbayev wanted to cultivate. In *Kazakhstan's Way* and elsewhere, the president tells of how he overcame major obstacles and saw his will prevail. Descriptions of the capital change decision sometimes temper that fact that he unilaterally made the move by pointing to technical studies conducted by a committee of experts and parliamentary debates. In one account, he even tells how he encouraged discussion within his own family about the move.[22] Yet these pretensions to democratic decision making are usually only footnotes to a broader narrative about the city as Nazarbayev's personal project: "It was a huge risk, and I took it intuitively. I put everything at stake, including my career and my name."[23] In the end, he explains, "I had to be the one to make the decision and answer for it."[24] And so he did.

In recounting the steps he undertook to move the capital, Nazarbayev invariably describes the political and logistical challenges he faced, with a common theme being the lack of support he received from parliamentary deputies. He describes those who opposed him as *politiki*, politicians uninterested in the good of the country: "There is a very specific boundary, differentiating politiki from responsible politicians and statesmen. If the former think about the next battle, then the latter think about the good of the people and the future of the country. Those who doubted the capital change did not want to understand the essence of the matter. It is very easy to spark hysterics [*razduvat' isteriyu*] surrounding an unpopular decision and present oneself as the 'voice of the people.' We have many such politiki in our country."[25] Here Nazarbayev demonizes the politicians who doubted his resolution to move the capital from Almaty, where they enjoyed a comfortable life in a pleasant city. He tells of his own love of Almaty and his reluctance to leave it. But unlike these politiki, he saw a higher calling and knew that "the interests of the country and objective factors" were more important than any "personal" attachments.[26] As Edward Schatz has argued, the capital change helped the government identify and subsequently weed out the disloyal cadres.[27] Having an immediate disciplining effect and quickly eliminating any dissenters, the move was perhaps more significant for its lasting didactic effect for elites. It was a rehearsal of how to demonstrate loyalty in the new configuration of power relations. Those who failed to support the decision swiftly learned the consequences of dissent and served as examples for others. As one of the few points on which Nazarbayev was challenged in his early years, it has defined his presidency since.

Furthermore, in describing his opponents, Nazarbayev was able to position himself as a fatherly guardian interested only in the "good of the people" and the "future of the country." Through setting up an opposition between politiki and "responsible politicians and statesmen," the official rhetoric endowed the president with an aura of paternal magnanimity and unparalleled visionary prowess. To moderate some of the self-aggrandizing rhetoric that imbues this state-building project, Nazarbayev has often assigned his own majesty to Astana. Yet the two frequently slip into each other in the official discourse: "In their hearts, our people have truly nurtured sincere love for our capital. Every year, thousands of people in Kazakhstan seek to come here just to see this majestic symbol of our state."[28] All over the city, citizens are routinely reminded that it is their "beloved city" on billboards, posters, and other placards (figure 2.2). And the pinnacle of any citizen's trip to Astana is placing one's hand in a

Figure 2.2 Billboard reading "My heart—Astana!" with Astana's skyline in the background and on the boy's shirt.
Source: Natalie Koch, 2009.

golden cast of Nazarbayev's handprint, located inside the golden orb of the city's gleaming Baiterek tower (figure 2.3).

While some Kazakhstanis remain deeply skeptical of the project, for many it truly is their beloved city. And in nurturing a love for the capital, these proud subjects simultaneously nurture a love for their paternalistic leader. In the capital change discussions, Nazarbayev enacts his benevolence not simply by presiding over the city's development but also in taming the politiki, who needed a reorientation of their priorities toward the "good of the people." All these conversations, from the banal to the stately, naturalize the idea that the country benefits from a strong leader who can subordinate parliamentary deputies and win the adoration of the citizenry—themselves passively supportive but ultimately excluded from decision-making processes. This is clearly an autocratic vision of politics. But it also describes a distinctly paternalistic relationship between the ruler and the ruled: the benevolent parent figure is imagined to look out for an infantilized population of thankful citizens, entrenching a relation of "childlike dependence on state power" to ensure that "the leadership could never be legitimately questioned."[29]

Beyond affirming a paternalistic vision of politics in the newly independent state, Nazarbayev's relentless discussions of Astana also worked to situate Kazakhstan within the imagined global community of states.

Figure 2.3 Visitors placing their hands in Nazarbayev's golden handprint
at the top of Baiterek's golden orb.
Source: Natalie Koch, 2015.

In response to some very concrete realities in the early years of independence (such as Russian claims on Caspian territory and hydrocarbon deposits and Russian nationalists advocating the annexation of Kazakhstan's northern territories), the president doggedly pursued recognition as a legitimate and sovereign state by the international community.[30] This is especially visible when he emphasizes how a prestigious capital is one of the most essential stamps of statehood. In his book on Astana, Nazarbayev evinces a fixation with the historical precedence of capital changes throughout the world and provides a lengthy exposition on other capital city relocation projects, going as far back as Alexander of Macedonia's relocation of his capital to Babylon.[31] According to him, the development of a capital city gains the credibility and aura of a time-worn tradition and hallmark of historically notable states.[32] For Nazarbayev and his supporters, Astana is narrated as a "proper" capital and thus serves as evidence of Kazakhstan's equivalence to other recognized states, thereby authorizing the state's legitimacy in the post-Soviet period.

In addition to making the decision to move the capital, Nazarbayev has narrated the visual image of the city as his own project. Describing the early planning, he tells of drawing sketches for various buildings: "I shared all my thoughts with the architects. The construction and constructional elaboration were done. I inspired the architects and they developed the actual projects." As if to confirm this guiding role, he is frequently photographed presiding over architectural models and traipsing through construction sites. Nazarbayev sees himself not as a naïve observer but as someone legitimately qualified to undertake such a project: "I myself started to research thoroughly the issues of city building. And what really helped me in this area was that I had gone through a very good management experience. In the past, while in diverse leadership positions, I also had to face the issues of city building and architecture." If, as he claims, "Astana is Kazakhstan in miniature," then he is the sagacious leader who can preside not only over the capital's construction but also over the construction of the new state.[33]

The construction site as a nation-building metaphor further emphasizes rapid, almost miraculous development. This is readily apparent in Nazarbayev's habit of underscoring the impressive speed with which the new capital has risen from a (not very) blank slate: "In a record short time, we have built the new capital city in the very heart of our nation. Every visitor to Astana is amazed by its transformation."[34] As if racing to fend off a utopian "moment of disenchantment—of recognizing the dream *as* dream"—Nazarbayev is eager to demonstrate that his dream has become a reality.[35] "Of course," he writes, "to only dream of building a new capital and realizing that dream are two different things."[36] But by his own account, he has already prevailed: "It was a dream. Now—it is a true [*chudesnyi*] city, the pride and heart of Kazakhstan." With a population of only 275,000 in 1998, reaching one million in 2017, for the new capital's founder, "Astana is a city-sign, a sign of dreams, incarnated in reality."[37]

Finally, paralleling Soviet discourses about capital cities as geopolitical shop windows, Nazarbayev has sought to position Astana as a means of attracting international capital.[38] For foreign audiences in particular, his government has tried to craft an image of Kazakhstan as market-oriented. The image of Astana as a site of economic opportunity is central to this effort to narrate the country as politically and economically reformed in the post-Soviet era: "Shifting the status of the capital city from Almaty to the new city that is open to the wind of changes has given a powerful impetus to the overall development of the country. The new capital should become the symbol of changes."[39] In elite narratives about the capital change, both about the decision to move the capital and the material shape it has taken, President Nazarbayev is clearly articulated as the ultimate authority in the country's political sphere. But if he is the supreme governor, then who and what constitute the governed?

In narrating himself as the father of the new capital, Nazarbayev, and sometimes the state more generally, is cast as the deliverer of these opportunities to a passive set of recipients, the social body. The benevolent provision of opportunity through the city's construction boom is indicative of the Nazarbayev paternalism, which has echoes and historical precedents in various other developmental regimes.[40] In the official rhetoric about Astana, Nazarbayev is not just overseeing the city's and the country's development. He is also described as managing a number of new entities: a wayward governmental bureaucracy; a sovereign territory with new borders and a complex demographic makeup; and an underdeveloped society. Each of these sites of government represents his own construction of the governed in his paternalist vision of rule in Kazakhstan. Yet the governor-governed or state-society relationship is certainly not the exclusive domain of elites.

The capital city project gains much of its traction and appeal from ordinary citizens of all backgrounds, whose own narratives and spatial imaginaries play an important role in confirming the spectacle at the center. Critical or oppositional narratives are common enough, but many people actively buttress the paternalistic manner of thinking about the state and authority in Kazakhstan. Sometimes this is conscious and other times it is not. For example, when discussing the capital change, people generally talk about "our" president as the sole decision maker in the process. By narrating Nazarbayev as "ours," the speaker situates himself or herself as a subject of his authority. But the speaker also locates himself or herself definitively outside the state apparatus and any relevant political deliberations. With Astana as a convenient icon and synecdoche of Nazarbayev's visionary acumen and interest in the "good of the people," it becomes a common reference point for citizens to affirm their gratitude toward "their" benevolent autocrat.

"It's for the People": Synecdoche and Subjectivity

"The monarch's person had a public aspect," writes Paul Veyne. "He enjoyed the private relationship of a father or of a patron with the plebs of his capital. The events of his family life were occasions for rejoicing or mourning for all his subjects and he accorded, or allowed to be accorded, divine honours from his favourites. He displayed in Rome and at the Circus a degree of pomp which turned the Eternal City into something like a king's court."[41] In many ways, Nazarbayev's relationship with Astana parallels the imperial Roman monarch's relationship with Rome. In Nazarbayev's court, Astana is where all of Kazakhstan's notable elites are gathered around him, where his birthday is celebrated with splendor on Astana Day, where the best entertainers and education can be found, where the modern architectural treasures are rapidly being constructed, where international delegations are hosted, and where the citizens receive special treatment. Like the emperor, Nazarbayev is the "sole *patronus* of his City," which is imagined to be the pinnacle of the country's politico-spatial hierarchy befitting his supreme political position. The splendor of Astana must not be the product of anyone else's generosity, as with its ancient prototype: "It was *urbs sua*, the city that was wholly devoted to the Emperor, wholly his," and "the jewel-case wherein the sovereign should shine alone."[42]

In both places, the recipients of the sovereign's munificence are the citizens of the capital; President Nazarbayev has no courtiers, just as the Roman emperors had none.[43] In imperial Rome, bread and circuses were for the masses, who were always accorded the role of passive recipients or spectators. The same paternalist relations are at work in Nazarbayev's

Astana, where the state's spending on bread and circuses is primarily reserved for the capital. And as in Rome, bread and circuses are *not* redistributive in Astana.[44] That is, if state benevolence were to serve the purpose of redistributing wealth, vastly different measures beyond building a beautiful new capital would be necessary. In their current spectacular configuration, by contrast, official investments in the city directly benefit only a tiny segment of the population. The overarching effect of Astana's development for the masses is thus more symbolic than material. To tap into the synecdochic imaginary, state beneficence is designed to give the *impression* that similar developments and generosity are found universally in Kazakhstan and that they are accessible to all. As I have already argued, it is less important to reject this narrative as false: that much is obvious. More illuminating is the question of how people take up such ideas and make them their own. In my conversations with ordinary people in Kazakhstan over the years, it is clear that they are well trained in thinking synecdochically about Astana and spectacle more broadly. Many certainly find the synecdoche to be unconvincing, but they are at least conversant in the metaphor's unique contours.

"*Eto dlya naroda,*" a taxi driver from southeast Kazakhstan once told me during the Astana Day celebrations in the capital city: "it's for the people." Astana Day is a holiday to commemorate the moving of the capital, and, not coincidentally, it is celebrated on President Nazarbayev's birthday, July 6. Every year millions of dollars are poured into an extravagant multi-day program of concerts, exhibitions, and official ceremonies in Astana in the days leading up to the holiday. Other cities and towns in Kazakhstan have celebrations, but they are generally held only on Astana Day itself, and are extremely limited by comparison. Many of the Astana Day festivities are the same as those of other official state celebrations, such as the country's Independence Day. But unlike at cultural or non-state celebrations such as Navruz (a Persian New Year celebration), which are quite popular, attendance at the Astana Day events is remarkably sparse. Nor is it accompanied by extensive family socializing and communal gatherings at people's homes. The anthropologist Mateusz Laszczkowski makes the important point that we should not immediately dismiss the possibility that ordinary Kazakhstanis "might actually enjoy such celebrations of statehood," but the relative unpopularity of Astana Day raises questions about the subjectivity of those *not* in attendance.[45]

If the festivities are "for the people," then where are all the people? How can we interpret their decision not to spectate?

Astana Day cannot be avoided in the capital, but the event itself is rarely the subject of much discussion. People are largely aware that the government spends extravagant sums of money on the festivities, but few raise vocal objections.[46] The vast majority of the city's residents, who do not attend the holiday's various events, would never explain their absence as an act of resistance or outright disapproval of its extravagance. If asked to reflect critically on their reaction, some people might be willing to characterize the events as a "sham," as one especially candid informant in Astana put it to me in 2011. But when asked why they do not attend Astana Day celebrations and other major state-sponsored events, the vast majority of my respondents would give mundane excuses: tickets were too expensive, they were busy with work, they had already made other plans, they were not interested, or they did not like mixing with the other people in attendance (the last being a particularly classist argument from the city's more affluent residents, who look down on the largely rural-origin demographic attracted to the state events).[47]

Such passive dismissals continue patterns that characterized celebration culture during Soviet times and actually represent a significant political practice. This argument is made forcefully by the anthropologist Alexei Yurchak, who explains that detached or minimal engagement with the state's celebration-mongering was a staple of late Soviet socialism, a time when people were constantly being forced to participate in mass events of one sort or another.[48] Soviet citizens understood that there were essentially three kinds of political subjects in the USSR: anti-regime *dissidents* and pro-regime *aktivists*, which were both fringe groups, and the "normal" subjects. The last designation represented most people—those who simply wanted to get on with life and stay out of politics to the greatest extent possible. When it came to celebration culture, Yurchak argues: "Participating in [ritualized] acts reproduced oneself as a 'normal' Soviet person within the system of relations, collectivities, and subject positions, with all the constraints and possibilities that position entailed. . . . These acts are not about stating facts and describing opinions but about doing things and opening new possibilities."[49] In the latter days of the USSR, when official ideology and rhetoric were so obviously out of synch with reality, "normal" subjects realized that "the only sensible behavior in the public sphere was the pretense that one did not see the falsity of the official claims." While these ritualized behaviors were *strategic,* Yurchak argues that they were not necessarily *calculated;* they simply "allowed one to live a 'normal' life and be 'left alone' by the system."[50] Living under a similar political system, most citizens in contemporary Kazakhstan would also identify as "normal" subjects, just wanting to get by. It is these subjects in particular who express indifference or boredom in explaining their failure to engage in political discussions or attend state spectacles.

On the basis of my participant observation experiences at the Astana Day events in Astana in 2009 and 2011, and in Pavlodar in 2011, I can empathize with their boredom. In Pavlodar, for example, the celebration of Astana Day primarily consisted of a series of live performances on the city's main square. The vast majority of these performances involved people of various ages singing about Kazakhstan and its new capital city. After a few hours of hearing one song after another with the same refrain, *"menim Astanam"* (my Astana), the repetition became tiresome—not just for me, but clearly for the rapidly thinning crowd of spectators. Writing on similarly repetitive spectacles in Uzbekistan, Laura Adams argues, "The production of kitsch allows the cultural elite to free themselves of the need to engage in a critical creative process; it provides them an easy and automatic route to a cultural product that will satisfy the only truly important audience: the political elite."[51] I would add that kitsch is simply safer and easier: following the official formula does not require extra thought, and it avoids any potential political risks.

Aside from watching the singers at Pavlodar's Astana Day celebration, there was not much for spectators to do besides walk up and down the main street, socializing with friends and family. The same can be said of many of the events in Astana. In both cities, most attendees at the Astana Day events are teenagers and young families with small children. The youth were invariably dressed to the hilt, on full display for one another. For them, the event was a social activity, which they experienced more in personal terms rather than in terms of political issues. Yet while many attendees at the Astana Day events might consciously or subconsciously tune out the political and ideological messages of the holiday (primarily glorifying President Nazarbayev and other nationalist clichés), their attendance nonetheless legitimates the event. By giving it life, any sort of participation opens the possibility that the celebration will gain the aura of being a "real" tradition, rather than an "artificial" event, as it is still widely considered. To illustrate the inauthenticity of Astana Day, ordinary Kazakhstanis would often contrast it with the country's ostensibly more "organic" New Year's Eve celebrations. Ironically, the way people celebrate New Year's in Kazakhstan today was a Soviet invention, designed to take the place of Christmas celebrations—"New Year's tree" and all.[52] Only with time did the holiday come to be seen as an authentic tradition.

In any case, when spectators say that it is simply boring, they are not necessarily (or at least directly) engaging the political issues surrounding the invented tradition. For them, it really is experienced as boredom. We would be led astray if we were to assume that there is some undercurrent of "true" political feelings that this narrative is strategically masking. This is the common liberalist interpretation of such acts of passive refusal, but it is problematic insofar as it tends to confine agency to subversive political action.[53] Yet the choice *not* to spectate has important political effects, even if it does not conform to liberalist notions of resistance. To interpret boredom as a code or veiled criticism would be to perpetuate a one-dimensional understanding of power as some force existing external to these individuals and their mundane practices.[54] The problem with this approach is that it positions Kazakhstan's citizens as—at least mentally—somewhere *outside* the structures of power that prevail in the country. On the contrary, their mere refusal to participate is a deeply political form of submission, which is crucial to the smooth running of a paternalist social order and to the system's perpetuation.

To see passive refusals to engage as instrumental to supporting unequal power structures is not a normative judgment. Rather, nonparticipation is a form of subjectivity that arises under specific political conditions. It even extends to many democratic countries, where it is commonplace for small percentages of the voting population to actually show up on election day. This is an issue famously addressed by Elmer Schattschneider in *The Semisovereign People*. Writing on politics in the United States, he begins by arguing that the political process can be understood as a sort of conflict consisting of two parts: "(1) the few individuals who are actively engaged at the center and (2) the audience that is irresistibly attracted to the scene."[55] The outcome of any given conflict depends on the extent to which the audience is involved, and, he suggests, this explains the long-standing struggle between conflicting tendencies in all polities to "privatize" or "socialize" conflict. Some actors benefit from involving more parties (socializing the conflict), while others would benefit more from restricting the scope of conflict, or even "keep[ing] it entirely out of the public domain," thus privatizing the conflict.[56] In the United States, politics is largely socialized because the masses are theoretically invited to join the conflict through the election process (albeit in an often distorted manner, as Gramsci would argue).[57] Under paternalist authoritarianism, such as we find in contemporary Kazakhstan, leaders are more inclined to privatize the scope of politics. In so doing, they actively cultivate a governmental style that hinges on promoting and colonizing the population's passive disengagement from politics. This is just as important as, or perhaps even more important than, the activity of the most engaged and enthusiastic attendees. So while the participants and abstainers choose a different relationship to themselves, they are ultimately both sideline spectators in the overarching structuring of politics in the country.

Even when people choose not to participate actively in celebrations like Astana Day, they do frequently consume and display the nationalist paraphernalia that is widely distributed surrounding state-sponsored spectacles. At the Asian Winter Games in January 2011, for example, authorities simply could not draw crowds, despite eventually giving away tickets for free. Yet the event was curiously accompanied by an overwhelming proliferation of miniature Kazakhstan flags mounted on the dashboard of Astana residents' vehicles. It was a small gesture, but it is exemplary of how citizens in contemporary Kazakhstan (and I would argue most countries) are happy to demonstrate their patriotic spirit in a manner that is not overly demanding. By simply displaying a flag, people can show they are good citizens in a manner that requires much less time, energy, and expense than attending a large event. Being born into a nation, citizen-spectators do not actually have to do anything to make the national team "theirs." It makes no difference that the spectators undergo none of the physical exertion of those athlete-representatives or political figureheads; their mere spectating validates them as supporters and members of the community. Of course, some may desire a more active role, and they will seek it out as athletes, performers, or politicians. Crucially, though, the synecdochic imaginary allows the actions of these few to be extrapolated to the remainder of the passive masses.

The more passive subjectivity of sitting on the sidelines also feels safer and more comfortable for many people. The desire to live a normal life means that they do not wish to engage with "political" (i.e., dangerous) issues. This was made clear to me when an informant in Astana once asked for my view on Kazakhstan's politics: "What do you think about it? We don't have democracy, do we?" I responded by saying, no, but it seemed to me that many people did not care because they have economic opportunities, and life in Kazakhstan is rapidly improving. "Yes, exactly!" she exclaimed. "I don't care what they do there [gesturing to the administrative center], because I have a good job and can live normally [*normal'no*]." When I gave the example of my travels to the poor and environmentally devastated Aral Sea region, suggesting that perhaps not everyone in the country has access to such opportunity, she responded, "Yes, I have heard that people in Semipalatinsk [Nuclear Test Site] have similar problems, that they are not happy."[58]

I have had this same conversation dozens of times. For this woman, as with many others, life is sufficiently tolerable that one should not rock the boat. Although there is a general awareness that the country's political system might not be acceptable for others in their country, Astana's residents seldom criticize the inequalities themselves; it is usually "hearsay" about others' concerns. Typically, the speaker mentions the nuclear-contaminated Semipalatinsk region and cites the critical narratives of the region's residents, but never claims to share their view. One young man from Oskemen, for instance, told me that many people in Semipalatinsk are unhappy (*nedovol'ny*) and *they* say, "Why do we need a new capital when we have to live as poorly as we do?" Or with another Astana informant's narrative: "Well, some people see that the government is spending millions of dollars on these celebrations, and that it is not right. But people don't like to talk about this, because what can they change? That is the way it is, and there is no point to speaking up. Some people may want to raise a criticism, but they don't speak." In these examples, the speaker never claims the dissident position; it is always someone else's. The unwillingness to own the critique may be a function of how well these respondents know me, a foreign researcher, but the uniformity of this narrative suggests that it has become a cultural trope that is repeated without thinking, "substituting cliché for thought."[59] In either case, the effect is the same: the speaker refuses the subject position of being an oppositional speaker. This relationship with the self is effectively one of self-preservation, even if it is rarely experienced as such consciously. In any case, it is still a way of critiquing the government and its policies. It bears repeating that such practices should not be construed as a "veiled" form of criticism; rather, they are a passive or indirect way of making the same point—just as a passive sentence construction says the same thing as an active construction, but in a different form.

Equally, for some urbanites, refusing to attend the Astana Day celebrations may be a passive form of critiquing the government. More often, though, people do not consciously experience it as an act of critique; they are truly bored or uninterested and attach no ideological weight to those sentiments. This is precisely the same dynamic that Schattschneider notes in his effort to explain the subjectivity of the 40 million nonvoting Americans who nonetheless typically profess deep commitment to democracy: "*The process is automatic, unconscious, and thoughtless. People reconcile their democratic faith and their undemocratic behavior by remaining comfortably unaware of the inconsistency of theory and practice.*"[60] Similarly, in Kazakhstan, many people are happy to display their national pride and take pleasure in the bread and circuses afforded to them, when it is not too taxing on their resources, inclinations, and ideological principles. Though it may change with time, the dominant form of citizen engagement vis-à-vis the state today remains one of "normal" subjects trying to stay out of politics. This is thanks both to inherited Soviet legacies that marked the lived experience of millions who grew up under the USSR, and to the experience of the millions more who have known politics only as the nondemocratic rule of Nursultan Nazarbayev. Although I have discussed nonparticipation in the context of spectacle, it reflects more broadly on subjectification practices under the paternalist Nazarbayev regime. The government's use of spectacle as a political technology both represents and materializes a sort of spectator citizenship, whereby state benevolence is something to be broadcast and observed but never substantively engaged. In this formulation, ordinary citizens are to be passive recipients and spectators, not active participants, in the affairs of the state.

As in Schattschneider's example, banal forms of disengagement are undeniably political. This is because silence is something that the government comes to count on and the overall quiescence of the population facilitates the implementation of elitist projects. Exemplified in the grandiose Astana development scheme, such projects are primarily funded by diverting money from state coffers that might otherwise go toward more redistributive measures (spatially and generationally). Till now, the profligacy of the government has gone widely uncriticized in Kazakhstan's major cities. Urbanites' oft-declared indifference to the spectacle-oriented policies which enrich elites rather than the masses are ultimately essential to supporting the system. Even if they represent an unreflective form of self-preservation, whether experienced as fear, aspiration, or fatigue, these relations *are* the system. Simply wishing not to rock the boat makes the elite's self-interested tactics easier to enact. Again, this is not a normative judgment: freethinking critics of the government cannot be blamed for looking out for themselves and their families.[61] And free-thinking supporters may indeed believe that elites at the top deserve more than others and feel contented with significant inequalities in their country. For these individuals, the spectacle of Astana represents a tangible symbol of the state's developmental ambitions and Nazarbayev's good intentions, and many are eager participants in the wider effort to build the city and feel part of the spectacle.[62] Through clinging to the synecdoche of the city, people are able to think about the capital as a "symbol of our high aspirations, our competiveness and unity," as Nazarbayev put it in the essay quoted at the beginning of this chapter.[63] The synecdochic imaginary alleviates the need to openly acknowledge the elitism of the regime's development policies, allowing people to articulate the official line that Astana's exclusive new buildings are "for the people." It thus helps them to overlook the incongruous facts that belie such a claim, which is essential to living problem-free, or "normally," under a regime they feel powerless to change.[64]

In this chapter, I have sought to illustrate how the capital city project in Astana, engaged by state-scale actors and ordinary citizens alike, confirms and constitutes certain arrangements of power in independent Kazakhstan. The country's paternalist state-society relations are undeniably rooted in the nature of Soviet power. But as Paul Veyne emphasizes, no structure can be "entirely explicable in terms of the preceding structure."[65] Post-Soviet Kazakhstan's elites developed a new set of political technologies to promote their authority and entrench nondemocratic configurations of rule—spectacle being foremost among them. The development of a spectacular new capital city, shining at the center of the state's territory, has been the centerpiece of the Nazarbayev regime's state-building agenda in the independence era. The simple act of discussing the spectacular city has important effects. The topic of Astana's impressive rise on the steppe of Central Asia has been a fixture of independence-era conversations about the country, even if sent somewhat off track by the Borat scandal (from the government's standpoint, at least). Engaged in by academics, politicians, journalists, and citizens alike, discussing the spectacular city creates a platform for people to negotiate the meaning of space and territory, as well as Kazakhstan's place in the world and its people's own role in the polity. For some, Astana may be home. For others, it might be a passing topic, far removed from their immediate experience and not given much thought. For yet others, such as state bureaucrats, it may be part of a political agenda that determines their entire career. Despite the fact that individuals are responding to a unique range of immediate stimuli, their manner of engaging the capital city project has contributed to an overarching effect of institutionalizing and naturalizing "Kazakhstan" as a discrete territorial state, and those acting in the name of the state as its legitimate representatives. In this sense, the ambitious effort to develop Astana has been a crucial element of the success of the post-Soviet government's state-making agenda.

The production of the spectacle at the center also has important subject-forming effects, as ordinary people come to understand their place in the country's new political order. Kazakhstan's citizens not only participate in weaving the state's myth of coherence but also position themselves as political subjects located within its geometrically conceived confines. In this spatial imaginary, they are separate from ("outside of") the state; they become the stuff that the state governs. So too are they territorially "inside" the state—a fact that is understood to give them privileged access to the Nazarbayev regime's benevolent provision of economic opportunity, stability, and celebrations "for the people." Just as with the case of Roman bread and circuses discussed earlier, the state's spectacle-based beneficence has never been intended to redistribute wealth. On occasion, such acts of giving might provide a certain material satisfaction, but these spectacles were largely symbolic, and allowed the sovereign "to prove to his capital that he shared popular feelings" and was not contemptuous of the masses.[66] The spectacle of Astana likewise hinges on the synecdochic imaginary: the city's elitist and point-based development projects reflect and constitute a particular geopolitical imaginary whereby they are metaphorically framed to represent state benevolence and progress in the entire country.

The discursive practice of framing the spectacle of the city as being for the people, on the basis of a (sometimes impossibly stretched) synecdochic imaginary, allows both elites and ordinary citizens to participate in a representational economy that forms the basis of the country's paternalist power relations. The synecdoche helps to divert attention from the elite-dominated nature of Kazakhstan's reconfigured political economy in the last quarter century of independence. And yet, by considering the broad *non*participation and political ambivalence of ordinary citizens, we can begin to see how their general passivity is a form of agency that is also implicated in state-society relations, whereby the regime is understood as benevolent and giving and the people passive and thankful. As with any economy of power, this relationship is inherently unstable, and to use Schattschneider's terms, the scope of political conflict may become more socialized in the future. This is true of all political systems that have a development-oriented *telos*, for the very impulse for progress necessarily brings social change. For now, the growing acceptance of the Astana development scheme suggests that Kazakhstan's government has successfully cultivated a sense of pride among ordinary citizens, which many people experience as gratitude and affinity toward the country's paternalist leader, President Nazarbayev.

But this is the view from the center. There are, unfortunately, certain segments of the population who have not felt the positive effects of the spectacular development agenda—or at least not to the same degree as their compatriots in Astana. Although large majorities of Kazakhstan's citizens look favorably on Nazarbayev and the central state, and have internalized the narrative that Astana is for the people, their numbers should not deflect our attention from the fact that this celebratory spectacle and other countrywide development schemes are intelligible only when contrasted with certain unspectacular Others. Metaphors in the political sphere, George Lakoff and Mark Johnson remind us, hide aspects of reality, and when such a metaphor does so, "by virtue of what it hides,

[it] can lead to human degradation."[67] To see how this works with respect to Astana as a metaphorical Kazakhstan-in-miniature, the following chapter moves beyond the center's celebratory narratives. Through the alternate perspectives found among residents of the Aral Sea region, the effects of the spectacle's slow violence unfolding in the country's hinterlands come into sharper relief. The story of Astana's spectacular rise on the steppe cannot be divorced from these unspectacular realities.

3

From Astana to Aral

Making Inequality Enchant in Kazakhstan's Hinterlands

On December 16, 2011, Kazakhstan's twentieth Independence Day, police forces opened fire on protesting oil workers in the Caspian coastal town of Zhanaozen, killing sixteen people and wounding about one hundred. Not many in the West noticed, but it is certain that the British musician Sting did. In July 2012 he unexpectedly canceled a concert in Kazakhstan for Astana Day. Just prior to his trip, Sting was given an Amnesty International advisory. The report detailed ongoing rights abuses in western Kazakhstan, where oil workers had been striking since May 2011, demanding wage increases, equal rights with foreign workers, and the lifting of independent labor union restrictions.[1] In 2009, Sting had been censured for performing for Uzbekistan's president, Islam Karimov, who was generally regarded as one of the region's cruelest despots until his passing in 2016. Sting was not eager to look supportive of yet another repressive Central Asian leader, so he canceled his trip to Kazakhstan.[2]

Unlike his Uzbek counterpart, President Nazarbayev is actually quite popular, largely because of his success in cultivating the image of benevolent paternalism discussed in the previous chapter. In fact, the Zhanaozen event appeared to be somewhat traumatic for the leader, and he was quick to reprimand local police officers and to shake up elite power circles. This is not the typical response of a despot. Karimov, by contrast, directly ordered a police crackdown on protesters in Andijon in 2005 and responded to their subsequently killing upwards of five hundred people by blaming "outside forces" for instigating the incident.[3] In contrast to the punitive spectacle of the Andijon massacre, Nazarbayev has preferred softer tactics to ensure his own authoritarian hold on power, embodied by the celebratory spectacle of state benevolence and modernization put on display in Astana. This is precisely what made the events in December 2011 so remarkable: progress-oriented and image-conscious regimes typically do not open fire on their citizens. Instead, the violence of developmental states tends to be more structural, more subtle, and in turn, more totalizing. As I have suggested in previous chapters, state-sponsored spectacle routinely diverts attention from the unequal power relations that make it possible. This is especially so in resource-rich states like Kazakhstan, where centralized control of extractive industries gives elites easy access to the state's wealth to produce spectacles and enrich themselves. By presenting themselves as the legitimate representatives of the state, ruling elites surrounding Nazarbayev have used their status as the sole arbiters and extractors of Kazakhstan's natural resources to achieve extraordinary wealth, while oil workers and other rural residents live in widespread poverty. The issue is not so one-sided as elites exploiting the poor, however, because, as in all political systems, a non-elite majority is also implicated in reproducing the system's economy of power. Even if it is only through their quiescence and desire to live "normally," ordinary citizens are caught up in Nazarbayev's developmental state ideal, and their mundane decisions help to perpetuate its structural violence.

Most of Kazakhstan's urbanites, who make up around 60 percent of the population, have experienced dramatic improvements in their quality of life in recent years. For them, the persistent challenges of the rural poor, such as the oil workers, are difficult to imagine. This was made abundantly clear to me in July 2011, when Sting canceled his concert in Astana. The news stirred a number of telling conversations among the city's young, middle-class Kazakh and Russian residents, who were uniformly irritated. This was on two accounts. First, they were outraged that Sting should liken Kazakhstan's political situation to that of Uzbekistan. Articulating a nationalist narrative of wounded pride at being compared to their "backward" neighbor, one informant exclaimed, "It's as if he thinks we are just another 'stan'!" Second, Astana's residents systematically trivialized the complaints of the oil workers. Assuming (incorrectly) that oil company employees had extremely well-paying jobs, they argued that the workers were the last ones who should be complaining about their pay. Overall, the sentiment in the capital was one of anger—not at the injustice of the government's massacre and ongoing repression of fellow citizens, but that Sting should cancel his concert for the sake of people so unworthy as oil workers. After all, these urbanites had paid good money for their concert tickets. In many ways, their demonization of the protesters points to the effectiveness with which Kazakhstan's leaders have been able to win over their support through its celebratory, spectacle-oriented state- and nation-building project.[4]

Kazakhstan is still challenged by various entrenched Soviet legacies, but the country has largely avoided the outright conflict and civil strife that have characterized many of its southern neighbors in the 1990s and since. Kazakhstan's relative stability has allowed elites to reap great profits, financially and politically, while ordinary citizens have been afforded at least a modicum of progress and comfort. Within this context, the urban population tends to see significant economic discrepancies that have arisen between the cities and the rural areas in the post-Soviet era as a nonissue. They believe that the benefits of a stable political situation far outweigh the threat of social disorder, and many today see those benefits as sufficient to justify their complacency about the country's considerable socioeconomic inequalities. This rationalization hinges on a certain degree of ignorance about how people outside the cities live. Often that ignorance is willful; other times it is merely naïve. In either case, Astana serves as an important reference point for the logic of complacency. With the city operating as a synecdoche for the country's rapid development and governmental benevolence, the narratives surrounding it are instrumental in allowing urbanites to avoid thinking about inequalities within their country: Surely the people in the hinterlands must also benefit from the government's newfound wealth? Like any good metaphor, synecdoche masks as much as it unmasks, helping people to forget that they already know the answer to this question is definitively *no*.

Even for Kazakhstanis who are not actively won over by the state's dazzling developmentalism, their relative prosperity (as compared to that of both their southern neighbors and their Soviet past) is itself grounds for political apathy. Popular attitudes in Central Asia are frequently characterized by what Anna Matveeva has termed a "hierarchy of regional disasters, making people think that 'here it is still not as bad as elsewhere.'"[5] Since the early 2000s, this has ossified into a "don't rock the boat" ethos, described in the previous chapter. It is a pervasive sentiment among most ordinary citizens, who overwhelmingly fail to see themselves—that is, their work, leisure, and consumption, and their overall prosperity in the independent state's new political economic order—as connected with the processes of resource extraction and uneven development in the state's hinterlands.[6] Yet natural resource exploitation, and its accompanying power inequalities, are the very condition of possibility for them to live "normally" under the independent state's current political configuration.

What, then, does it mean to live normally in the spaces *beyond* the privileged center? Much of the liberal commentary about nondemocratic states like Kazakhstan tends to fixate on the fact that citizens lack free expression and are often subject to systematic violations of certain political civil liberties. Important as these issues are, a liberalist lens can obscure other challenges that do not easily slot into media scripts about press freedom and human rights. These narrow scripts also mean that when the few local opposition figures do choose to critique the government, they emphasize issues that they know will get Western media attention. Environmental issues are almost never on this list. In the early 1990s, some international attention was given to Central Asia's environment because observers feared that the region's newly independent states would go to war over shared water resources. That prediction never materialized, and since the Soviet Union's dissolution, the Western press and policy circles have paid almost no attention to the severe environmental challenges that continue to plague Kazakhstan and nearly all of the Soviet successor states.[7] Editors and journalists instead seem to have preferred more sensational and, frankly, less depressing topics like the spectacle of Astana's development.

But environmental challenges have dramatic consequences for people in Central Asia, and they are, it turns out, part and parcel of the story of

Astana. This is largely because the city and other elite-centered development projects have worked as something of a vacuum, sucking in state resources that might be distributed otherwise. Critics can (and do) easily lodge this complaint, but its ramifications are rarely followed through with questions such as: What would a more just distribution of state funds do? What issues are *not* being addressed because of the uneven distribution of state funds? And what does this mean for how the Astana project is understood elsewhere in the country? This line of inquiry demands a comprehensive view of political geography in Kazakhstan that accounts for the multiple constructions of place, scale, and time beyond Astana. As the case of the environmentally devastated North Aral Sea region shows, the spectacle of Kazakhstan's grandiose new capital is inextricably connected to certain unspectacular Others: the everyday realties and slower, less eye-catching forms of structural violence that are most evident in the territorial peripheries.

Social marginalization in Kazakhstan comes in many shapes and forms. Environmental pollution is among the most significant issues, owing to the tragic environmental legacies of the Soviet Union now combined with the independent state's reliance on extractive industry. The effects of severe ecological degradation are usually concentrated at the local level, not just in Kazakhstan but around the world. Scholars have long shown that *who* feels these effects and *where* are questions inextricably tied to larger issues of social marginalization, such as racism, income inequality, and other forms of structural violence. And when marginal groups are subjected to environmental contamination, this in turn reinforces their social marginalization.[8] For various reasons, including their marginality and frequent lack of time and resources to raise their concerns, the plight of marginal groups often goes unheeded. Calling attention to cases of environmental injustice is a strong focus in critical social science research, but for many other actors, especially journalists and politicians, these more mundane geographies are easily overwritten by sensational issues, such as election results or territorial conflict.[9]

The nature of slow, silent, or structural violence is unspectacular, meaning that it is easily ignored or sidelined as marginal—in headlines and policy agendas alike. Yet the temporally elongated and unspectacular nature of structural violence from environmental degradation does not make it any less politically salient. A geographic approach thus demands a broader perspective than the simple then-and-there tack that predominates in the literature on spectacle. It requires a deliberate effort to account for spectacle's unspectacular Others. As with so many places, a view from Kazakhstan's periphery brings the environmental consequences of local and global structural inequalities into sharp focus. Accordingly, I aim to decenter the spectacular view from Astana by contrasting it with one from the North Aral Sea in the country's western hinterlands. The unspectacular challenges unfolding there are not a story apart, but are fundamental to the geopolitics of spectacle in Astana and the country as a whole.

Unspectacular Others

Kazakhstan's resource wealth and the leadership's ability to navigate away from most serious forms of civil strife have served many of its citizens quite well. Yet the country continues to be plagued by major center-periphery inequalities, which are manifested primarily in its stark urban-rural divides.[10] To understand these divides, we cannot simply focus on the urban *or* the rural, but must see how they work in tandem, as well as how they are rooted in the historical legacies of Soviet rule in Central Asia. In 1924 Leon Trotsky wrote, "Under socialism a man will become a Superhuman, changing courses of rivers, heights of mountains and nature according to his needs and, after all, changing his own nature."[11] Part of a high-modernist imaginary, the image of the Soviet man conquering nature figured centrally in the USSR's nationalist tropes. Spectacular projects to control landscapes and natural forces were seen as advertisements for the glories of the communist system over that of capitalism.[12] Improbable cities were built in the Arctic; plans were laid to reverse the Siberian rivers; and no water was spared to cultivate cotton, wheat, and rice for Khrushchev's Virgin Lands campaign on Central Asia's arid steppe. This conquering ethos gained even more significance when the Cold War spirit of competition brought the pursuit of nuclear dominance. Under socialism, "man" did indeed become Superhuman, as landscapes and bodies were tragically exposed to nuclear radiation, both intentionally and accidentally. The environmental legacies of Soviet efforts to conquer nature continue to plague countries across Eurasia today, though their effects have not been experienced evenly.

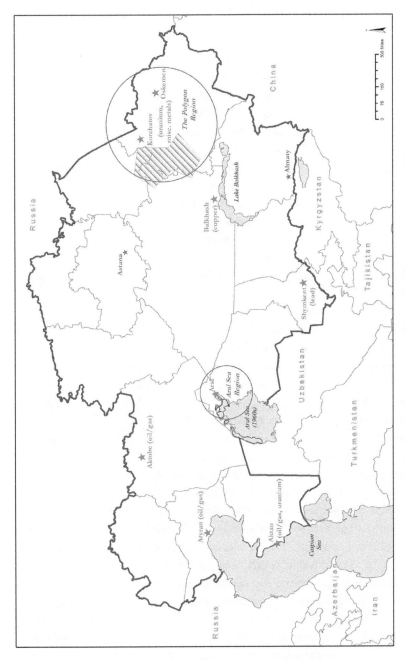

Map 3.1 Major resource extraction sites and ecological disaster zones in Kazakhstan.
Source: Natalie Koch, 2016.

Like many of its post-Soviet neighbors, Kazakhstan is now facing a dual burden combining these inherited environmental legacies with the impacts of the state's increasing reliance on extractive industries in the era of independence (see map 3.1). The effects of this burden are felt minimally in the urban centers, while socially and spatially peripheral regions bear the brunt of the country's greatest environmental challenges. This is most evident in Kazakhstan's officially designated "ecological disaster zones" (*zona ekologicheskovo bedstviya*), which include the Soviet-era Semipalatinsk Nuclear Test Site and the North Aral Sea region.[13] Situated in the western reaches of the country, the North Aral Sea region has been overwhelmingly neglected by government authorities since independence. Facing serious environmental and health issues related to the desiccation of the Aral Sea, communities in this area represent some of Kazakhstan's most marginalized citizens. Yet residents do not always hold the state responsible for the region's present condition. Nor do they always see themselves as victims of locally-manifested problems. In fact, they are often dismissive of the severity of ecological and health issues, and sometimes deny their existence altogether. By examining the unspectacular daily challenges in the hinterlands, we can begin to shed light on why this is, and what factors shape local residents' scalar and temporal attribution of responsibility for environmental stewardship and social welfare. We can also ask how residents understand their relationship to the spectacular center. That is, when viewed from Aral, does the Astana project indeed possess what Clifford Geertz has called the "semiotic capacity to make inequality enchant"?[14] If Kazakhstan's leaders have worked to promote the impression of a benevolent if authoritarian state through positive, feel-good projects, what does this mean for the people and places that are *not* directly included in the spectacle at the center?

I first traveled to Aral in 2005, where I encountered some of these individuals and their stories about the sea that disappeared. The desiccation of the semi-saline Aral Sea was one of many outcomes of the Soviet Virgin Lands campaign, which began in 1953 and became a hallmark of the bureaucrats' efforts to manage people, territory, and resources in much of Central Asia.[15] The region specialized foremost in cotton, but also produced other water-intensive crops like rice and wheat. To bring vast swaths of territory under cultivation, the Amu and Syr Darya rivers were diverted to the region's new collective farms.[16] The Aral Sea had previously been a slightly brackish lake, but because of these diversions, too little fresh river water was reaching the sea, and it became increasingly saline. Native fish species were wiped out, and the region's once booming fishing industry crumbled. The sea's water levels started to decline after 1960 and, by the late 1970s, no water from the Syr Darya reached its shores. Meanwhile, under pressure to meet state agricultural production quotas, and facing popular distrust in the quality of Soviet products, farmers and their collectives were applying excessive amounts of fertilizers, herbicides, and pesticides. Leaching into groundwater supplies, these chemicals resulted in water contamination across the entire region. Moreover, as the shoreline retreated and the bed of the Aral Sea slowly became exposed from the 1970s onward, massive dust storms came to plague the entire basin. These storms picked up sand, salt, and toxic pesticides, which were inhaled by residents all over Central Asia and spread over crops and fields, exacerbating already troubling salinization problems and further depressing agricultural yields.[17]

When I first visited in the summer of 2005, I interviewed locals in Aral and surrounding villages about the impact of the sea's desiccation on their livelihoods.[18] I asked them why they had stayed in the largely abandoned region and what they made of the "water wars" thesis which had prevailed in outside accounts of their local tragedy.[19] I was profoundly challenged by all that I saw and heard and struggled to make sense of the curious mix of fact, rumor, pride, and despair in people's narratives about the sea, their health, and their attachment to their tragically altered homeland. At the time, international attention had already started to wane after the initial rush of concern in the 1990s. And during my last visit in 2015, it was abundantly clear that the disaster had been all but forgotten by international observers. The sea's disappearance is now little more than a curiosity for the occasional journalist or disaster tourist. The fleeting nature of international concern for the Aral Sea region was expressed most succinctly by a schoolteacher I met in Aral in 2015, who exclaimed: "You came back after ten years?! *That* is a heroic deed. I've met many foreign journalists and researchers here, but I have never seen their second visit."

Although the communities in the Aral Sea region have not been able to maintain the attention of global observers, they have attracted some small investments from the central government in Kazakhstan. This support notwithstanding, they have not experienced anywhere near the same improvements in their quality of life and material infrastructure found in Kazakhstan's cities since the late 1990s. This fact alone may seem to suggest that rural residents would not share in their compatriots' predominantly positive interpretation of Astana and Nazarbayev's urban-focused developmental agenda. Yet rural residents are also affected by the prevailing discourse in Kazakhstan, which has been characterized by a hegemonic script in which citizens, unthinkingly or otherwise, praise Astana as a welcome site of economic opportunity and a place where they feel renewed pride in their young country. There are undoubtedly segments of the population that do *not* look favorably on recent developments in the capital, but people are acutely aware that public criticism of state policy is not tolerated by the government. In the effort to locate these critical perspectives, then, the problem is not simply that they are shut out of public spaces, but that they also come in the form of indirect criticism. These are the passive-voice critiques highlighted in the previous chapter, wherein Astana residents occasionally note that they have heard of complaints about government spending that prioritizes the capital vis-à-vis the country's impoverished or environmentally devastated rural areas, such as the Aral Sea region and Semipalatinsk. Having heard this formulation numerous times in the city, I began to wonder, do people actually say such things in the hinterlands?

In 2011 I had a countrywide, demographically representative survey administered in all sixteen regions of Kazakhstan. With a sample size of 1,233 people, the survey included a number of directed questions about Astana, such as whether people agreed with the decision to move the capital, how they thought the move was funded, and so on. Unsurprisingly, the survey response about the capital change was overwhelmingly positive: 69 percent claimed to favor the decision to move the capital, 11 percent were opposed, and 20 percent either refused to answer or were unsure. The results showed, however, that the urban-rural divide was *not* a significant predictor of support for the Astana project, nor of support for the government more generally.[20] Kazakhstanis are quite skilled at reproducing the officially promoted perspective, so it is hard to invest too much credence in a formal survey, which respondents likely experienced as an official interaction.[21] But, in light of my other experiences of hearing and feeling true support for Astana's grand development over the years, it is hard to dismiss these results entirely and assume that people are merely dissimulating. In any case, a practice-based research approach suggests that it is unhelpful, if not entirely futile, to fixate on uncovering whether people "really" believe in state-sanctioned narratives. To get a better sense of how people in Kazakhstan's periphery perceive the government's development efforts in Astana, I therefore returned to Aral to see how people's everyday lives had changed since 2005 and ask about their challenges, hopes, and experiences, as well as what connections they drew between themselves and the spectacle at the center. From the western periphery, we can begin to see the Astana project relationally and account for some of its diffuse Others. Among the most visible of these are the people and places plagued by environmental degradation in the Aral Sea region.

Life in the Zone: The North Aral Sea Region

It was only in 1986, with the introduction of glasnost-era press freedoms, that the international community became fully aware of the severity of the Aral Sea's desiccation. Once the fourth-largest lake in the world, the sea is now split into two sections, referred to as the Small Sea to the north and the Big Sea in the south. The southern section, much of which lies within Uzbekistan's territorial jurisdiction, now consists of only a few highly saline lakes that form seasonally. The fate of the sea was sealed by Soviet-era agricultural plans for Central Asia: irrigated agriculture had been practiced locally for millennia, but the state's "cotton at any price" agenda destroyed traditional water management systems and the local ecological balance.[22] Its social costs for people in the region were significant. In Kazakhstan, these issues have all had serious consequences for the inhabitants of the so-called "ecological disaster zone," which covers about 400,000 square kilometers surrounding the sea and comprises a population of about 4 million.[23] Included in this zone is the North Aral Sea (NAS) region, anchored by the town of Aral, which was once a port on the sea and a major hub for the fishing industry. Already suffering from poverty, the town's residents and those in surrounding fishing communities were ill-equipped to cope with the loss of their livelihoods when the sea started to dry up. And as regional air and groundwater supplies became contaminated by industrial chemicals and pesticides, local troubles were further compounded by rapidly expanding rates of respiratory illness and cancer, among other maladies.

When I visited Aral for the first time, the town was marred by a strong sense of abandonment—a sense especially reinforced when juxtaposed with vibrant images of its former glory on display in the local museum. In my 2005 interviews, I heard a wide range of responses to the question of what caused the area's ecological troubles, though most people agreed that it was rooted in the ill-advised agriculture and water policies.[24] They also agreed that the sea's desiccation still presents many of the same challenges faced in the last decades of Soviet rule. When I asked about the region's current ecological problems, people named the level of the Aral Sea as the most serious issue, followed by the wind and salty dust storms. Other major concerns included access to drinking water, the impact of environmental degradation on the health of the people, the ability of trees and crops to grow, and extreme weather.

Infrastructural shortcomings and poverty were also a major concern in 2005. The old port held no promise for economic revival. Nothing more than an empty harbor, it was fortified by rusting and rotting cranes that once unloaded cargo from the now beached ships into adjacent train cars (figure 3.1). The roads at that time were covered by sand in parts and elsewhere were in utter disrepair. So bad was their condition that drivers seldom drove on them, but instead took a series of dirt paths around them. When I returned to Aral in 2015, the town's sense of absence and longing for its namesake sea were equally visible from certain vantage points. The same cranes stood rusting, trash still littered back alleys, and camels and stray dogs still wandered the unpaved roads. From other angles, however, Aral felt utterly transformed—prosperous almost. Along the main street running through the town, a new mosque was going up, cafés and shops had opened, and KazMunaiGaz had just built a sparkling new gas station on the town's outskirts, where more prosperous locals were beginning to develop large modern homes. But beyond Aral, scattered throughout the region were small villages that exhibited some of the worst material standards of living in Kazakhstan today. Most homes still did not have running water or indoor plumbing, for example. Indeed, villagers in Raim, which I visited in 2005 and 2015, had not received water connections until 2013 (and then they came only in the form of

Figure 3.1 Empty harbor in Aral.
Source: Natalie Koch, 2005.

an outdoor spigot). Unemployment also remained pervasive, and those without state jobs (primarily as schoolteachers) could find only intermittent work in agriculture, fishing, and animal husbandry. Wages were predictably meager. And given the region's environmental degradation, combined with the fact that most villages lacked a trained physician, so were health indicators.

Life was not always so difficult in the North Aral Sea. One of the fishing villages I visited, Tastubek, was at the height of its glory in the early years of the USSR. Labeled a "millionaire village" because of its record-setting fish exports, it was among the first in the area to receive paved roads, electricity, and special food rations.[25] Once the fishing industry began to collapse, however, residents lost their electricity, and with it, their ability to get what fish they could catch to market before it would rot. Many such villages were slowly abandoned over the course of the Soviet era. The most significant exodus from the NAS came in the 1990s, however, when people were suddenly afforded more freedom of movement in the newly independent state.[26] Apparently Kazakhstan's government had also tried to introduce a program to move everyone in the Aral region to other cities. "But," explained Aral's vice mayor (*viz-akim*) V. M. Kemalashev in 2005, "the people were against it."[27] Part of the reason, as I also discovered in the course of my interviews, was that people had a very strong attachment to their homeland. For many residents, the idea of leaving the area was completely outside their thinking; they demanded to know where else they could possibly live and why they should even consider doing such a thing. As one elderly man asked, "If we were born here, and lived here, where would we go?"

Residents often described a similar sense of attachment to the place because they were born and raised there, just like their ancestors for generations before. One respondent told me, "The ones that stayed, their souls still long for their homeland." Another asserted: "We live here! We're used to it! We'll never abandon our homeland." Many people had a similar reaction and claimed that people who stayed were simply accustomed to life as they knew it in the NAS area. For example, one common response was, "We were born here, we live here. So it's fine." Or in the words of another resident:

> We've grown accustomed to being right here, to this town, because we've lived here since childhood. It doesn't depend on whether the sea is here or not. There are people here who move to other towns, but then they return, because they are already used to this town, to the nature here. They would move elsewhere in good weather but then return here. . . . They can't acclimate, get sick a lot, so they move back here. This is why we don't want to leave, because we are used to it. This is our favorite town . . . even though there is no sea here.

Although many NAS residents expressed an extremely positive attitude about their home, others were less effusive and simply stated that they "could live." This resignation is notable in one man's description of life in the "ecological disaster zone," when he said: "I was born here, I live here, and I am used to life here. An ecological tragedy or not—we live [on]. You have to survive. One has to live on."

Various respondents in 2005 also felt that ecological problems simply did not bother them. For instance, a man in his early thirties asserted: "I, for example, was born here, and I want to live here. I do not think

Figure 3.2 View of the Kokaral Dam sluice letting water from the
Small Sea into the Big Sea.
Source: Natalie Koch, 2015.

that the ecology affects me. I feel good and I live here and I am happy."
Others argued that the region was not as bad off as observers have made
it out to be, and mixed this with a strong degree of hope for the sea's
eventual return. Said one: "A lot of experts call this an 'ecological [disas-
ter] region,' but I personally don't agree with this because Aral's region is
getting better every day—better, better, better. And in the future when the
sea comes back, Aral's region will be the best." Was this hopeful narrative
simply wishful thinking, or did locals have a reason for believing in the
sea's return?

In the early 2000s, Kazakhstan's government accepted a World Bank
loan to build the Kokaral Dam, an eight-mile-long dike between the Small
Sea and the Big Sea, with a sluice that allows excess water to flow into the
Big Sea (figure 3.2). In an effort to save this small section (amounting to
only 10 percent of what was once the Aral Sea), the structure retains the
water from the Syr Darya in the Small Sea. Experts promoting the dam
project had already deemed the Big Sea's demise a foregone conclusion.

The World Bank project's justification states: "Experts and practitioners agree that full restoration of the Aral Sea is impossible and act accordingly. . . . Full restoration through water savings is also unrealistic. At best, what could be expected is a retardation of the state of the Sea's decline and future maintenance of the Sea at a sustainable level."[28] In the NAS region, which stood to benefit most, government actors were keen to sell the project as a local cure-all and a way to slow out-migration. Vice Mayor Kemalashev, who was particularly absorbed by the prospect of the sea's return, related these benefits to me in 2005: "The first phase in the construction of the dike was finished in August, and the sea is day by day coming closer to town. So the people don't have to leave the place where they were born. After completion of the second phase of the project, the sea will come back to the town and the social conditions of the town will be improved."[29]

In April 2005 President Nazarbayev visited Aral. In the midst of a reelection campaign, Nazarbayev had traveled there to initiate a drinking water project and to visit the recently completed Kokaral Dam. The dam was, he declared at the time, "a modern hydro-technical installation [that] will breathe new life into an entire region plagued by environmental problems, promote economic growth, and improve life conditions and wellbeing for the people there. Let your work be a symbol of the man's victory over environmental problems and forces of nature."[30] Engaging the familiar modernist tropes of "man" conquering nature, Nazarbayev's message to the NAS communities stressed hope, optimism, and revival.[31] Through his praise for the dam project, the president positioned himself as a trusted guardian who would help local residents in the pursuit of future prosperity. By the time of my arrival a few months later, in August, people were still abuzz with excitement over the attention he had given them. Nazarbayev's image was still plastered all over the town's public spaces, including one billboard in the central square, which depicted the confident leader striding through beautifully green grass and smiling benevolently. The grass may have been foreign to locals, but its symbolic promise of prosperity and a thriving environment was not lost on them. When I returned ten years later, that presidential visit had come to be regarded as a major milestone in the town's history. It was also his last.

In discussing the president's visit to the NAS in 2005, it was clear that his message of paternalistic care resonated with my informants. Many of them were taken in by his optimism, which they so desperately wanted to share, and they claimed that he had given them hope for the sea's return and the improvement of conditions in the area. In the words of one respondent: "Yes, we have hope, expectation that the sea will come back. And the president came here in April, and he said a lot of things about the sea, and the sea will come back. And he is sure that the sea will come back, and [I believe] the president." While some said that Aral would never return to what it once was, most felt certain that the dam project would at least bring back the Small Sea. "We hope, we hope. Of course, we hope," said one resident. "But now, with this Kokaral, the problem is being solved, and tomorrow the river will flow. With time, it should return. It should return." Some residents were less quick to pin their hopes on the dam as a source of the sea's revival, but discussed long-term historic variation of water levels and trusted that time would restore it, though perhaps only "after a few millennia." As one old fisherman put it: "Our parents told us that the sea will come back in a few centuries. Now it is only up to God if the sea will come back. I believe that the sea will come back. When I was a small child, I heard that the sea disappeared once, but it came back. I heard this from the old people." Even though both these respondents were aware of the role of poor water management in causing the sea's disappearance, they still drew a degree of optimism from the idea that there might be enough historic variation to return the sea to what it once was.

The idea that the sea's return could suddenly solve all the social ills in the NAS is deceiving. But strategically so: the political focus on the dam diverts attention from regional challenges with far deeper roots than the sea's disappearance. The region's widespread social and political troubles are largely the result of governmental neglect and unequal development policies. But the language of ecological tragedy and techno-fixes such as the Kokaral Dam imply that the sea itself can be faulted for these woes. This is not to diminish the significance of the local ecological issues, or even to say that the dam was ill-advised. On the contrary, the environmental challenges are real, and so too are the benefits that the dam has brought to segments of the local population in the NAS.[32] It is to say, rather, that just as rhetoric surrounding Astana synecdochically paints a picture of prosperity and benevolence of the state that supposedly characterizes all of Kazakhstan, rhetoric surrounding the Aral Sea disaster synecdochically paints a tragic environmental legacy as the sole source of present-day challenges. This picture changes when we start to ask what keeps people in the NAS, and what visions they harbor for the region's future.

The Politics of Neglect in the Periphery

In the 1990s, staying in the NAS region was not always a voluntary choice but rather the result of insufficient resources to leave. Those who had resources in the form of a job and livestock could choose to stay, while others lacking resources felt they were forced to stay. For example, one respondent explained that the currency change from the Russian ruble to the Kazakhstani tenge was another reason people stayed: "Before the tenge appeared, we could leave. Some saved and saved money, then the ruble turned into the tenge and the sharp money devaluation came, and their large savings turned into nothing, and many people stayed because they could not [afford to] leave. . . . My neighbor wanted to leave for Astrakhan. She saved and saved money all her life—then the money changed. Where would she go now? Stayed here. Lives, still, alone. She wanted to go to her sister and she could not leave." As with this woman's neighbor, efforts to leave the NAS to reunite with family were a common theme in my interviews. Concern for their children's future was also a major concern for some. One woman's lamentations about remaining behind illustrate the sort of reasoning families must have gone through when faced with the decision to stay or go:

> I support those that left. I support—they did they right thing. It is we [who remain], who are, so to say, fooled. Like, they tell us: "Everything will be okay, the sea will come. You will live long yet, and in good health." This is just a lie, it turns out. They simply lie to us. We simply sit here, wait for the sea . . . we're clueless. Simply, you can see what I have become. When I look at the future of my children, I simply . . . I pity them. I think . . . and their father thinks: What have we done to them? It turns out we should have left sooner. We should have left sooner. You can see for yourself: we have no greenery, nothing. See for yourself. It's very hard.

Regrets abounded as people realized that the new regional disparities in the wake of Kazakhstan's postcommunist transition imperiled their own and their children's life chances. Though I did not again meet the woman just quoted when I returned in 2015, I learned that at least one of her daughters was no longer "sitting and waiting" for the sea to return but had already moved to the city.

Apart from family ties, most people explained that those who had left did so primarily in search of work, which they could not find in the region's post–Aral Sea economy. Not only were the fisherman thrown out of work, but also boat factories and various other related industries had been almost entirely shut down. Overall, economic troubles ranked high among the concerns of my 2005 respondents, and despite some superficial improvements in Aral's local infrastructure, this certainly had not diminished by my second visit.

Rumors in 2015 also suggested that some local fishermen were beginning to make large sums of money as Small Sea levels started to rise and fish returned—although the living conditions I encountered in the small settlements adjacent to the sea suggested that this was more local lore than reality. Though many people had expressed concerns in 2005 about the eventual out-migration of educated youth, by 2015, young people in Aral and surrounding villages were extremely pessimistic about their chances of finding work in Kazakhstan's major cities. This is because having social and family networks is key to one's success in moving to the country's urban centers, and those who remain in Aral tend to lack strong connections to draw on. Some also expressed a fatalistic attitude about being tied to the region because of family responsibilities and cultural norms. For example, the eldest son in a family is seen as the designated caretaker of the family home and is responsible for its upkeep. This obligation was constantly referenced by young men and their wives, who asserted a desire to move to the city but deemed it unrealistic. Even when NAS locals had left, I found that this rarely meant complete abandonment: family relations and expectations continued to bind people to their hometown, and it was only when children moved their parents to the city that ties to the area were completely severed.

By and large, though, younger residents of the Aral Sea region were fearful of leaving for the city and failing. Having to face the shame of returning unsuccessful was a terrifying prospect. In 2015 I was given diverse examples of people who had moved to cities like Astana, Almaty, or Shymkent, but later returned to Aral because they couldn't "make it." For instance, on several occasions, I was told about the owner of a well-known restaurant, who had leased the business and moved to Almaty in the early 2000s. After a decade away, he and his family had just returned to Aral. Their motives for coming back were unknown, but speculation varied between a patriotic longing for their native homeland and the mere inability to stay afloat economically in Kazakhstan's largest and most expensive city. Regardless of the actual reasons, recounting the stories of returnees functioned as a cautionary tale about the difficulties of making it in the city. The act of speculating was a regular reminder to residents of the shame of failure. Evincing the complex mix of emotions inherent in schadenfreude, many Aral residents seemed to revel in these tales of out-migrants' failure. For one thing, it made those who stayed look superior, when they had previously felt inferior. That is, whereas they had previously seemed to fall short by not taking a risk and trying their luck in the city, this could now be framed as wisdom: they had known "all along" that it was better to stay. Similarly, these narratives inverted the role of Aral in the spatial hierarchy of valued homelands. Whereas the NAS is typically relegated to the bottom rung of poor and backward places in Kazakhstan, the tales of return migrants patriotically position the provincial town as superior to the big city. These stories thus served the dual purpose of raising up Aral as a desirable place to live and of reinforcing the fear of a shameful return if one failed to succeed in the big city.

Perhaps more troubling for NAS locals when they move to the cities, however, is how they are received by urbanites. Like their compatriots from the Semipalatinsk area, people from the Aral region are well aware of the stigma that is attached to those hailing from a "disaster zone," who are often treated as contaminated or dangerous.[33] As one respondent put it in 2005: "Well, when I go to other cities, many people ask, 'Where are you from?' I say, 'From Aral.' They all get scared, thinking that in the 'ecological disaster zone' we are all sick." Or in the words of another: "Some people from other parts are afraid of Aral. They say, 'Well, it's an ecological [disaster] region. If we go to Aral, we will get some disease.'" I also encountered the dehumanizing effects of this label when traveling in Kazakhstan's cities and discussing the rural regions with my urbanite interlocutors. In Almaty in 2005, people were alarmed at my intent to travel to Aral and expressed a general distrust of people from the Aral Sea region. As one ethnically Russian friend advised me, "Seriously, do your interviews as fast as possible and get out of there!" And later, on the train, a man from Kyzylorda told me upon hearing my destination, "In Kazakhstan, we have good people and bad people," and warned me to be on guard for the disproportionate number of "bad people" in the Aral Sea region. After I returned to Almaty that year, I found most people to be less interested in hearing my take on the experience than in my response to their question "It was scary, wasn't it?" They were shocked to hear that the people were friendly and open—as if living in such an environmentally degraded and poverty-stricken area made them incapable of such human qualities as generosity and kindness. This manner of stigmatizing the poor has a long history in Kazakhstan, which spatializes intolerance through urban narratives about the rural hinterlands.[34] When stigmatizing traits are ascribed to people from a particular place, such as the NAS, the effect is to deflect attention from what is base prejudice. Through such language, however, it is not *people* who are being critiqued but *regions*. Of course, people are the ones affected by such rhetoric, but regional stigmas conveniently erase the actors—and their political decisions—that are responsible for Kazakhstan's stark urban-rural inequalities.

When I asked NAS residents in 2005 who was responsible for addressing the country's inequalities and local troubles, there was a consensus that it was a governmental obligation.[35] Many people placed their utmost confidence in President Nazarbayev, such as one fisherman who told me: "I trust in God that Nazarbayev is doing his best to improve the conditions of the people. People are getting their pensions on time, they are building houses in the villages. . . . Now he is solving the problems with the unemployment, and the government is building houses in the villages for young teachers and doctors." Such faith in the president's leadership was common, but people clearly saw themselves as separate from the state apparatus and uniformly rejected the idea that they could personally effect change. In explaining why not, many simply reiterated that they were powerless.

Others claimed that they were too old or too young, or lacked the financial resources or the necessary skills. Several people also asserted that one person cannot do anything alone—that effective solutions must be implemented by an entire community working together, since "one man, in any case, can never resolve anything. One man is never listened to here." Today as in the past, communities of the NAS have learned that the individual is seldom empowered to make change happen. One fisherman illustrated through a historical example: "The local people and local authorities in the early 1960s, they wrote a letter to the government that the level of the Aral Sea was decreasing every year . . . some twenty, thirty [centimeters], then up to one meter per year. And all the fish, of course, when the water becomes more salty, all the freshwater fish die; they didn't exist anymore. The government didn't pay attention to the scream of the local people." The Soviet-era valorization of communal governance may explain in part why local residents have not felt personally empowered to effect change, but many of these narratives reveal a sense of popular disenfranchisement in the context of hierarchical political structures that disregard what this man calls the "scream of the local people." Equally dismissive of the government, albeit in a different manner, was one woman, who said: "I don't think that [we] need to turn to the government or our leaders. It all depends on God, if you will." This sort of fatalism, whatever its roots, relinquishes both individual and governmental responsibility for finding a positive path forward.

Another difficulty with solving local problems, respondents emphasized, was the lack of financial resources. For instance, one man claimed, "If the government takes it into their hands, then in a year or two you can solve everything . . . but everything depends on money now." Or as another argued: "The first thing, the authorities should learn to care. But still, in the end, everything depends on finances—if there are finances. . . . What are the authorities for? To oversee all of this. So that the people live well. They should do all of this. . . . If the people choose them, then they should do their job." So while most people agreed that the government was responsible for implementing solutions, there was less consensus about whether it was actually fulfilling its obligations at the local level. Some respondents adamantly supported the government's social and environmental remediation efforts, whereas others attributed any shortcomings to financial restrictions and affirmed that government officials provided assistance "as they can."

Only a handful of NAS residents explicitly critiqued the central government for doing too little to address local challenges. One man rejected the argument made by several others that the government's ability to help was dependent on finances, saying: "The money is there, and you can just sit there and not do anything. That's another way to use it. The government, they work like this—whether the money is there or the money isn't, they still do nothing. Therefore, to achieve their goals, to solve the problem, you have to give money to those who will work on this." Another respondent, an elderly woman from Aral, described her experience:

> We have to fight this ourselves, yes? Because we need our children, but as for our superiors—like our president—they don't really pay us any attention. We have to fight for this ourselves. Yes, we're living in an ecological tragedy, and so, we live. There are people even worse off than us. And if you only saw how they lived, you would be afraid to look at them. They don't have anyone at all to help them. What our president is concerned with I, for instance, do not know. Sometimes medicine is bought. They say, "So you live in an ecological [disaster] zone, get your medicine free by prescription." But this is all bogus; there is no such thing.

Forceful dissenting views about the government's alleged magnanimity, such as this woman's, were rather uncommon, even if people recognized the shortcomings of local development policies. More common were echoes of President Nazarbayev's standard rhetoric about progress in Kazakhstan necessarily being gradual, as with one respondent who acknowledged that the government's effort to provide assistance "doesn't happen right away. Step by step it's trying, but there is no such thing as immediately." He is surely correct, but this official narrative about gradualism is notably reserved for everywhere *but* Astana, which is in fact steeped in the language and spectacular imagery of immediacy.

Enchanting Inequality: Viewing Astana from Afar

In light of prevailing assumptions that the government should take care of local issues, but the persistence of significant social and ecological challenges decades later, how have NAS residents viewed Astana, the government's favored and opulent project of state-making in the country's center? When I visited in 2015, I sought to answer this question by simply asking people, "Have you been to Astana?" As I have learned over the years, the topic serves as a key platform for much wider discussions about politics, economics, and social affairs in Kazakhstan today.[36] Some people were more willing than others to discuss the capital, but among those who were less willing to do so, there was a subtle yet clear affective dismissal. This was exemplified in one short response that I received from a young man in his early twenties about whether he had been there: "No, why go to Astana [*Net, pochemu v Astanu*]." Though formulated as a question, his reply was a declarative statement, manifested in the disdainful and annoyed tone that seemed to come less out of irritation with the question than with the city itself. He then proceeded to tell me all about the positives of his own hometown. He never directly contrasted its pros to the cons of Astana, though this comparison was implied. Similarly, one woman in her late thirties wanted me to compare Astana with other cities in Kazakhstan. I gave some noncommittal responses, and since she had been to Shymkent and liked the city very much, she pushed this comparison. She never said anything explicitly negative about Astana, but she was dismissive of it and took great pains to emphasize how Shymkent has excellent weather, a better environment, and so many nice places to walk, eat, and enjoy oneself. Again, the cons of Astana were implicit. These are the silences that flag dissenting views, which cannot be publicly expressed in authoritarian settings, but wherein "meaning itself is made possible by what is missing."[37]

Odd as it may seem to people unfamiliar with Kazakhstan, to critique Astana is to critique the president.[38] It is *his* city, *his* project, and *his* birthday that is celebrated on Astana Day. Outside of the public sphere, explicitly contrarian views in Kazakhstan, as elsewhere in the post-Soviet space, are largely confined to private spaces—primarily shared among family and close friends at the kitchen table.[39] This is not to say that the kitchen is a space exclusively for dissenting opinions, for even there, people will express the state-promoted discourse and certain majority opinions. The case of Aigul and Nazgul is exemplary. The two sisters were both in their late twenties in 2015 and have always lived in the NAS.[40] I met them originally on my first trip to the region and spent much of my later visit with them. Neither had been to Astana, but both were familiar with it on the basis of images and stories on the Internet, on television, and in newspapers. Aigul was firmly opposed to the government's concentration of national resources in the capital. Sitting with me, indeed at her kitchen table, she was very open about her critical stance: "It's my personal opinion, but I don't see why they put all that money there and don't help people in the rest of the country." I asked if others thought like she did, but she evaded the question and underscored that it was just her "personal opinion."

Some days later, Aigul asked me for my thoughts on the upcoming EXPO-2017 event, a second-tier world's fair exposition hosted in Astana in the summer of 2017, and in which the government has already invested billions of dollars in facilities and infrastructure development. I turned the question back to her instead, and she again expressed her disappointment that the government was spending so much on the event. "But why?" she wanted to know. Aware that many foreigners would come to Kazakhstan for the exposition, she told me that she hoped to organize some tours for foreigners wishing to see the Aral Sea region during their travels. She wished she could attend the EXPO herself, but she knew that she would not be able to participate personally in the spectacle. Not only was she working as a schoolteacher, but also she lacked the substantial time and money it would take for her to get to Astana from Aral. She also had several small children and a husband to tend to. And though they already had three beautiful girls, her husband still wanted a boy; Aigul knew she was likely to be pregnant with or caring for yet another small child by the time of the event. The most she could hope for, it seemed to her, was a trickle of overflow from the spectacle to come to her.

Aigul's sister Nazgul, by contrast, had long been fascinated by Astana, and when I spoke with her in 2015, she desperately wanted to move there. She knew this would be an extremely difficult dream to realize, but she was finally planning to travel to the city a few weeks after my visit to Aral. She and Aigul had an aunt who lived in Astana. She expected to stay with her for a short time to assess her job prospects and hoped to remain, if she could. Although Aigul had her own frustrations with her life situation in Aral, Nazgul was far more discontented than her sister. She had recently separated from her husband, who was an abusive alcoholic. Her family supported her in living apart from him at the time, though they put constant pressure on her to return to her marriage. She was also frustrated by her work situation. She had been trained specifically as a physical education teacher, but the only employment she could find was serving food in a cafeteria and occasionally selling odds and ends in the bazaar. Nazgul was very entrepreneurial and she wanted so much more for herself. She had higher aims and aspirations than she felt could be achieved in Aral, but she was nonetheless largely reluctant to aspire to bigger things. The aura of Astana, however, helped give her the courage to dream—not just for the prestige of making it in the city, but mostly for what she perceived as its transformational potential. She longed for a chance to feel challenged and fulfilled, and to break out of her domestic struggles.

For many in the NAS, travel from one of the region's small villages to the town of Aral alone can be a major leap. So expensive is such a move that few villagers can even fathom being able to afford living in Aral permanently. For them, it already feels like a big city. Considering a move to any of Kazakhstan's larger provincial towns, such as Kyzylorda, then, is even more remote. And Astana sits at the top of this urban hierarchy, well beyond these major centers. Anyone who succeeds in "making it" in the attempt to climb to the towering heights of Astana is thus clearly an impressive individual worthy of respect. Even traveling there was enough to confer a certain prestige. Typically my foreignness masked this effect for me, though in one case a woman in Aral in her early thirties asked me about Astana. "So, you've been to the big city, huh?" she said with a heavy inhalation as if to imply "respect!" "How is it?" This woman, Zhanat, was especially keen to move to Astana. She felt tied to Aral, however, because her husband had a job as a policeman and many family obligations as the eldest brother among his siblings. Like Nazgul, she did not like Aral and wished for more from her life, including the possibility of escaping a marriage that was not only constraining but also abusive. For Zhanat, a move to Astana would have meant a radical change in her life circumstances, an escape from her family troubles and boredom at work. Perhaps more than anything else, the simple *idea* of Astana represented the hope for prosperity, fulfillment, and material comforts unattainable in Aral. She was thus not envious of me as an American; she knew my citizenship privileges were unattainable. But she was envious of my having experienced the Astana dream, which she did consider, if only remotely, personally attainable.

In considering the spectacle of Astana, outsiders can begin to understand its attraction for Kazakhstanis only by exchanging their own spatial hierarchies for those of the country's rural residents. For example, Western observers might rank Astana within a set of experiences with other major cities, whether Chicago, Istanbul, Dubai, or Kuala Lumpur, and then their experience of reaching the Aral Sea would map onto the country's descending urban hierarchy, with Astana and other large cities like Shymkent and Almaty at the top, followed by regional capitals, such as Kyzylorda, a step down from this, a provincial hub like Aral being another step down, and a small village like Raim or Tastubek at the farthest reaches from the capital. But when one is thinking in reverse, from the vantage point of villagers, the experience of *ascending* Kazakhstan's urban hierarchy to reach Astana is radically different from the descent. To *descend* Kazakhstan's urban hierarchy implies the loss of status and certain material comforts, but to *ascend* implies the possibility of attaining status and its indicators.

All this is to say that people in Kazakhstan's periphery understand the city relationally—as a site of prosperity vis-à-vis their own relative poverty, as a site of opportunity and work in contrast to their local challenges with unemployment, and as a site of uncommon celebrations and opportunities unparalleled in their small communities. Viewed relationally and as a synecdochic icon for socioeconomic prosperity, the spectacle of Astana is designed to make inequality enchant. The question, though, is whether the metaphor is stretched too far, and whether people are actually able to envision all the wondrous possibilities of Astana as being within reach for citizens *like them*—or not. For those from the rural hinterlands, regardless of whether they have the additional stigma of hailing from an ecological disaster zone, the social stigmatization that they have encountered in urban areas has largely taught them that people like them are not readily welcomed. This has certainly not stopped the heavy rural migration that has characterized urban change in Kazakhstan since the early 1990s. But actual (rather than aspirational) urban migrants are a special population. As we have seen, Zhanat and Nazgul wanted something more than they could find in Aral. In contrast to Aigul, however, they were not contented with the spectacle's overflow: they longed for the "sense of being near to the heart of things," as Geertz puts it.[41] In his effort to understand this "paradox of charisma," Geertz draws on the work of the influential sociologist Edward Shils, who describes the contrasting ways that people relate to the spectacle at the center. Some, he says, feel a strong, positive draw to be close to the center, while others are largely indifferent or experience only an "intermittent, occasional, and unintense" desire to be part of the center's value system, while yet others are strongly opposed. Generally, the farther one moves from the center of society, the more one's "attachment to the central value system becomes attenuated."[42]

Shils makes it clear that this attenuating effect characterizes both the territorial margins of a political system *and* marginal individuals within given societies. For him, the center is not a "spatially located phenomenon," having "nothing to do with geometry and little with geography." Rather, centrality is foremost a symbolic ordering according to a society's prevailing "central value system." As seen in the case of capital cities, this central value system is often mapped onto places and territories—the values imagined to manifest themselves spatially, with the sovereign power of the state deemed most intense in the capital and territorial "heartland." For those at the spatial or social margins of society, Shils argues that their distance from the center is often not experienced in a negative light: they do not feel "their remoteness from the center to be a perpetual injury to themselves." Most, he says, hardly notice. That is, their ostensible alienation from the central value system has not been "active or intense, because, for the most part, their convivial, spiritual, and moral center of gravity has lain closer to their own round of life." But for some people, their distance from the center is experienced as a negative sense of exclusion. It can lead to "an acute sense of being on 'the outside,' to a painful feeling of being excluded from the vital zone which surrounds the center of society." Different people, says Shils, have different ways of responding to this feeling of exclusion.[43]

To this I would add that different people have different means or resources with which to respond to this sense of exclusion. For the vast majority of NAS residents, an intimate connection to the spectacle in Astana is out of reach. Yet this situation does not trouble many of them at all. They may be contented with the yearly Astana Day celebration in the Aral town square, if even that is of interest. More often, they are simply focused on their own "moral center of gravity," such as the problems and prospects of their hometown, and they do not naturally draw the connection between the state of affairs there and the spectacle at the center. Others, like Aigul, may feel indignant about policies that prioritize Astana's development over more meaningful investments in Kazakhstan's most needy places. And yet others, like Nazgul, may feel enticed by the hope and courage that the sparkling image of the city offers.

Just as with the costs and benefits of the Astana project, those associated with environmental change in the Aral Sea region have historically been unevenly distributed. Elites with the power to determine Central Asia's water policies have historically benefited from them, while the periphery has tended to bear the brunt of their harms. According to the early scholarship on environmental politics in the newly independent states of Central Asia, ecological degradation and water scarcity were expected to transform the region into a tinderbox for conflict.[44] These commentators, however, made too many ill-founded assumptions about the values and attachments of those most affected by environmental problems. As we see in Kazakhstan (and in much of the world), rather than being characterized by widespread conflict, people and places affected by long-term environmental pollution generally suffer slowly and quietly, accumulating the effects of slow violence over decades and generations.[45] If we view this issue from the perspective of some of Kazakhstan's most marginalized citizens in the western periphery, and the way they narrate their personal challenges and affinities, it becomes forcefully clear that their unspectacular realities are not merely the byproduct of the spectacle at the center. Rather, the two produce each other.

In considering the various ways in which people relate to the center, we must bear in mind that these are only snapshots of any individual's views on Astana, the state, and environmental challenges in the North Aral Sea. Malte Rolf stresses this point in his work on mass festivals in Soviet times, noting that people's views may change and shift over the course of their life, or even the course of a day or week. In analyzing the diary of one Soviet citizen, he writes:

> Stepan Podlubny's life story reads radically differently depending on whether we focus on the period of the early 1930s, when he was trying to recast himself as a Soviet "New Man," or on the phase of critique and detachment toward the regime during the terror he experienced, or if we further pursue his life story to when he sought reintegration into the community of Soviet citizens as a medic. . . . Which of his celebration experiences over the years are the "real" ones? It depends on the observer's perspective, which crucially predetermines how we interpret personal experience.

Rolf argues that the subjective nature of these experiences does not make a dated analysis insignificant or false, just as it does not render the interviews and ethnographic material presented here unhelpful. Rather, it hints at a much larger, theoretical point that participants in celebrations or onlookers at a spectacle do not "experience a celebration just once, or in one particular way, but many times and in many different ways." It also suggests that scholars need to abandon the classical view of the "unity of self":

> What we encounter in the behavior of celebration participants are fragmented identities of the individual through time and space. Individuals are involved in several contexts and constitute themselves and their subjectivity through different actions and by reference to different discourses. It annoys the researcher, of course, that individuals do so without trying to resolve the conflicts between their different selves. Individuals take up various roles and adapt themselves to their surroundings without deciding which of these roles constitutes the "real self." As observers, historians should not attribute to individuals a clarity that those individuals did not attribute to themselves. A person always had different, coexisting impressions of celebrations. The same people who yesterday were thrilled by the fireworks may tomorrow see the whole event critically, or vice versa.[46]

And so it is for Aigul and her sister Nazgul, Zhanat, and all the other NAS residents and their compatriots in Astana. What may enchant people today may not enchant them tomorrow. But to the extent that Kazakhstan's leadership has been able to promote the positive affective response of people like Nazgul and to silence the more critical narratives of people like her sister, it has—at least publicly—been able to effectively mobilize Astana as an icon, as a synecdoche for the supposedly benevolent state and future prosperity, to make inequality enchant.

Like so many large-scale development projects, Kazakhstan's spectacular capital city simultaneously represents an intense idealism and an intense brutality. The latter is simply obscured by the spatial and temporal disjuncture between spectacle and slow violence. Rather than investing state funds in social welfare agendas, which might result in more diffuse and concrete improvements in the population's living conditions, elites have been enticed by their own spectacles. In their schemes to develop Astana, they have sought rapid, dazzling rewards, while externalizing the impact of these decisions, both spatially and temporally. Indeed, spectacles seduce. Crucially, though, the general apathy bordering on lukewarm support of those who do not feel "their remoteness from the center to be a perpetual injury to themselves" is fundamental to the perpetuation of structural violence, manifested in the state's neglect of marginal people and places.[47] While some Kazakhstanis may be drawn in and awed by the spectacle of the city, most are far too wise to be convinced of the sensibleness of these agendas, even if the country's political context proscribes their ability to expressly say so. Yet it is truly painful for many people to think about this injustice actively and constantly. This is equally so in Kazakhstan and in any other place.

The stories recounted here may feel exceptional and far from the personal experience of many readers, but the case of Kazakhstan has much to teach us about power, technologies of government, and subjectivity in many other corners of the world. Most pointedly, taking this authoritarian context seriously challenges liberal understandings of agency as subversive action: regardless of whether citizens of nondemocratic regimes consciously agree with state-initiated development projects, people invariably work opportunistically within them. In so doing, they ultimately constitute the resulting networks of political and economic relations. In their everyday life, people in Astana and well beyond are active participants in a political system that is possible only through deep structural inequalities. To be sure, the paternalist, elite-dominated structures of the state can never be total; there is inherently space for overflow, exemplified by the actions of both the protesters and the police forces in Zhanaozen described at the beginning of this chapter.

But state power is *not* something external to the citizens of the authoritarian state of Kazakhstan. Through their political and economic behaviors, they are instrumental in constituting it, even if this looks, more often than not, like the pursuit of a "normal" life and a desire not to rock the boat. Complacency and indifference are in fact agencies—and they are strategically colonized and technologized by certain regimes. Though this may be more visible in paternalist and illiberal systems, it is undeniably applicable in liberal democracies as well. This is exemplified, if nothing else, in the 103 million Americans who did not vote in the 2016 U.S. presidential election, despite being eligible—the successors to Schattschneider's 40 million nonvoters of the 1960s, "remaining comfortably unaware of the inconsistency of theory and practice."[48] Comfortable unawareness, willful ignorance, oversight with or without malicious intent: they all tend to blur together. Though perhaps appropriately so, because the outcome is often the same: "Structural violence is silent, it does not show—it is essentially static, it is the tranquil waters. In a static society, personal violence will be registered, whereas structural violence may be seen as about as natural as the air around us."[49]

4

FROM ASTANA TO ASIA

Spectacular Cities and the New Capitals
of Asia Compared

Astana is probably not the first city that comes to mind when most people in Europe or North America imagine spectacular cities in Asia. They
are more likely to conjure images of places in East Asia or the Arabian
Peninsula, such as Taipei, Kuala Lumpur, Seoul, or Dubai. This is largely
the result of a deliberate strategy: boosters in each of these cities have
actively pursued spectacular urban development, as well as a diverse and
wide-ranging international campaign to broadcast their achievements by
hosting global events and disseminating images of new architectural icons
in the foreign media. So impressive have these place-branding campaigns
been that many international observers have a hard time imagining large-
scale urban development schemes in Central Asia as spectacular. They
might wonder how a city like Astana could be deemed legitimately spectacular when it pales in comparison to more globally renowned spectacles.
This skeptical perspective assumes a spatial hierarchy particular to certain
hyper-mobile foreign audiences, but which neglects alternatively imagined

urban hierarchies among locals and other individuals with different cultural, political, financial, or moral centers of gravity.

Dismissals of Astana's claim to being "legitimately" spectacular are underpinned by an objectivist understanding of spectacle rather than a relative one. That is, while they may seem to be objective statements, these judgments actually touch on political questions of who gets to decide what is spectacular and what is not. Indeed, my interlocutors in Kazakhstan emphasize that their own sense of regional identity usually does not align with how foreigners understand their country's place in the world. As noted in the previous chapter, many people would become irritated when they heard descriptions of Kazakhstan that grouped it with "all the other 'stans'"—a classification they resent as a label of backwardness. Instead, internationally-minded Kazakhstanis now tend to express their geopolitical affinities beyond the post-Soviet space, increasingly turning toward other parts of Asia and the Gulf—places they consider to be more prosperous and forward-looking than their regional neighbors.[1] At the center of these regional identity narratives, Astana has become a key site for individuals to narrate their competing aspirations for the country's geopolitical orientation. Each person is working with different material and rhetorical resources to advance his or her ideas about how this should look, but as Astana has been imbued with immense symbolic significance, the city-as-icon synecdochically works as a rhetorical platform for ordinary citizens and elites to narrate *their* personal vision of Kazakhstan's place in the world—rather than having one imposed from outside.

Beginning from this relative understanding of Astana as a site of competing identity narratives, rather than a place that can be objectively read and interpreted by foreigners, the geopolitics of spectacle and spectacular cities can be cast in a more critical light. To further explore the contingent temporalities and spatialities of urban spectacle, I examine several additional cases around the key questions I posed in chapter 1: Who uses spectacle, for whom, and when and where? I adapt Jan Nijman's method of "multiple individualizing comparisons," which integrates individual cases of a comparative study by focusing on one primary case and drawing out the connections around this central node.[2] Astana is the central case here, joined by similar developments in Central Asia (Baku, Azerbaijan, and Ashgabat, Turkmenistan), as well as cross-regionally in the Arabian

Peninsula (Abu Dhabi, UAE, and Doha, Qatar) and Southeast Asia (Naypyidaw, Myanmar, and Bandar Seri Begawan, Brunei). It is impossible to present a comprehensive view of each of these spectacular capital city projects. And while my goal is to suggest how their differing political geographies can extend our understanding of how spectacle becomes intelligible through its unspectacular Others, it is equally impossible to consider the full range of Others that give meaning to a spectacular city. By examining a small sample, however, we can begin to appreciate the relative nature of spectacle—and how it shapes and is shaped by regional geographies.

The verb *compare* means to examine multiple objects or ideas to note similarities and differences. In academic practice, the key word *differences* sometimes gets dropped, and scholars can lapse into assumptions that the goal of comparative research is to look for similarities alone.[3] Not only does this represent an impoverished understanding of the comparative method, but also it risks entrenching power-laden assumptions about geography and power. Exploring differences and disjunctures is and should be an important element of any comparative study that aims to reveal new insights about the world rather than merely recounting our perceptions of it. Integrating "unexpected comparisons" into academic practice requires, Garth Myers notes, "continual reflexivity, consciousness and humility, as well as some systemic changes in research development sympathetic to the cause, en route to transnational postcolonial cosmopolitanism."[4] Suggestive of what such an approach might look like, this chapter brings together examples stretching across Central Asia, the Arabian Peninsula, and Southeast Asia as an invitation to other scholars to consider how they might challenge their assumptions about what constitutes legitimate grounds for comparison. On the surface, many of the capital cities I discuss may look remarkably similar, but they all arise from unique political and geographic confluences. Their diverse geographies should not be viewed as an apples-and-oranges problem. Instead, they offer a unique opportunity to understand the highly divergent political effects of spectacular urbanism across and within various world regions. While their commonalities are important, examining these divergences can offer exceptional insights about power, spatial imaginaries, and the geopolitics of spectacle. If, as I have been arguing, spectacle is relative and intelligible only when contrasted with its unspectacular Others, this means that both will take many different forms and occupy starkly different places in the spatial imaginaries of their diverse audiences.

Political geography is thus the necessary foundation for interrogating how spectacle works in one context versus another and what spatial and temporal underpinnings make the projects spectacular. Because my approach is more cursory than exhaustive, I cannot detail the similarities of recent developments in Astana, Baku, Ashgabat, Abu Dhabi, Doha, Naypyidaw, and Bandar Seri Begawan. Any casual reader of the news will easily find information about these spectacular cities, but as I noted in the introduction, there is some important common ground that gives rise to this particular set of comparisons. Specifically, each is the capital of a nondemocratic state, which also has access to substantial natural resource wealth (see table 4.1). The cities themselves are spectacular insofar as they (1) have been developed on the basis of strong state planning, quickly, and on an unprecedented scale for their region; (2) boast lavish built landscapes and celebrations that represent a stark contrast with their surrounding context; and (3) are designed to display the government's prosperity and ostensible beneficence in a manner that contrasts significantly with other forms of state austerity and violence. With all of these elements coming together, each of these cities plays an important role in institutionalizing and legitimating local power relations.

Across the diverse cases in Central Asia, the Arabian Peninsula, and Southeast Asia, capital city development projects are founded on various unspectacular spaces, temporalities, embodied experiences, and forms of slow or structural violence, which are felt most in the territorial peripheries and among marginalized populations. They also largely depend on the synecdochic imaginary, with the cities serving as both icons and material platforms for elites to promote a paternalist image of the benevolent state and to make "inequality enchant" by engaging ordinary citizens in the spectacle at the center. Yet not all metaphors are successful, and they constantly risk being stretched too far. For the synecdoche of the city to be taken seriously, for its rhetorical claims to come across as accurate, "the facts must not contradict it too flagrantly, there must be no insuperable credibility gap."[5] President Nazarbayev's government has largely been able to overcome, or at least peripheralize,

Table 4.1 Demographics and economic indicators of the case countries, 2015–2016 estimates.*

Country	Total population	Percent urban	Avg. life expectancy	GDP per capita & world rank	UN HDI Index & world rank
Kazakhstan 2,724,900 km²	18.4 m	53.2	70.8 years	$ 25,700 (74th)	0.788 (56th)
Turkmenistan 488,100 km²	5.3 m	50.0	70.1 years	$ 17,300 (96th)	0.688 (109th)
Azerbaijan 86,600 km²	9.9 m	54.6	72.5 years	$ 17,700 (94th)	0.751 (78th)
Qatar 11,437 km²	2.3 m	99.2	78.7 years	$129,700 (1st)	0.850 (32nd)
UAE 82,880 km²	5.9 m	85.5	77.5 years	$ 67,700 (13th)	0.835 (41st)
Brunei 5,765 km²	.43 m	77.2	77.2 years	$ 79,700 (8th)	0.856 (31st)
Myanmar 676,578 km²	56.9 m	34.1	66.6 years	$ 6,000 (162nd)	0.536 (148th)

*United States Central Intelligence Agency, *The World Factbook,* https://www.cia.gov/library/publications/the-world-factbook/ (accessed January 30, 2017); United Nations Development Programme, *Human Development Report, 2015,* http://hdr.undp.org/sites/default/files/2015_human_development_report.pdf (accessed January 30, 2017).

the flagrant contradictions in Astana's being "Kazakhstan in miniature." Some of Asia's other spectacular cities may be stretching the synecdoche beyond its limits, however.

Central Asia: Developmentalism and Soviet Others

Like Kazakhstan, Azerbaijan and Turkmenistan are Caspian littoral states with access to the significant oil and gas reserves in and around the sea. Since the collapse of the Soviet Union in 1991, governments in all three countries have remained firmly authoritarian and have been quick to orient their economies toward hydrocarbon exploitation. Political and economic elites in Turkmenistan and Azerbaijan have used these resources to fuel spectacular development agendas in their capital cities, similar to what we have seen in Astana—albeit each with its own flavor.[6] The language of their presidents also parallels Nazarbayev's descriptions of

Astana's beauty, as they routinely underscore the impressive aesthetic transformations of their capital cities in the independence era. Here is Ilham Aliyev, the president of Azerbaijan:

> Baku has a historical beauty. Ancient Baku has its own beauty, and it is a source of our pride. At the same time, the rejuvenating and modernizing Baku has already secured a rightful place on the world map. . . . We are turning Baku into a city of gardens, parks, and boulevards. Baku is our beautiful city, and I can say with full responsibility today that it is one of the most beautiful cities around the world. . . . So we are creating an unprecedented environment in the city that will be very difficult to match. Such development and such investments really show the dynamic development of our country over a short period of time.[7]

Aliyev's sentiment and rhetorical flair is echoed in a statement from Turkmenistan:

> Ashgabat gets new breath and according to many indications has been achieving the level of world standards; our President Gurbanguly Berdimuhamedov has done a great service for this. It is the result of his political will, diplomacy, distinguished organizational skills, and permanent attention to the problems of the capital and, of course, to architecture. The love of each Ashgabat inhabitant to native city doesn't leave his heart. And it is [a] huge [testament] of success that the city in spite of any difficulties will overcome all obstacles and will confidently make a step into future.[8]

These official accounts of Baku and Ashgabat transcend mere lofty rhetoric. Neither capital was moved, as happened in Kazakhstan, but their built landscapes have undergone significant transformation since the Soviet era (see figures 4.1–4.2). Because of their access to resource wealth, unparalleled in other Soviet successor states, leaders in Kazakhstan, Azerbaijan, and Turkmenistan have quickly set themselves apart from their poor, politically weak, and unstable regional neighbors. Indeed, their shared Soviet past is central to how Astana, Ashgabat, and Baku are understood locally and regionally as spectacular. This is because their impressive capitals are all framed as marking a radical break with the Soviet past. An imagined version of that past is a central Other that makes the urban spectacle intelligible, as it is mapped onto the built environment and even entire countries across the border.

Figure 4.1 Monumental boulevard in central Ashgabat.
Source: Natalie Koch, 2014.

Figure 4.2 The Flame Towers in central Baku.
Source: Natalie Koch, 2013.

Local elites in Ashgabat and Baku argue that investing in lavish urban redevelopment schemes is necessary to capture the attention of global audiences, build international prestige, entice foreign capital, and advertise the countries' emerging market status. The significance and scope of this global audience can often be more fiction than reality—especially in the case of Turkmenistan, where recognition in the *Guinness Book of World Records* is frequently used to illustrate how attentive the world is to developments in the country.[9] Planners are practiced in fashioning the *image* of a highly attentive global audience, which they then harness to justify more and more costly development projects. Such international imaging projects are thus a common thread uniting Astana and Central Asia's other spectacular cities. When elites build up the image of their capitals as icons of the state's prosperity, they are also positioning themselves as beneficent. Who else besides a generous and caring leader, they ask, would work so hard to provide his citizens with a beautiful new capital?

The paternalist image of the benevolent state is a staple of developmental regimes, which stake their legitimacy on a goal of propelling a particular polity, nation, or other imagined community on a path of progress. The notion of "progress" is a troubled one, but as many scholars have suggested, its vagueness is precisely the source of its power: individuals in a position to define it are also in a position to define the agenda of any given group. Developmental regimes thus actively seek to dominate the very definition of progress. Given the hegemony of market capitalism in today's geopolitical system, developmentalist leaders generally define it in economic terms rather than in terms of other values such as social welfare, justice, or sustainability. Critically, in monopolizing the right to define progress, elites seek to obviate the need for competitive politics by establishing a pre-political consensus about the validity of this "inarguably good," if nebulous, goal.[10]

Efforts to define progress necessarily have a spatial and social extent. Temporally, development discourses are characteristically future-oriented: desired social arrangements absent today are temporally imagined and located in a utopian future.[11] Some progress-oriented regimes may hark back to an ancient golden age, but this is typically set in stark contrast to a more recent past of decay or backwardness that needs to be overcome. Spatially, narratives about modernity and progress are often inscribed onto material sites and landscapes or mapped onto entire countries or continents. We have already seen that cities are especially important sites for elites to materially inscribe their developmental narratives. Sometimes, though, the existing fabric, either material or social, may not align with their idealized visions. When this happens, some elements of a city or country, or certain members of a social group, might be categorized as backward or unmodern. Such anxious modernity narratives typically involve both temporal *and* spatial references, situating people and places as "outmoded" in an imagined time horizon oriented toward achieving future progress.

Developmentalism in Central Asia evinces the jointly temporal and spatial nature of imaginaries about modernity. In recent years, leaders in Kazakhstan, Turkmenistan, and Azerbaijan have considered their post-Soviet modernization agendas by looking at examples of other countries around the world. And because of their substantial hydrocarbon reserves, they have given special attention to similarly endowed places that have successfully mobilized their revenues to achieve development. Predictably, their attention has been fixed squarely on the former British protectorates in the Arabian Peninsula. The UAE, Qatar, Oman, and Bahrain all gained independence in 1971—only twenty years before the dissolution of the Soviet Union—and they have undergone tremendous growth since then. Development indicators in Central Asia still lag far behind those of the Gulf monarchies today, but elites and ordinary citizens consistently look to their remarkable transformation as a promise of what their own future might hold. Progress for these individuals is largely understood as equivalence with other highly developed countries.

In Kazakhstan, for example, Astana's master plan chief Amanzhol Chikanayev once told me in an interview, "The goal is to have people talk about Astana like Dubai." Not to *copy* Dubai, he emphasized, but to be *talked about* in the same terms as Dubai.[12] Meanwhile, in Azerbaijan, one local oligarch, Ibrahim Ibrahimov, told the *New York Times Magazine* about his plans to develop a series of artificial islands for luxury residences and entertainment venues outside Baku, to be called Khazar Islands. Although he admitted that the idea came to him as he was flying back to Baku from Dubai, Ibrahimov was adamant that he had not modeled his project on Dubai's strikingly similar "Palm" and "The World" artificial island archipelagos.[13] Khazar has since been abandoned, with little more than an entry arch and some dead palm trees to show for Ibrahimov's grand vision. Although elite projects in Central Asia often fall short of the standards of spectacle in the Arabian Peninsula, the broader aspiration of achieving equivalence with the prosperous Gulf states remains pervasive in Kazakhstan, Turkmenistan, and Azerbaijan. And for many of these political and economic elites, the built landscape of a country's capital is one of the most important measures of this prosperity. In seeking equivalence with Gulf capitals, Central Asian elites' visions of modernity on display in their own capitals are simultaneously future-oriented and geopolitically oriented—specifically geared toward the oil- and gas-rich Arabian Peninsula.[14]

Spatial imaginaries valorizing Gulf development stand in stark contrast to geopolitical narratives about the Soviet past. Being considered a "Great Power" was so central to nationalist pride in the USSR that many leaders and citizens throughout its successor states felt deeply humiliated at their lost status. This is especially so in Kazakhstan, Turkmenistan, and Azerbaijan because, unlike Russia, which still claims this status, these smaller states suddenly became geopolitically "peripheral" after 1991. No longer part of a global superpower, they have all positioned recent development agendas as a way to efface the shame of this lost glory and, perhaps, reclaim global prestige. Elites in Central Asia's resource-rich states were aided immensely by high hydrocarbon market prices from 2001 to 2015. Having at their disposal the funds from resource revenues and related speculative loans, local leaders were able to transform their countries rapidly (if selectively) in a way that their poorer neighbors, such as Georgia, Tajikistan, or Kyrgyzstan, simply could not. Viewed from Astana, Ashgabat, and Baku, those countries and their run-down cities look remarkably outdated and mired in the Soviet past.

The heavy investments in revamping the physical appearance of Kazakhstan, Turkmenistan, and Azerbaijan's capital cities in the post-Soviet era must be understood in this context. The regimes have overseen the development of hypermodern new architectural icons and consumer centers, torn down old Soviet structures and infrastructures, and otherwise beautified many decaying or neglected public spaces, squares, and parks (figures 4.3–4.5). The scope of these investments, begun in the 1990s, generally struck foreign commentators (and some domestic critics) as ill-advised in the broader context of poverty and political turmoil that prevailed at the time. Yet these urban development schemes were strategically calculated by local leaders. After the collapse of the Soviet Union, the transition was indeed a turbulent time. It is widely remembered across the post-Soviet space for being a period of complete disorder

Figure 4.3 Lavishly planted park at the foot of the "Healthy Path" mountain trail on Ashgabat's outskirts.
Source: Natalie Koch, 2014.

Figure 4.4 View of Baku's revamped Caspian Sea promenade, the "Bulvar," ending with the iconic new Crystal Palace arena, adjacent to the flagpole that was once the tallest in the world.
Source: Natalie Koch, 2013.

Figure 4.5 The Khan Shatyr entertainment complex in Astana, designed by Foster and Partners.
Source: Natalie Koch, 2015.

and social upheaval—popularly referenced as *bardak* (chaos).[15] The surface image of a beautiful, orderly new or otherwise overhauled capital city in Astana, Ashgabat, and Baku thus operates as a highly charged symbol of the ability of new state leaders to effect change and ensure effective governance.[16] By conjuring the visual appearance of order, even if it permeates no deeper than a building's façade, they have sought to instrumentally deploy their cities' material transformation as a synecdoche for the progress and order provided under their strong-handed but "benevolent" rule. Overall, official urban planning in each of Central Asia's three spectacular capitals is coordinated to evoke an emphatically *post-Soviet* vision of modernity.

For local elites, leveraging the image of a beautiful city is a form of nation-building. The spectacular city projects in Astana, Ashgabat, and Baku provide ordinary people the chance to see themselves as newly "modern," insofar as the cities are no longer mere monuments to Soviet architectural dogma and urban planning. As in so many other parts of the world, citizens in Central Asia are repeatedly taught to feel proud of their country because they now have a beautiful capital city—and one that is distinctively *national* rather than *Soviet*. For many, the synecdochic jump is persuasive: citizens frequently speak of their capitals with great pride, even if they disagree with the precise policies of their government. Just as their leaders do, citizens want to feel modern and proud of their national heritage, to be taken seriously on the world stage, "a recognized and respected somebody in the world who counts and is attended to."[17] Iconic capital city projects appear to offer just that. In the region's resource-rich states, the beautiful capital city allows people to speak positively of their country *without necessarily hailing the government itself*. This is especially important for skeptics of the authoritarian regimes: spectacular urban development creates opportunities for them to praise the capital itself rather than the elites presiding over its development. The cities in turn create a platform for citizens to express their national pride without the cognitive dissonance that comes with forced expressions of support for the autocrats at the top. In this respect, spectacular urbanism in Central Asia has facilitated and buttressed state-scale actors' efforts to mobilize popular support. Even if that support takes the shape of nationalist pride geared toward the homeland or the city, it is still a form of support that naturalizes the statist agenda of territorial sovereignty and newly configured visions of post-Soviet modernity.

In articulating their visions of what this post-Soviet modernity should look like, local leaders have tended to treat the Soviet past as an outdated Other to be materially expunged. For example, Astana is consistently portrayed as marking a clean break from the Soviet past, and representing all that is modern and forward-looking about the independent state of Kazakhstan. Countless Soviet buildings have been destroyed since Astana became the capital. Though many of the Soviet-era structures remain, large parts of the original Tselinograd settlement have been, and continue to be, razed, as prescribed by the official master plan, which is closely supervised by President Nazarbayev himself. Nazarbayev once explained his demolition orders when the capital moved to Astana by saying: "There were a lot of old, decrepit buildings, which were spoiling the look of the new capital. We had to demolish them. Instead, we have built new ones. For example, the building of the Ministry of Finance replaced old wooden houses. They did not match the look of Kazakhstan's new capital at all. As to my views on Soviet architecture, I will say that each epoch leaves its creations. Some of them live forever, others do not pass the test of time, quickly become morally outdated and wear out physically."[18] For Nazarbayev, Soviet urban landscapes were physically and morally outdated, as was the principle of standardization, which was a hallmark of Soviet urban development. Official planning and rhetoric have thus consistently underscored the need to make Astana's urban form unique, to preserve through architecture the "national coloring" (*natsional'nyi kolorit*).

Astana's Left Bank administrative center is intentionally eclectic, with its iconic buildings designed in a colorful assortment of styles and shapes. The city's skyline is a coordinated pastiche, which government leaders narrate as a symbol of the state's newly modern identity, definitively marking it as *not* Soviet. One of the government's most acclaimed projects in recent years has been the Khan Shatyr shopping mall, which was designed by the world-renowned architect Norman Foster (see figure 4.5). The values and wealth represented by the Khan Shatyr are not accessible to the vast majority of citizens, as we have already seen. Yet for many urbanites, Kazakhstan's iconic new consumer sites are understood less in terms of their exclusionary or elitist nature than as icons of the country's rapid development in the years since independence and its now legitimate claims to modernity. Many people therefore look positively on these sites, even if they cannot afford to participate in or enjoy their luxuries. Astana's iconic buildings, and indeed the city's development as a whole, offer a material reference point for Kazakhstan's rapid progress. Yet by defining the shining new spaces and structures as icons of the state's newfound prosperity, elites appropriate the language of modernity to de-stigmatize the practice of exclusion and to recast elite fancies as popular desires. As a geopolitical imaginary with wide resonance, Astana has thus become a salient metaphor for what many citizens understand to be their great fortune in living in a country that has successfully moved beyond the Soviet past.[19]

Monumental urban planning serves a similar purpose in official narratives in Turkmenistan, though it has taken a rather different form in Ashgabat than in Astana. While President Nazarbayev openly criticizes Soviet architecture for its uniformity, Turkmenistan's first president, Saparmurat Niyazov, desired precisely this and famously mandated that all Ashgabat's buildings be clad in white marble. Niyazov felt that the standardized façades would lend the city a dramatic feel—one of opulence in the post-Soviet period, which would be visually stunning when contrasted to the hulking gray concrete blocks that were the hallmark of Soviet housing in the years after Stalin. Perhaps the most dramatic element of the city, however, is the sense of abandonment in contrast with the scope of recent development. Nearly everywhere in the new quarters, the city is devoid of the chaotic movement of street commerce, traffic, and pedestrians (see figure 4.1). As in Astana and, increasingly, Baku, enormous distances between major buildings and broad multi-lane avenues mark Ashgabat as a car-oriented city, where pedestrians and a lively street life are not welcome. There are, of course, large areas that do not conform to the monumental image that is usually projected of all three cities. Having some of the liveliness of a less planned city, such spaces are coded as not "really" part of the new, modern capital, but rather unofficial developments or holdovers from the old Soviet urban fabric (figure 4.6). These unspectacular Others are, in short, cast as morally outdated—even if (or perhaps because) they are the spaces that most ordinary citizens inhabit in their day-to-day life.

Figure 4.6 "Unofficial" view of a Soviet housing block in Baku.
Source: Natalie Koch, 2013.

Figure 4.7 The Heydar Aliyev Cultural Center, designed by Zaha Hadid, in Baku.
Source: Natalie Koch, 2013.

Baku's city center and surrounding neighborhoods have also undergone a dramatic transformation, geared toward creating the impression of modernist order and post-Soviet prosperity similar to that of its neighbors across the Caspian Sea. It has quickly become home to many hypermodern skyscrapers, sports stadiums, and other sites of entertainment and consumer culture (figure 4.7; see also figures 4.2 and 4.4). Yet the vision of modernity enacted here is unique to Baku because of its history as the birthplace of the oil industry in the late 1800s. Supplying half the world's oil by 1901, Baku was settled by many newly rich oil barons (notably including the Nobel brothers). Most hailed from Europe, and they brought their architectural traditions with them, transforming the city center by building numerous grandiose mansions in an eclectic mix of European styles.[20] Most of these buildings were preserved during the Soviet period, but because this architectural legacy predated the Soviets, Baku's *post*-Soviet leaders did not embark on the same sort of demolition agenda seen in parts of Astana and Ashgabat. Many Soviet-era structures throughout the capital have in fact been removed, but just as many or more have simply been plastered with vaguely neoclassical façades to create a sense of unity with the mansions of the early 1900s and expand the city's "European" image. The practice of covering large Soviet apartment blocks and other structures with new façades is also common in Kazakhstan, Turkmenistan, and much of Eurasia, but in Baku it is widely interpreted as a return to the pre-Soviet glory days. In all these cases, though, it entrenches an image of the Soviet past as an undesirable Other.

Leaders in Kazakhstan, Turkmenistan, and Azerbaijan have consistently stressed the risk of turning back the clock and returning to a time when the national community lacked proper sovereignty. Similarly, the post-Soviet governments draw on the collective memory of their populations about the more proximate past—the period of *bardak* (chaos) which marked the transition to statehood after 1991. No one among presidents Nazarbayev, Aliyev, and Niyazov was keen to accept democracy after the fall of the Soviet Union. Instead, they all argued that strong authoritarian leadership was needed during the transition and that any political liberalization should come only gradually. Even today, local politicians and state-controlled media outlets consistently warn citizens that more liberal political configurations are a recipe for disaster by drawing from and embellishing on popular narratives about the wild 1990s. They constantly return to the negative collective memory of collapse and *disorder* in the past to condition how people understand and relate to affirmative political values of *order* in the present. Raising the specter of returning to the Soviet past and the *bardak* of the transition period is one of the most potent political discourses in the resource-rich states of Central Asia. This temporal narrative is also mapped onto particular places, as their poor and conflict-ridden regional neighbors serve as convenient spatial referents for these claims: the turbulent past is vividly located just across the border.[21] So in addition to building on a stigmatized vision of Soviet urbanism, these cities also build on a stigmatized vision of the contemporary situation in Central Asia's poorer republics—Georgia, Kyrgyzstan, Tajikistan, and Uzbekistan.

When citizens of the wealthier, resource-rich states look over the border, the lack of extensive state-led redevelopment is glaringly obvious; they quickly note crumbling infrastructure, ramshackle dwellings, and rapidly deteriorating Soviet structures, which their own governments have actively sought to destroy, replace, or at least hide. As residents of Almaty will often proclaim, "Bishkek [in Kyrgyzstan] looks like Almaty did twenty years ago—it's amazing!" Thus, even those urbanites in Kazakhstan, Turkmenistan, and Azerbaijan who are not pleased with their state's development priorities can readily visualize their own prosperity relative to that of their poorer neighbors as well as the Soviet past. The resulting attitude that "at least it's not as bad as over there" often serves as grounds for political apathy while also validating the efforts of political elites to position their spectacular capitals as a touchstone to validate their claims about the merits of illiberal governance.

Regardless of their accuracy, interpretations of regional urban geographies work through an interlocking set of spatial and temporal imaginaries. To fully internalize them, citizens must actively be instructed about their relative prosperity. Much of this learning happens through daily conversations and interactions among individuals, as well as personal travel experiences. It is also built into the material landscapes of their capital cities and manifested in the prolific official discourse that praises the beauty of the capital. By looking across the border to places like Bishkek or Dushanbe, the capital of Tajikistan, and thinking back to the extreme hardships of the 1990s period of *bardak*, ordinary people are able to measure the progress proffered by their governments. Their neighbors, it seems, are woefully mired in the Soviet past. This is a deeply geopolitical imaginary because, in thinking synecdochically about capital cities as markers of an entire country's progress, they believe they can *see* the difference that their leaders have made through their benevolent, if heavy-handed, development agendas in the post-Soviet period. This is not an apolitical act of seeing, but one that has been strategically coordinated and guided by the political elites in Kazakhstan, Turkmenistan, and Azerbaijan. But as Michael Mann underscores, "In politics, minimal but resonant plausibility—never some higher standard of truth—rules."[22] Likewise, metaphors are only ever judged on their plausibility, and here, the synecdoche generally seems to work.

The Arabian Peninsula: Hinterlands beyond State Borders

As we have seen in the case of Kazakhstan, spectacular urbanism is intimately bound up with structural violence in the country's hinterlands, and this *spatially peripheral* deprivation is key to sustaining the fiction of the capital city as a wondrous site of opportunity and state benevolence. The synecdochic imaginary is readily apparent within the state's large territory. By contrast, in smaller states with little territorial differentiation, questions arise regarding the spatial, social, and political extent of the "periphery." Indeed, when considering the case of two of the world's smallest states, Qatar and the United Arab Emirates, we find that a territorially focused approach can hinder our efforts to conceptualize the social and political Others that give spectacle meaning locally. As with the Central Asian states just considered, these two monarchies on the eastern Arabian Peninsula are both nondemocratic and rich with hydrocarbon reserves. They are, however, territorially small and almost entirely urban (see table 4.1). This, combined with their unique histories and demographics, demands a broader understanding of the hinterlands that make their spectacular city projects possible—and intelligible. In short, the Gulf Arab states' peripheral Others extend well beyond state boundaries.

As with the Central Asian states, narratives about the past are also highly politicized in the Arabian Peninsula and figure centrally in local spectacular city development agendas. Formerly Trucial States under British protection since the early 1800s, Qatar and the UAE became independent in 1971, when the United Kingdom decided not to renew its protectorate treaties with the eastern sheikhdoms of the Arabian Peninsula. The UAE declared its independence on December 2 as a federation of smaller emirates: Abu Dhabi, Ajman, Dubai, Fujairah, Sharjah, and Umm al-Qawain. A seventh, Ras al-Khaimah, joined the federation several months later. Qatar initially considered joining the UAE but ultimately declared its independence separately on September 3 of that year. The British were aware early on that the region was rich in oil and gas reserves, but hydrocarbon-funded development was minimal in Qatar and the UAE until after independence. People in the area had traditionally led subsistence lifestyles along the coast or in the desert interior, oriented around herding, trade, seafaring, and pearl diving.

Whether referring to Bedouins or coastal residents, popular narratives about the pre-independence era consistently recollect the humble origins of these two now prosperous states. In addition to being among the world's wealthiest countries, Qatar and the UAE also have some of the highest urbanization rates: those living in cities constitute

Figure 4.8 Downtown Doha's iconic skyline.
Source: Natalie Koch, 2014.

Figure 4.9 Downtown Abu Dhabi's skyline.
Source: Natalie Koch, 2013.

98.8 percent of the total population in Qatar and 84.4 percent in the Emirates. It was not until the 1950s and 1960s, however, that urbanization processes in Qatar and the UAE began in any meaningful fashion, essentially starting with the introduction of the countries' first water desalination plants in 1953 and 1960, respectively. As in Central Asia, the two capital cities, Doha and Abu Dhabi, and their carefully choreographed skylines are synecdochically framed as a testament to the countries' stunning growth since independence (figures 4.8–4.9).[23] The cities' impressive rise has consistently been a central theme in official rhetoric, which highlights the contrast between the image of ultra-modernity today and their countries' humble past. This is especially visible in formulaic descriptions of each capital targeted at foreigners. The official Doha tourist website declares:

> Qatar is situated at the cross-roads of East and West with its strategic location between the Americas, Europe and Asia. Its social warmth provides the foundation for the country's hospitality. The country offers world-class facilities with a deep traditional cultural experience. Home to more than one hundred different nationalities, from the moment you land, you can sense diversity in all its aspects. Accordingly, Qatar has become a popular hub for regional and global cultural, intellectual, artistic and sports events. . . . Qatar is one of the few countries that were able to mix between modernity, with its gleaming skyscrapers and advantageous gas industry, and history.[24]

According to the Abu Dhabi tourist website: "Abu Dhabi's culture is firmly rooted in Arabia's Islamic traditions, creating a shining example of Islam's true commitment to tolerance and hospitality. The combination of international influences and a strong commitment to local heritage has created an intriguing mix of new and old."[25] The website elsewhere explains: "Meaning 'Land of the Gazelle' in Arabic, Abu Dhabi was founded when a young antelope led a wandering tribe to fresh water, on an island with no more than 300 palm ('barasti') huts, a few coral buildings and the Ruler's fort. This simple island settlement has since been transformed into the modern, cosmopolitan city of Abu Dhabi and the high-rise capital of the United Arab Emirates."[26]

The contrast between local traditions and globally oriented modernity is synecdochically mapped onto the image of the spectacular capital cities, encouraging observers to think about their gleaming skyscrapers and cosmopolitan character as representative of the progress and values found across the entire country and its populace. Also notable in these descriptions is the focus on *diversity*, as in the proud proclamation that Qatar is "home to more than one hundred different nationalities." This is paralleled in the Emirates, where during the 2014 National Day celebration, for example, the country was proudly reported to have broken the world record for the most representatives of different nationalities singing one anthem (that of the UAE) simultaneously: 119.[27] Who are all these non-nationals residing in Qatar and the UAE? And why is the official discourse about the capital cities so permeated with references to national diversity?

Neither Qatar nor the UAE is very populous today. Both have grown dramatically since the middle of the twentieth century, however: Qatar's population is up to 2.3 million from 25,000 in 1950 and the UAE's to 5.9 million from 70,000 in 1950. But of these total populations, passport-holding ethnic nationals represent under 15 percent of the entire population in both countries. The remaining 85 percent of residents are non-nationals and, because of citizenship laws, noncitizens. Like the other Arabian Peninsula states, Qatar and the UAE have *jus sanguinis* (right of blood) laws, which determine citizenship by lineage or ethnic identity rather than place of birth, as in *jus soli* (right of the soil) regimes.[28] Most states with *jus sanguinis* citizenship laws have mixed regimes that permit naturalization on the basis of residency, marriage, or other allowances. The Gulf states are particularly strict in that they do not permit naturalization, and only children with *both* parents of the official nationality (that is, Qatari or Emirati) have a juridical right to citizenship. Children with only one parent who is a citizen-national, along with all other non-Qataris and non-Emiratis (or "expats," as they are locally called), are never legally entitled to become citizens, regardless of how long Qatar or the UAE has been their home.

The two monarchies' unique demographic situation is not merely a passing phase but is *integral* to the entire political economic system advanced by the ruling families and their governments. Though noncitizens make up the overwhelming majority of the two countries' total population, and though many were born in the Gulf into families that have even been there for multiple generations, they are only ever accorded temporary residence permits based on employment. This may seem to imply that local governments do not desire the presence of large numbers of foreign residents. In reality, precisely the opposite is true: promoting the in-migration of foreign residents has been a major (if not *the*) driving force in the Gulf monarchies' recent development policies. As elsewhere across the Arabian Peninsula, growth agendas are built entirely around and upon the labor of noncitizens. Local development would be impossible without a vast population of migrant workers of all professions, nationalities, and socioeconomic backgrounds. They include highly educated and highly paid "knowledge economy" workers from other Arab countries, Europe, and the Americas, as well as India and other parts of South Asia. Among the lower-paid ranks, such as in the construction and tourism sectors, migrants come from all over South and Southeast Asia (but especially India, Pakistan, Sri Lanka, Nepal, and the Philippines), and increasingly Africa.[29]

Citizenship rights understandably dominate discussions about politics in the Arabian Peninsula. Although an exclusive focus on the citizen/noncitizen binary can obscure many important social and political processes in the region, the juridical categorization is nonetheless tremendously important because it has concrete implications for who is entitled to substantial state-sponsored welfare benefits.[30] Noncitizens are not wholly excluded from certain state benefits, but they do not have access to the same social welfare benefits granted to passport-holding citizens. These can include free or subsidized education, free health care, privileged access to state-sector jobs and state-mandated higher salaries than for noncitizens in equivalent posts, and much more. These dispensations, combined with the substantial informal benefits of social networks among ethnic nationals, ensure that citizens are almost uniformly well off. This privileged minority is predictably keen to preserve their countries' strict citizenship regulations; the state's political and financial rewards would only be diluted by a larger citizenry.

A prevailing narrative about resource-rich countries is that their governments use extensive state welfare to "buy off" their citizens and deter opposition. Social benefits are certainly a powerful stabilizing force in many countries, but this narrative obscures the fact that citizens are not merely passive recipients but rather active promoters of such a system. In fact, citizen-nationals have been vocal proponents of the Gulf states' nondemocratic and largely exclusionary political configuration. Much of this support can be traced to how the countries' exclusivist citizenship models are applied to corporate ownership policies and property rights. Noncitizens do not have access to the same social welfare benefits as citizens, nor are they allowed to own land outside a handful of special zones. Consequently, citizens have a near monopoly on land- and property-based revenues, which they derive from renting to foreign workers and companies. This situation has fueled the rapid expansion of the two countries' already substantial foreign resident population, which contributes to an expanding market of renters and further fuels the building booms in Doha and Abu Dhabi.

Corporate laws in Qatar and the UAE also require that small businesses have at least 51 percent ownership by a citizen. When a foreign resident wants to open a business, then, a citizen sponsor must sign off on the paperwork. This individual typically refrains from engaging in actual business operations, but the ownership structure creates the opportunity for idle profits and adds to the financial benefits citizen-nationals reap from the expanding presence of noncitizen residents. This system is inextricably linked to spectacular urban development in the region. Combined with property rights and citizenship regimes, citizens have substantial incentives to support the continued expansion of their capital cities. More buildings and urban infrastructure, as well as more foreign workers and companies, translate into more prime profits. Sporadic murmurs about the demographic "imbalance" between citizens and noncitizens notwithstanding, Qatari and Emirati citizens largely favor state-promoted urban development, seeing spectacular city schemes in Doha and Abu Dhabi as a welcome economic opportunity. For them, the rewards are quite tangible. In this respect, they occupy a place more or less analogous to that of Central Asia's elites. In the Gulf countries, however, there are no national masses who are obviously shut out from the benefits of the state's developmentalist agenda. There are masses, to be sure, but they have no legitimate claims to these rewards: they are not citizens.[31]

Furthermore, because of their small territorial size and high urbanization rates, in Qatar and the UAE there are no rural poor who are excluded from the states' city-focused modernization agendas. In the Central Asian states, this is quite different. There, for both historical and contemporary reasons, being an urban resident is already to be privileged; those in the rural hinterlands have significantly lower living standards and are subjected to various forms of social exclusion and structural violence. As I have shown, while urbanites are generally aware of these differentials, cultural and economic stereotypes work to stigmatize poor individuals in the periphery. Mundane practices of stigmatizing the rural poor are not imposed by state authorities, of course, but they do help to naturalize the governments' overwhelming bias toward urban development at the expense of more territorially expansive development agendas. At first blush, the situation would appear fundamentally different in the Gulf states, which lack any major discrepancies between the cities and their hinterlands.

If, however, we broaden our understanding of the center and periphery to include the noncitizen residents who are the majority in Qatar and the UAE, we can begin to trace their hinterlands far across the region. Unskilled workers, predominantly hailing from Asia and Africa, are important political subjects both in the Gulf and beyond. Extensive research and investigative reporting have illuminated the plight of the poorest of the region's expats, many of whom experience extreme injustice on the job.[32] Yet precisely because of their labor and their earning potential in the Gulf, they are also vital conduits of power relations between the resource-rich Arabian Peninsula and their places of origin. These power relations are not uniformly negative or oppressive; they are also built on pleasure and pride. The spectacle of Gulf urbanization enchants, entices, and draws in even the most marginalized individuals—not only through the material opportunities it is imagined to offer, but also through the symbolic-cultural values ascribed to places like Dubai and Abu Dhabi in popular imaginaries in India, Pakistan, and beyond. Among low- and middle-income expats in the Gulf, there is even an urban hierarchy akin to that discussed in the previous chapter: Dubai is definitively at the top, being the most desired destination for living and working, followed by the other larger Gulf cities Abu Dhabi and Doha. Smaller cities, such as Ras al Khaimah or Kuwait City, as well as places in Saudi Arabia, rank much lower, and many expats feel ashamed if they can find work only in one of these "lower-tier" Gulf destinations. However this hierarchy is imagined for a given individual, the important point is that foreign workers attach a great deal of pride to their place of residence, in no small part because of the prestige it accords them back home in their sending countries.

While spectacle in the Central Asian cases was shown to work largely through a synecdochic imagination of the capitals as symbols of benevolent state developmentalism and opportunity for all, in the Gulf, the synecdoche has a different balance between the social and the spatial. In this regional configuration, noncitizen residents, who face a perpetually liminal political status in the Gulf, are structurally barred from reaping the full material rewards of the region's spectacular urban development. Yet, in the official discourse, expats are taught to focus on the benevolence and *inclusion* being offered by the government, rather than the long list of social *exclusions* they face on a day-to-day basis, which silently circumscribe their potential. The official narratives that are mobilized through the spectacle of the city in Qatar and the UAE systematically downplay these structural exclusions and instead emphasize the governments' generosity and magnanimity. These projects are politically effective to the extent that they can successfully narrate such spatial and temporal displacements, institutionalizing the cognitive frames that allow people to focus on the positive and the spectacular, and overlook its negative and unspectacular elements. And this is largely why the official discourse about the capital cities, quoted earlier, is saturated with references to national diversity.

To see how these positive, inclusion-centered scripts get internalized by expats, one need look no further than the yearly National Day holidays in both Qatar and the UAE. The December celebrations are greeted with tremendous enthusiasm by many of the lower-class residents of Doha and Abu Dhabi (though, precisely for this reason, they are held in contempt by middle- and upper-class expats). Throngs of workers eagerly join the festivities, including the most popular event of the holiday in both countries, the evening car parade. Many attend in casual attire, but some decorate their cars and their bodies with Qatari or Emirati nationalist paraphernalia. Certain participants simply attend for want of another weekend diversion, while others are eager to demonstrate their reverence for the state and what they describe as its leaders' "generosity" for allowing them to live and work there. In either case, the overarching effect is one of grounding this population's understanding of place and subjectivity in a manner that reinforces statist discourse about the capitals as bastions of diversity and cosmopolitan ideals and, by implication, definitively *modern.* Ephemeral as it may be, expat enchantment on display during National Day also seems to suggest that the spectacle of the city is working its synecdochic magic. Just as with the residents of Aral who were enticed by the spectacle at the center, many of these poor migrant workers exhibit a substantial degree of fervor for the celebrations and actively mobilize the nationalist frames that they afford.[33]

This dynamic extends well beyond the National Day holidays, but it is difficult for outside observers to imagine that noncitizens in Qatar and the UAE might experience an emotional connection to a country that explicitly bars them from becoming full-fledged members of the nation. Nonetheless, expats are often extremely proud of their adopted home and view their ability to "make it" in a Gulf capital with just as much pride as someone moving from Aral to Astana might. It may not persuade everyone, but the spectacle at the center can indeed make inequality enchant among some of the region's most politically, socially, and financially marginal expat populations. Viewed beyond statist thinking, the center-periphery relations that are conjured through the spectacular city schemes in the Arabian Peninsula begin to look rather more like those we have considered in Central Asia, here encompassing not the rural hinterlands but the many places that send thousands of migrant workers, stretching across Asia, Africa, and the greater Middle East. Ultimately, though, it is the logic of the territorial state, combined with the state's power to designate who *is* and *is not* entitled to citizenship, that makes this extended understanding of the hinterland so crucial. Beyond territorial delineations, citizenship regimes also hinge on a binary between the *legal* and the *illegal*: Who is legally counted as "one of us" and who is excluded? Who is legally entitled to the benefits of state resources and services? And who is legally entitled to an opinion about these very questions? The different manner in which these borders are drawn in the Arabian Peninsula and Central Asia is what makes the comparison between spectacular urbanism in the two regions particularly illuminating.

On the surface, spectacular urbanization agendas in Qatar and the UAE look quite similar to those in Central Asia's capitals. In the Gulf, however, citizens, residents, and foreign observers all tend to interpret local building booms as "legal," and thus legitimate, investments on the part of citizens. In Central Asia, by contrast, they are largely coded as "illegal." One of the primary ways for Central Asia's elites (and especially the presidents and their families) to enrich themselves and distribute patronage to their allies is through the allocation of sizable construction contracts. Large-scale developments funded by the state are typically awarded to a handful of elite-controlled shell companies headquartered abroad (e.g., Sembol in Kazakhstan, Polimeks in Turkmenistan, and DIA Holding in Azerbaijan).[34] But because all citizens in Central Asia ostensibly have an equal right to the state's resource rents, and because government leaders claim to be fairly distributing this wealth to their citizens, privileging a select group is understood as a form of cronyism and thus an illegal and corrupt practice. This interpretation hinges on a basic understanding of *who* is legally entitled to state resources, as dictated by the official citizenship regime.

Spectacular urban development in Abu Dhabi and Doha is also a way to distribute resource rents, but elite patronage politics are not tied to offshore money-laundering schemes, as in Central Asia. Rents in the Gulf monarchies are instead primarily made accessible through the granting or denial of citizenship. Inequalities among citizen-nationals notwithstanding, their profits from the capitals' building booms are deemed legal and appropriate because the official citizenship regime accords them, and them alone, the entitlement to rewards from state resources. So while Qatari and Emirati citizens may occupy a place analogous to that of Central Asia's elites in terms of their privileged access to the benefits of the spectacle at the center, it is resident foreigners in the Gulf and ordinary citizens in Central Asia who cannot reap the same rewards. The vastly different citizenship regimes explain the discrepancy in how spectacular cities are understood to be legal/legitimate in one context and illegal/corrupt in another. The cities in both regions may operate through many of the same aesthetics and spatial imaginaries, but local demographic, territorial, and political-economic configurations influence how foreign observers and citizens alike interpret their justness—and locate their unspectacular Others. If we do not take a statist perspective for granted, we can begin to see how spectacular cities in the Arabian Peninsula operate through similar forms of structural violence but with a different geopolitical scope.

Southeast Asia: Spectacular Cities in a Less Exhibitional World

The East Asian capitals of Naypyidaw, Myanmar (Burma), and Bandar Seri Begawan, Brunei, like their counterparts farther west, are made possible by local resource economies. As capital cities, they are necessarily positioned as sites where outside observers look to understand the ruling regimes and their priorities. "The modern capital is expected to be, above all else, the seat of government and the focus of its symbolic presence," Lawrence Vale reminds us.[35] In many respects, however, the cases of Naypyidaw and Bandar Seri Begawan represent a marked contrast to the form of spectacular urbanism in the cases just discussed. In particular, neither city is currently configured to project a coherent image of the city-as-icon, to circulate internationally as a "floating signifier."[36] In contrast to the intense city-branding exercises seen in Central Asia and the Arabian Peninsula, spectacular urbanism in Myanmar and Brunei works through a different "representational economy."

Representational economies are those practices involved in repre-senting and interpreting space and the material world, including urban landscapes. As discussed in the introduction, the dominant way of seeing urban landscapes as "picture-like and legible" requires think-ing abstractly about space, separating the observer from the material world.[37] Though they are frequently taken for granted and naturalized as apolitical, representational practices that position the façade of a build-ing as a sign of some reality underneath (modernity or backwardness, perhaps) arise and are reproduced through deeply political processes. In exploring how these forms of abstract thinking arrived in Egypt, Timo-thy Mitchell argues that prior to being subjected to the colonial gaze, Cairo's built environment had not been organized representationally. That is, the city was not seen as a text to be read and interpreted for some fundamental realities about Egyptian culture, values, or modernity. As Mitchell's work illustrates, people must *learn* to think about and read urban landscapes as symbols of an abstract ideology or developmental status. So while it is not natural to consider a city skyline or a skyscraper a representation of a nation's modernity or progress, doing so is now globally pervasive.

In Southeast Asia, this manner of reading the urban landscape as a set of signs has long been at work and continues today. Architects, planners, and other expert elites across the region readily participate as consumers and producers of symbolic meanings by inscribing them onto building façades and launching them into international discourse through city-branding schemes. The shape of spectacular urbanism in Southeast Asia amply attests to its pervasiveness, as city planners from Singapore to Kuala Lumpur and Taipei all compete with one another to position their city as *the* leading icon of modernity, development, or innovation.[38] But not all places and people operate with such enthusiasm in these representational economies. Some state and urban planners lack either the interest or the resources to compete over their city's image.

The two cases at hand, Bandar Seri Begawan in Brunei and Naypyidaw in Myanmar, have the resources but apparently not the desire; their built landscapes have *not* been organized as iconic images for international circulation. But why is this the case? And what can it tell us about local representational economies and the place of spectacular urbanism in Myanmar and Brunei?

Some observers might simply dismiss Bandar Seri Begawan and Naypyidaw as non-spectacular capitals. Unique as it may be that they are not accorded the same degree of iconicity as seen in the Central Asian and Gulf cities, I believe they are indeed spectacular. This is not just because they boast impressive urban landscapes with monumental architecture, water features, greenery, pomp and circumstance, and amenities, as we have seen elsewhere. It is also because, regardless of the fact that these luxuries are not advertised internationally, they represent a stark contrast with the unspectacular realities and hardships one encounters in the two cities' hinterlands. Beginning from the assumption that the spectacular and the unspectacular are contextually co-produced—that the spectacle of the center can only ever be intelligible when contrasted with something markedly different beyond its spatial and temporal confines—political geographic context again illuminates the unique contours of the geopolitics of spectacle in these two Southeast Asian capitals.

Bandar Seri Begawan is the capital of Brunei (officially Negara Brunei Darussalam, or Nation of Brunei, Abode of Peace). The country is territorially minuscule (at 5,765 square kilometers) and has a population of only around 436,000. It was a British protectorate like the Gulf states, from the late 1800s until formal independence in 1984. Thanks to the country's significant oil and gas reserves (which account for over 90 percent of its exports) and its small population size, Brunei's GDP per capita is among the highest in the world (see table 4.1), and citizens have access to a range of generous social welfare benefits.[39] Brunei is an absolute monarchy, presided over by Sultan Hassanal Bolkiah, who came to power at age twenty-one, after his father's 1967 abdication.[40] For an extraordinary length of time, from 1962 until 2004, the country was managed under a state of emergency, which was renewed every two years. A new constitution was introduced in 2006, as part of the transition away from emergency governance. It declared the sultan infallible, stating that he "can do no wrong in either his personal or any official capacity."[41] Sultan Hassanal Bolkiah's rule has been both severe and quixotic. He and his family are also known to have amassed huge fortunes, including his famous collection of over seven thousand luxury cars and exclusive properties around the world. When they are not traveling, the royal family live in the world's largest residential palace, the Istana Nurul Iman, in Bandar Seri Begawan. Allegedly costing over $1.4 billion to build in 1984, the opulent palace is but one symbol of the degree to which Brunei's wealth has been concentrated in the hands of the royal family.[42]

Over two-thirds of Brunei's residents, or approximately 280,000 people, live in the metro area of Bandar Seri Begawan, Brunei's longtime capital and largest city. In recent years, large-scale development has begun to transform its urban fringes, which are now dotted with a wide range of new government ministries, mosques, hotels, and palaces (figures 4.10–4.11). Nevertheless, the city's built landscape has not historically been organized to promote an iconic image for foreign circulation. Nor are recent developments designed to do so. Bandar Seri Begawan's newest buildings are certainly monumental and have cost state coffers large sums to build and maintain. They are also surrounded by carefully manicured roadways and grounds, promoting both the image of opulence and the clear visual order

Figure 4.10 Central Bandar Seri Begawan.
Source: Natalie Koch, 2015.

Figure 4.11 The prime minister's office (jabatan perdana menteri) in
Bandar Seri Begawan.
Source: Natalie Koch, 2015.

common to modernist urban planning. The city draws much of its spectacular nature from the visual impressiveness of these sites, but because the buildings are decentralized and accessible only by car, they are not strategically coordinated to develop an iconic image of the capital's skyline.[43] Given this orientation, the spectacular nature of Bandar Seri Begawan is most intelligible for domestic audiences rather than international observers. This is because the city's primary Other is an entirely different urban form: the water village.

Bruneians traditionally lived "on the water" and reserved their contact with land for burials. Communities of homes were built offshore on stilts and connected via gangways. Still pervasive today, these settlements have electric and telecommunication connections, as well as schools, mosques, hospitals, and police and fire stations—all on stilts. The largest discrete settlement is Kampong Ayer in Brunei Bay, with over 39,000 residents, or approximately 10 percent of the country's entire population (figure 4.12). From the time of British rule, the sultans of Brunei have tried to encourage people to move to the land, believing that "modern" Bruneians should abandon their old-fashion living patterns and the associated fear of land as harboring dangerous spirits. Yet these beliefs and cultural inclinations,

Figure 4.12 The Kampong Ayer water village offshore from Bandar Seri Begawan.
Source: Natalie Koch, 2015.

combined with strict limitations on property ownership in the capital, mean that this push has not translated into complete success in eliminating water villages. Settlements such as Kampong Ayer continue to expand, and people are reluctant to leave. Because of the interconnected nature of the communities and unsafe electric connections, they are sometimes destroyed by fire. In such cases, the government has largely refused to permit reconstruction, opting instead to raze the site entirely. Otherwise, though, it can seem that the government has given up on its modernization agenda to relocate the water village populations.

In some respects, the status quo may be desirable for Bruneian authorities. Akin to many of the newly planned sites across Central Asia and the Gulf, parts of Bandar Seri Begawan can have an eerie sense of abandonment. Its monumental buildings, mosques, and hotels on land stand largely in quiet isolation, in contrast with the lively communal environment of the water villages. There are no teeming masses to be found anywhere in the city, leaving its modernist order largely unchallenged by dense layers of social activity and exchange. If the spectacle of the capital city becomes intelligible in contrast to an unspectacular Other in the form of the water village, another aspect of that relationship is the fact that the government's largely laissez-faire attitude has ensured a population largely unconcerned with how the state operates and uses its vast resource wealth. By allowing people to continue practicing their traditional ways of life, "unmodern" as it may look to foreign observers, Bruneian authorities are avoiding a sensitive issue that might provoke wider civic engagement. They are also advancing, if only implicitly, an image of the sultan as a benevolent ruler because of his refusal to take a heavy-handed approach to relocating people to the land, uprooting them from their social and community attachments.

As we have seen in Kazakhstan and elsewhere, the paternalist image of the considerate leader can foster a complacent, or at least a silent, citizenry. In Brunei, popular disengagement has similarly allowed the sultan and his inner circle to amass tremendous fortunes. The result is that, as local elites monopolize land markets across Brunei, Bandar Seri Begawan truly becomes the *sultan*'s city—a dynamic also seen in Astana, which I described earlier as paralleling Veyne's characterization of ancient Rome as the *urbs sua,* "wholly devoted to the Emperor, wholly his," and where he alone should shine.[44] The spectacle of the sultan's city on land is made possible by the state's monopolization of rents from oil extraction, from which the sultan benefits inordinately. Although it can be difficult to discern when contrasted with more familiar forms of spectacular urbanism, globally and regionally, the structural violence inhering in Brunei's development priorities is definitively tied to the highly unequal distribution of benefits from the state's resource wealth. In sum, the representational economy of Bandar Seri Begawan may not work explicitly on the basis of the synecdochic imaginary, but the capital's development exemplifies the paternalist power relations and structural violence that we have seen in other countries in Central Asia and the Arabian Peninsula, insofar as it reflects an intense concentration of the state's resources in the hands of a small elite around the sultan and his family.

In Myanmar, the image of its capital, Naypyidaw, also does not circulate as spectacular icon for foreign consumption, though it has much in common with the states in Central Asia. Like Astana, Naypyidaw was a greenfield capital, moved to the center of Myanmar from a more southern capital, Yangon (Rangoon). It was relocated suddenly in 2005, after the government had been secretly constructing the city for three years. The new capital was conceived by the eccentric Senior General Than Shwe, who ruled the country from 1992 to 2011. Than Shwe was the latest in the line of military leaders in charge of the country since General Ne Win's coup d'état in 1962. The most brutal phase of military rule in Myanmar began with Than Shwe's predecessor General Saw Maung, who introduced martial law after his own coup in 1988.[45] Under both generals, Myanmar came to be seen as an international pariah because of its record of gross human rights violations and increasing closure and hostility to the outside world. After nineteen years in power, Than Shwe stepped down in 2011. That year, some political reforms were introduced, including a transition away from military rule and the first multi-party elections since 1990. Most observers see the country's recent "opening" as far from complete, and many obstacles to democratization remain firmly in place.[46] One thing that has not yet been challenged is the decision to move the capital to Naypyidaw. For now at least, Than Shwe's successors are retaining its place at the top of the country's urban hierarchy.

Meaning "the abode of kings," Naypyidaw was reportedly designed for a population of 1 million and covers more than 4,600 square kilometers.[47] Over this sprawling area, the city is split into various zones, including separate commercial, hotel, and civilian housing zones, a sport zone, a central park, golf courses, a zoo, an enormous new airport, and a military zone. A network of tunnels purportedly connects the most exclusive sites in the city, and the military elite are understood to have built multimillion-dollar mansions on the outskirts. Foreign embassies have yet to move (with the exception of Bangladesh's), and indeed the city was largely closed to foreigners until the post-2011 reform period began.[48] The secrecy of the project, combined with the fact that photography and video was banned from the city, clearly indicates that Naypyidaw was not designed to serve as a visual icon for international—or even domestic—consumption.

Naypyidaw is a work in progress, but over fifteen years since construction began, it still has little in the way of monumental architecture. One iconic site does stand out in the new capital, however. The Uppatansanti Pagoda is a replica of the country's most venerated site, the Shwedagon Pagoda in Yangon. It is only one foot shorter than the original and, when it was developed under Than Shwe, was ostensibly aimed at legitimating "the regime, the capital, its leader, and his family."[49] What the leader could not replicate, however, is the organic social milieu of the

Shwedagon Pagoda, and Uppatansanti feels strikingly empty and artificial by contrast. In addition to this site, the handful of structures that can be found in Naypyidaw have been funded largely by Chinese companies, including the city's enormous parliament building (figure 4.13). In the absence of access to any concrete data, estimates suggest that Myanmar's government has invested billions of dollars in developing the city, presumably funded with rents from its natural resource sector, which includes natural gas, timber, gems, and hydropower.[50] Much as in the Central Asian cases, backroom exchanges with private firms interested in related extraction contracts are certain to play a major role in enabling Naypyidaw's construction.

What Naypyidaw lacks in monumental buildings it makes up for in an astonishing number of monumental roads: sixteen- and twenty-lane highways have been constructed all over the city (see figure 4.13). Despite being almost entirely unused, save for the occasional motorcycle in an outside lane, they are meticulously kept up. Gardening crews carefully maintain the landscaping in the medians and roundabout islands, while teams of women can be spotted all over the city ensuring that the alternating red-white and black-yellow color schemes on the curbs are always freshly painted. These vast, empty roads are the counterpart of the iconic skylines in Central Asia and the Gulf states, which are more often than

Figure 4.13 Myanmar's Parliament building on the left, situated in an otherwise abandoned government sector in Naypyidaw.
Source: Natalie Koch, 2015.

not populated by an array of empty, if visually impressive, towers. Like those empty buildings, Naypyidaw's roadways represent a stark visual contrast to other sites around the country. Part of the spectacle of Naypyidaw therefore hinges on the overwhelming sense of order that comes from being intensely underpopulated and devoid of the chaotic congestion of the former capital, Yangon. Although the government has never offered an official rationale for the capital change, one exceptional comment from Myanmar's information minister, Brigadier-General Kyaw Hsan, in 2006, is suggestive: "The government needed to expand and there simply was not room or a good environment in congested Yangon," and officials "wanted a 'garden evergreen city' where everything is neat, tidy and organised."[51] In addition to being exceptionally tidy, Naypyidaw is notable for being a place where the lights are always on: it is the only city in Myanmar with reliable twenty-four-hours-a-day electricity. (Other localities reportedly have power only two to twenty hours a day, and only 26 percent of the country's population have access to any electricity at all.)[52]

Naypyidaw's unspectacular Others are not just limited to those places lacking its modernist order and functioning infrastructure, but also encompass the structural and direct forms of violence that have defined the brutal and capricious military dictatorship over decades. This has left the general population in extreme poverty and subject to arbitrary torture. Meanwhile, minorities in the territorial peripheries (especially the Karen and Rohingya) suffer from the most brutal repression, which human rights groups declare amounts to genocide.[53] Than Shwe's government also famously oversaw one of the most tragic disaster responses in May 2008, when Cyclone Nargis hit Myanmar's southern coast. Insulated from the storm in centrally located Naypyidaw, the leader refused to acknowledge the event for days. His government also repeatedly rejected outside help for many weeks, allegedly fearing a foreign invasion backed by aid groups and the United States Navy. This resulted in an inordinately high number of fatalities, with estimates ranging from 100,000 to 140,000 people dead or missing.[54] In addition, the government is known to use forced labor for its major infrastructure projects, including developing Naypyidaw.[55] And more broadly, the substantial diversion of state funds to develop the new city has, as David Steinberg notes, "undercut the government's interest or capacity in improving the exceedingly low level of social services provided to the general population."[56]

The ruthless disregard for human life evinced by Myanmar's successive military governments, and that of the Than Shwe government in particular, makes the spectacle of Naypyidaw intelligible. The city is a spot of modernist order, in stark contrast to Yangon and everywhere else in the poverty-stricken country. Its opulence brazenly proclaims the wealth of a country that is not substantiated anywhere else. Synecdochically projected as a capital to propel Myanmar forward in its pursuit of independence and progress, the development of Naypyidaw represents a glaring case of structural violence, and one that likely stretches the metaphor too far for even the most optimistic of its citizens. As in the spectacular cities of Central Asia, the elitist nature of the project comes into sharp focus when contrasting the selective appropriation of state resources to benefit only a handful of political-economic elites with the extreme poverty and brutal violence found elsewhere in the country. By portraying the capital change as a means of protecting the country from foreign invasion, Than Shwe's government also framed Naypyidaw along a similar logic of being "for the people" as that described in Kazakhstan. Yet "guarding" the country against outside influence, regardless of whether that comes in the form of aid or military intervention, is precisely the means by which ordinary citizens remain victims of the state's overt and structural violence. The supposed public benefits of the grand urban spectacle are, for most observers, an overextended political fiction. Perhaps it is because the synecdoche of the new capital has so obviously failed that the transitional government has not endeavored to build up the city beyond its massive roads. Or perhaps the money simply ran out, with the mid-2010s dip in hydrocarbon prices. At least on this account, Myanmar would have much in common with the other resource-rich countries across Asia, which are now facing budget shortfalls that are putting their spectacular development schemes in question.

Why has constructing a spectacular capital city been such a common tactic among autocratic rulers? And why do we see it used so readily in the authoritarian and resource-rich states of Asia today? Considered comparatively, the spectacular new capital cities in Asia can be seen as largely connected to elite-dominated patronage politics. Ordinary citizens are generally aware of the elitism of spectacular urbanism, but not everyone perceives this as a form of social injustice or a problem to be solved.

For many, the capital is read as an uncomplicated sign of their nation's newfound prosperity. Meanwhile, critics are keenly aware of the limits on free expression, which circumscribe open debate over their government's development priorities. They recognize that raising questions about the spectacular building underway in their capitals can be extremely hazardous and largely avoid vocalizing the questions they have about social justice in their countries.

In many encounters over the years, I have found that supporters and detractors alike are quick to direct our discussions to the new beauty of their capital, the international prestige it is garnering, and all the new opportunities opened up to them. This rhetorical pattern in part reflects the hegemony of official discourse. This should not be read simply as an instance of "dissimulation" or "preference falsification," however.[57] In some cases it could be, but positive reactions to these grand capital city development schemes also reflect the power of spectacle to capture people's imagination and to structure their vocabulary: "They ground political thinking in the images and symbols the regime puts forth, framing the ways people see themselves as citizens."[58] This structuring effect is, in itself, the very instantiation of the state's power.[59] By territorializing the official representation of the state and providing discursive openings for people to engage in (often deeply felt) nationalist rhetoric, the spectacular city becomes an important way for government leaders and their variously defined subjects to understand their political relationship to one another and to the different places they inhabit.

The synecdochically imagined cities of Asia similarly construct a convenient fiction about the promise of large-scale, elitist urban development. As metaphors that mask just as much as they reveal, iconic capitals in the region are characterized by many social and political displacements that are hard to trace. In this chapter, I have attempted to illustrate some of the analytical insights to be gleaned from tracing just a handful of them. Despite the many similarities between the spectacular urban developments in the three regions examined here, the state-society relations they sustain and materialize are quite different. This is not, as I suggested at the outset, an apples-and-oranges problem to be solved but the very heart of political geography as a discipline and a worldview. From their remarkable convergences and divergences, the impressive new capitals of Asia considered *together* offer many useful lessons about the geopolitics of spectacle.

By treating capital city development schemes as a form of spectacle, we can begin to understand how the tactic unfolds in diverse moments, places, and saturations. Large-scale infrastructure projects have long been a staple of resource-rich states, but if scholars dis-embed these tactics from their spatiotemporal context, they risk missing a wider set of logics and political technologies that are decidedly geographical. Aiming to preserve some of this contextual contingency, I have endeavored to expand my analysis of spectacle and its unspectacular Others to encompass a wider range of vantage points and geopolitical settings. The seven cases in Central Asia, the Arabian Peninsula, and Southeast Asia give us clues as to how different actors use and respond to spectacle as a political technology in many ways that are similar but in others that are quite different.

Local and regional differences among the various capital city projects notwithstanding, it is clear that spectacular urbanism is both made possible through *and* materializes deeply contextual power relations. This is especially important in our contemporary era of consultant-driven development, whereby self-proclaimed experts at McKinsey, Boston Consulting Group, and Bain advocate large-scale urban (re)development schemes, which planners can apply at will. Readymade solutions, whether adapted from consultant plans or history books, and whether for maintaining autocratic rule or establishing tighter integration with the global economy, hold immense sway among international elites. This is because simplicity is seductive: free-floating plans or tactics, like the idea of a centrally located capital city, strip away the complexity of a place's historical and geographic specificity. This chapter has been one modest attempt to decenter and empirically ground such depoliticized, disembodied, and anti-geographical understandings of superficially similar phenomena like spectacular urbanism.

CONCLUSION

Synecdoche and the Geopolitics of Spectacular Urbanism in Asia

Spectacle is no mere relic of the past, but an important element of political systems all around the world. In examining the practice of constructing spectacular capital cities in Asia, I have asked: What makes a capital spectacular? How do such projects factor into illiberal power configurations and state-making agendas? What are the spatial imaginaries, tropes, and metaphors they build and build upon? And why do we see this tactic in such diverse places around the world? In the case of Kazakhstan, the government's development of a new capital city in Astana has been central to the authorities' effort to institutionalize the newly sovereign state in the post-Soviet period. Although the Astana project may seem to be a decidedly illiberal, top-down decision imposed on the country, the support (both active and passive) of ordinary citizens suggests that it is not just about elites imposing a particular vision. Spectacular urbanism in Astana has come to be both representative and constitutive of the political order in the highly centralized state. Urban residents are active participants in bringing the spectacle of the city to life, and their agency is necessary to sustain the system. Sometimes their agency takes the shape of mere apathy. Other times, citizens subject themselves to the state's authority through an enthusiastic embrace of its political agenda and development initiatives. The ultimate effect, however, is one that confirms prevailing patterns of structural inequality that have come to characterize the state in the post-Soviet period.

As Edward Shils argued some time ago, individuals at the spatial or social margins of society often do not experience this exclusion in a negative light: they do not feel "their remoteness from the center to be a perpetual injury to themselves."[1] In Kazakhstan, we find this to be manifested in the prevailing attitude among those who simply want to live a "normal" life and actively guard against any behavior that might be considered rocking the boat. Alexei Yurchak's formulation regarding political subjectivities in the USSR as being split between *aktivists, dissidents,* and *normal* subjects is still relevant in Kazakhstan, with the last being the most common subject position today.[2] For these individuals, the capital city development scheme more or less *is.* They actively take advantage of the opportunities it has opened up, but otherwise tend to refrain from reflecting critically on what conditions have made its spectacular rise possible, and at what cost. The other groups have contrasting views of the spectacle at the center: the positively inclined *aktivists* are truly enchanted by the capital, while the *dissidents* tend to feel their exclusion from the spectacle at the center as an injury.[3] To the extent that those individuals invested in orchestrating the spectacle are able to enlist the *normal* and *aktivist* positionalities and downplay the significance of the *dissenters'* narratives, they may in fact succeed in making "inequality enchant."[4] Indeed, many people in Kazakhstan today experience and perform their political subjectivity as one of real love, appreciation, and respect for the homeland and its benevolent leader, President Nazarbayev.

Spectacle here operates as a crucial political technology in both materializing and institutionalizing these varied subject positions in Kazakhstan's post-Soviet political order. As I have shown, this set of political relationships is built upon and builds specific spatial imaginaries that give meaning and purchase to prevailing illiberal power configurations. So while the case of Astana demonstrates how certain governments work to make inequality enchant through the use of spectacle of the center, it also highlights how such regimes are founded on unspectacular spaces, temporalities, embodied experiences, and forms of slow or structural violence—the impacts of which are felt most in the territorial peripheries and among marginalized populations. The local context in Kazakhstan is essential to tracing the political geographic implications of the spectacular capital city project, but the center-periphery relationships that give it meaning are not unique. When Astana is put in comparative perspective, we can begin to unravel key axes of similarity and difference between the geopolitics of spectacle in Kazakhstan and those elsewhere in Central Asia (Ashgabat, Turkmenistan, and Baku, Azerbaijan), the Arabian Peninsula (Doha, Qatar, and Abu Dhabi, United Arab Emirates), and Southeast Asia (Bandar Seri Begawan, Brunei, and Naypyidaw, Myanmar). Perhaps the most important axis of similarity is the idea of a benevolent state offering up the spectacular city as a space and symbol of progress and future development. Synecdochically imagined to represent the magnanimous paternalism of the state, this spatial metaphor is strategically designed to obscure the temporally elongated and unspectacular forms of structural violence that otherwise prevail.

Illiberalism, Paternalism, and Developmental Logics

Contrary to popular assumptions in liberal democratic states, authoritarian governments usually make a concerted effort to minimize their use of the most punitive tactics, or "sticks," and focus on more positive methods of persuasion and co-option, the proverbial "carrots."[5] Yet even the ostensibly positive tactics or technologies of government can have corrosive effects. These are especially visible in places dominated by developmentalist and paternalist power structures, as with the countries discussed in this book. Elites promoting developmental discourses frequently fashion the people's happiness as an element of their own prestige, and in this paternalistic vision, the parent figure is made proud by the progress of an infantilized group of thankful citizens. Ostensibly well-intended, infantilization can rapidly take on pernicious effects, which Yi-Fu Tuan classically explores in *Dominance and Affection*. One particularly striking example he gives is that of a white woman in slaveholding America who kept a black boy as a pet. He asks, *Was she right to do so?*

She thought so, for did she not dress the boy in finery and allow him special privileges? Of course, some of us are now inclined to disagree, arguing that the boy's dignity was compromised by his pet status and even by his mistress's acts of favor and indulgence. Affection mitigates domination, making it softer and more acceptable, but affection itself is possible only in relationships of inequality. It is the warm and superior feeling one has toward things that one can care for and patronize. The word *care* so exudes humaneness that we tend to forget its almost inevitable tainting by patronage and condescension in our imperfect world.[6]

Even if it is not experienced as such, the humiliating and degrading nature of paternalism arises from the vast power differentials between the parent and child figures, which can operate at any scale, from broad structural inequalities to the most intimate interpersonal interactions. And when this caretaking is not acknowledged in the desired manner—when it is acknowledged not as a form of love but as a form of domination—when the child figure revolts, paternalism can take on a characteristically punitive dimension. In colonial tutelage of native populations, for example, the allegedly sympathetic giving of European overseers was always in danger of withdrawal should it go unacknowledged: "How easily so much could be compressed into that simple formula of unappreciated magnanimity!"[7] And furthermore, how easy and seemingly humane the punishment constituted by merely withholding benefits of the state's magnanimity. It truly is a slippery slope between naked despotism and "good" despotism targeted at nobly improving or "caring for" a given population.[8]

Historically rooted and entrenched as these practices are, paternalism, like all broad governmental *ratios*, is anything but static. Paternalism takes many forms, its logic pervading any range of political technologies—state-led urban development included. Across Asia, paternalist logics have grown together with the region's cities. As urbanism has become increasingly significant on the global stage, cities are rapidly becoming more and more entrenched as synecdoches or markers of a country's status or international prestige. State-scale actors worldwide have consequently been quick to tap into the symbolic repertoire of iconic urban development to further their political agendas, progress-oriented and otherwise. With respect to the spectacular capital cities across the region, it is clear that they align well with the broader concerns of authoritarian leaders, who are eager to put their countries' resource wealth to use in a manner that can enrich them and their cronies, while simultaneously crafting an image of the state as legitimate, if not benevolent.

Yet, as Paul Veyne has emphasized in *Bread and Circuses,* "self-justification is not universal." That is, elites could wantonly steal the riches of the state without trying to apologize for their behavior by describing multimillion-dollar celebrations or iconic buildings as "for the people." Nor are such apologetics always "a rational form of behaviour: very frequently it fails in its effect."[9] For Veyne, what drives leaders to publicly proclaim their benevolence—whether through bread or circuses or monuments—depends on the prevailing economies of power, which I discussed in the introduction. This is why it is so important to approach spectacle geographically: as a political technology, it never has an inherent logic. It can be useful to paternalist leaders in one historical or spatial instance and fail utterly in another. Insofar as the capital city projects I have explored here continue to work in making inequality enchant, and as they have access to the material resources needed to realize them, leaders will continue to use spectacular urbanism.

Outright forms of violence and other exclusionary and repressive tactics of political control have not been the focus of this book. Such practices are perhaps most visible in places like Myanmar and Turkmenistan, but all the developmental regimes considered here use them to some extent. By employing a sort of scalar logic, however, they all downplay or peripheralize the use of violence or oppression, often reacting to outside criticism of human rights abuses as exaggerated. Celebratory spectacle, by contrast, is played up, centralized, embellished by local media. By scaling up the celebratory and scaling down the punitive, the regimes work to produce an image of the state's benevolence. Political elites' success in engineering popular support in these settings is thus largely tied to their success in dictating the cognitive frames that allow people to focus on the positive and the spectacular. But as with any metaphor, the trope of synecdoche at work here is always in danger of being stretched into the realm of incredibility.

As the case of Kazakhstan illustrates, it is not enough simply to erect iconic structures and populate the city with marble-clad signs of splendor; the government's spatial narratives and practices must confirm that it "cares" or is "good" through creating for its people, at minimum, an impression that this opulence is or should be within reach of citizens *like them.* Synecdoche here works as the fundamental metaphor that allows the population to overlook inconsistencies in the narratives about any given spectacle, and take to the fiction of the part representing the whole. The broader population may be apathetic or indifferent to the capital city project, but making inequality enchant requires that people think synecdochically about the spectacle at the center in order to then transpose this to an image of the state as benevolent. The ability of specific governments to engineer popular support through spectacle is thus tied to precisely this question of whether or not people come to believe this narrative fiction—to overcome what Veyne terms the "credibility gap."[10] When they fail to do so, when spectacle is not coupled with a wider set of experiences and spatial realities that support the "benevolent dictator" narrative, the synecdoche fails. In Kazakhstan, Nazarbayev's government has largely been able to avoid the problematic credibility gap, though in some cases, such as Myanmar, the spectacular capital city synecdoche has been much less successful. Broadly speaking, the issue for these countries' leaders is whether the celebratory spectacle at the center can sufficiently hold sway among the general population: Does it bolster their position within the prevailing economy of power?

The *spatial* question of vision and visibility is of utmost importance in whether the geopolitical imaginaries of spectacle work because the more that slow or structural violence comes into popular sight, the more the metaphor is at risk of failing. Time is also central to the effectiveness of metaphor in politics. In *The Magical State*, Fernando Coronil describes a political dynamic in oil-rich Venezuela that is quite common in resource-rich states. He illustrates how local elites crafted an image of the state as a magnanimous provider for its people during the 1970s boom years and themselves "as powerful magicians."[11] These self-styled magicians were eventually exposed as tricksters when their initiatives failed to deliver the promised progress and citizens came to realize that the country's oil wealth had been squandered. This is the familiar boom-bust cycle in many resource-dependent economies. But politicians riding its waves are not naïve. They are always aware of the risk of the magician being exposed as a trickster and thus actively seek to cultivate an aura of permanence. One favorite method for crafting the impression of permanence is to materially inscribe their developmentalist visions through various spatial strategies.

Using the same focalization strategy discussed in this book, leaders in Venezuela also sought to develop their capital, Caracas, as a spectacular city. In the boom years, they transformed Caracas to impress the onlooking world and physically manifest their narrative of magical progress: the capital was to be a glittering icon of the luxury made possible by oil wealth.[12] Later, it was to become an icon of excess: the leaders' progress-oriented iconicity allowed only for boom-time imaginaries. The cities considered in this book have much in common with Caracas. In any resource-rich country, there is no telling how and when the mythical narrative of resource-fueled development will rupture. With global oil prices collapsing in around 2015, the cracks are already visible across the three regions I have discussed, as leaders are tightening budgets, imposing new taxes, and putting some of their spectacular projects on hold.[13] It is too soon to say whether the synecdoche of spectacular urbanism will completely fail in the years to come, but the important point is that the effectiveness of the metaphor depends just as much on time as it does on space.

Spatial Imaginaries and Metaphor

A geographic approach to spectacle raises questions about how it operates as a political technology on the basis of spatial metaphors such as synecdoche. Metaphors do not have any free-floating meaning. They are intelligible only within ever-shifting and multiply experienced political contexts. Yet there are some commonalities in the use of metaphor in Asia's spectacular capital city schemes. Using synecdoche in contrasting ways, they are ultimately positioned as wondrous sites of opportunity, progress, and paternalist benevolence, allegedly reflecting the nature of the state's governance across its *entire* territory and for *all* its subjects. This synecdochic imaginary is not neutral because it systematically obscures the challenges and daily realities of those who are *not* privy to the benefits of staging the spectacle. Spectacle here works through a series of spatial and temporal displacements, strategically "smoothing the way for amnesia" about these structural inequalities. The "consequential forgettings" that Rob Nixon describes in *Slow Violence* have figured centrally in my account of the lived experiences of marginalized communities in the North Aral Sea region.[14] Although it is tempting to view the hardships faced by residents there as a sort of byproduct of unequal power relations, they are actually fundamental to the system. This is the political work of an effective metaphor. By fixing the gaze on one aspect of a concept, metaphors keep us from "focusing on other aspects of the concept that are inconsistent with that metaphor."[15] If synecdoche is the root metaphor underpinning spectacular city projects—the key to sustaining the fiction of the capital city as a wondrous site of opportunity and state benevolence—then the celebratory spectacles of the center need to be examined alongside their unspectacular Others.

A critical geographic approach to spectacle would therefore join conventional questions about the "who, when, and where" of these episodic events and exceptional spaces, with analyses concerning unspectacular dimensions that condition something as "spectacular." The case of spectacular cities and their geography offers a particularly useful window onto the way illiberal states govern through multiple logics that are experienced differently by their subjects. That is, the very same project may simultaneously be deemed oppressive and unjust by some but liberating and worthy by others. What makes the particular cases that I consider in Asia so troubling to outside observers is that they seem to symbolize so many obvious injustices. In Central Asia, for example, urban showpiece projects—from stadiums to palaces to universities—are instrumental to the elites' system of laundering natural resource rents. In the Gulf monarchies, impoverished foreign workers have their passports taken away and their wages withheld, and are confined to labor camps as they build fancy new towers on the cheap. And in places like Myanmar and Brunei, popular opinions on matters like urban development are not merely discouraged but actively and violently suppressed. But by critically interrogating the geopolitical imaginaries that underpin these injustices, we find that they can be glossed over and ignored by ordinary citizens when they are taught to focus on the spectacles at the center and think synecdochically about them as positive symbols. When synecdoche is used effectively, elites can obscure or divert attention from their failure to distribute the country's resource wealth in a more egalitarian manner.

For this reason, considering only critical narratives about paternalist or illiberal rule would skew the picture. It would mask the fact that many people are truly proud of their cities, their leaders, their countries, and by extension themselves. To understand the spectacular capitals of Asia, scholars need to take them seriously as sites where people with contrasting resources pursue competing interests and agendas, and articulate conflicting and dynamic geopolitical affinities. Doing so requires not just great patience and empathy for (not to be confused with agreement with) people whose values can be diametrically opposed to our own. It also requires that we think reflexively about our own spatial imaginaries and how we may also fall into the trap of synecdochic thinking when we reduce the Gulf region to "slave labor" or Central Asia to "money laundering," as in the many tired clichés that masquerade as critical analyses of politics in these regions.

This is not to dismiss these issues; they are, no doubt, important and pressing social justice challenges. But if we are to understand why illiberal practices and modes of governing are so pervasive, and even popular at times, we need to remove our liberalist lenses and examine their inner logic, appeal, and embodied performance. For this reason, it is far too simplistic to unmask the truth claims of the synecdochic imaginary as "false." Unfortunately, this is often what an analysis of metaphorical thinking amounts to, because, as Clifford Geertz points out, what troubles people most about metaphor is that it is inherently "wrong." It is by definition the act of comparing two unlike things. But worse yet, he adds, "it tends to be most effective when most 'wrong.'" He continues: "The power of metaphor derives precisely from the interplay between the discordant meanings it symbolically coerces into a unitary conceptual framework and from the degree to which that coercion is successful in overcoming the psychic resistance such semantic tension inevitably generates in anyone in a position to perceive it. When it works, a metaphor transforms a false identification into an apt analogy; when it misfires, it is a mere extravagance."[16] When metaphors work, they transform a falsehood into a seeming truth. And when they do not work, they come across as entirely depoliticized semantic play.

But all metaphors are deeply political, as George Lakoff and Mark Johnson suggest, because they structure our everyday functioning, perceptions of space, how we move around, and how we relate to others.[17] In analyzing metaphor, therefore, scholars must not stop at the moment of deconstruction. In asking who gets to impose their metaphors, when, where, and for whom, we find ourselves back at Harold Lasswell's classic questions of political analysis: Who gets what, when, how?[18] And—the addition of political geographers—where? These are all important questions to start from in approaching spectacle geographically: as a context-dependent political technology. From here, even more targeted questions can open up crucial issues about power relations at work in specific contexts, such as Kazakhstan, and around specific political tactics, such as the government's effort to build a spectacular new capital city in the middle of the Eurasian steppe. In analyzing city-building projects like that of Astana or Doha, many observers often assume that the spectacle is part of the illiberal elites' effort merely to buy the complacency of their citizenry. This book has shown that we need to subject this claim to more scrutiny, and ask more incisive questions about the geographies and spatial imaginaries implicated in how certain political technologies slot into state-society relations. It also shows the need to take certain places and people seriously. Academics and non-academics alike often dismiss smaller and lesser-known countries, like Kazakhstan, as peripheral or irrelevant to the core concerns of international affairs. The dynamics explored in the previous chapters push against the implication that such places cannot offer any new insights about contemporary geopolitics. In fact, Kazakhstan, and its grandiose urban development scheme in Astana, has a great deal to teach us about power, spectacle, and authoritarianism today.

The political logics at work in the Astana project also have much in common with spectacular capital city projects in other illiberal and resource-rich states of Asia. So too does its uniqueness help us to understand the role of geography in shaping how spectacle is used by different actors as a political technology. The degree to which this spectacle is successful as a tactic varies from country to country, from project to project, and from citizen to citizen. The geopolitics of spectacle thus demands that we study the practices (rhetorical and material) of both elite *and* popular actors. Doing so implies a comprehensive approach to power that does not fixate on elites alone, but takes the agency of ordinary people seriously—even in the most nondemocratic of countries and places where they lack citizenship rights. A relational approach to power as capillary thus sheds light on the differential *kinds* of agency of political subjects, as well as their multiple, often contradictory perspectives on structural violence and inequalities in their societies. More often than not, people in illiberal societies simply want to live "normally," without directly engaging in the public political sphere. This sort of passive agency promoted under paternalist regimes is precisely the condition of possibility for the persistence of illiberal systems. But it is crucially underpinned by synecdochic modes of thinking about space, power, and subjectivity.

The Geopolitics of Spectacle

Central to my approach to the geopolitics of spectacle is the effort to account for the relative nature of spatial imaginaries. That is, while synecdoche may be a common trope invoked by spectacular city projects across Asia, it takes a somewhat different shape and does different political work in each of the regions considered, from Central Asia to the Arabian Peninsula to Southeast Asia. Homing in on these differences, as well as their commonalities, a cross-regional approach offers a unique opportunity to explore the divergent political effects of spectacular urban development across and within various world regions. For example, in seeking to explain the differences in the representational economies of Southeast Asia's capitals, we are forced to recognize that international iconicity is not a requisite for spectacular urbanism and that domestic audiences might be more determinative of the spectacle's intelligibility. And in seeking to understand why superficially similar urban development projects are coded as legal and legitimate in the Gulf and illegal and corrupt in Central Asia, we can glean important insights about the differential roles of citizenship regimes in justifying who is "rightfully" entitled to benefits from any given spectacle and who is not.

Extending well beyond resource-rich states, this points to broader questions about the structures, institutions, and spatial imaginaries that underpin and structure assumptions about who has a legitimate claim to benefits from the state. Unfortunately beyond the scope of this short conclusion, these broader questions shed light on the structural violence of state-defined citizenship regimes, which are made possible by the hegemonic geopolitical architecture of the territorial state system—a system that institutionalizes, rationalizes, and naturalizes the unequal distribution of natural resources globally. Although this book makes no pretensions to presenting a more just architecture, I have sought to at least shift my analytical lens beyond prevailing state-centric imaginaries of global space to see how power and political technologies produce inequality at variable scales. Such inequalities can of course be manifest within a state's borders, as with social disparities in Central Asian states. But in other cases it takes on a more regional character, as with spectacular urbanism in the Arabian Peninsula, where expat workers feel the brunt of the structural inequalities produced by aggressively elitist development—just like their counterparts in the North Aral Sea and the minority regions of Myanmar.

As a study in political geography, this book marks one small step toward a more global conceptualization of space and power. Methodologically, this may need to begin by challenging academia's conventional world regional designations, which can sometimes obscure the very workings of these structural inequalities. The point is not that we should abandon them entirely or develop more "accurate" regional designations, but rather that we need to be more attuned to how they are mobilized and by whom. Only with this attentiveness, together with a wider definition of comparison that embraces difference, is it possible to challenge those "hierarchies of judgement" that are so easily reproduced through the "basis and form of comparison."[19] Exploring divergences in cross-regional research, I suggest, is one such way forward. In asking how Kazakhstan's spectacular capital city compares to other urban development schemes elsewhere in Asia, I have sought to develop a more nuanced approach to spectacle that accounts for state- and region-specific political geographies. I have not attempted a comprehensive survey of these nuances, but by highlighting some of the forms that spectacular cities' Others might take, I have endeavored to show how a geographic approach to spectacle and the unspectacular can bring them into sharper focus.

This geographic approach also offers important insights into how various political subjects are called upon, and called into being, in illiberal settings. Indeed, as we have vividly seen, nondemocratic states are not homogenous; rather, they actively engage their citizens through many different technologies of power. Although, or perhaps because, they do not use free and fair elections, they nonetheless seek to cultivate legitimacy among their subjects. Spectacular urbanism is just one way that state leaders work to create the image of benevolence and govern through people's pleasure. I have accordingly stressed what Foucault in *Discipline and Punish* describes as a *positive* economy of power, or what Gramsci in the

Prison Notebooks terms the "prize-giving" functions of state power.[20] As both great thinkers highlight in these works, the positive and negative economies work in tandem.

I am arguing that the passive and negative economies of power are reflected not only in the government of *others* but also in how people choose to govern *themselves*. Here too the active and the passive work together. Individuals have highly unstable styles of reasoning about the self, which arise and subside in response to an infinite number of inter-actions and stimuli. As we have seen in Kazakhstan, though, the active supporters of the regime and its passive opponents (who might even be the same persons at different moments) are ultimately all part of the same system of power. This system, we must note, is *not* as self-contained as the statist modes of thought would suggest. The persistence of the Naz-arbayev regime's hegemonic position in Kazakhstan's web of power rela-tions is made possible not just by these domestic arrangements—of the developmental and paternalist state objectivizing a passively accepting citizenry—but also by the contemporary international arrangements of a world still stuck in the "territorial trap."[21]

NOTES

Introduction

1. On Asia's recent urban market-oriented transformations, see especially Catherine Alexander, Victor Buchli, and Caroline Humphrey, *Urban Life in Post-Soviet Asia* (London: University College London Press, 2007); Tsypylma Darieva, Wolfgang Kaschuba, and Melanie Krebs, *Urban Spaces after Socialism: Ethnographies of Public Places in Eurasian Cities* (Frankfurt: Campus, 2011); Yasser Elsheshtawy, *The Evolving Arab City: Tradition, Modernity and Urban Development* (London: Routledge, 2008); Ananya Roy and Aihwa Ong, *Worlding Cities: Asian Experiments and the Art of Being Global* (Malden, Mass.: Wiley-Blackwell, 2011).

2. An extensive interdisciplinary literature has long considered statist urban development projects, but see especially Sibel Bozdo an, *Modernism and Nation Building: Turkish Architectural Culture in the Early Republic* (Seattle: University of Washington Press, 2001); James Holston, *The Modernist City: An Anthropological Critique of Brasília* (Chicago: University of Chicago Press, 1989); Paul Rabinow, *French Modern: Norms and Forms of the Social Environment* (Cambridge: MIT Press, 1989); James C. Scott, *Seeing Like a State: How Certain Schemes to Improve the Human Condition Have Failed* (New Haven: Yale University Press, 1998); Lawrence Vale, *Architecture, Power, and National Identity* (New Haven: Yale University Press, 1992).

3. Stephen Daniels, "Geographical Imagination," *Transactions of the Institute of British Geographers* 36, no. 2 (2011): 182–87.

4. For this reason, among others, I deliberately do not engage with Guy Debord's analysis in *Society of the Spectacle* (Detroit: Black & Red, 1970) and *Comments on the Society of the Spectacle* (New York: Verso, 1990). Nor do I engage the work that follows the spirit of his analysis, such as, in a themed issue of the journal *Geoforum*, Cecilia Chu and Romola Sanyal, "Spectacular Cities of Our Time," *Geoforum* 65 (2015): 399–402. Not only is Debord's capitalism-centric approach unhelpful in accounting for statist spectacle, but it also tends toward the sensational and editorial, and rather less toward the analytical and critical approach that I adopt.

5. Lily Kong and Brenda S. A. Yeoh, "The Construction of National Identity through the Production of Ritual and Spectacle: An Analysis of National Day Parades in Singapore," *Political Geography* 16, no. 3 (1997): 213–39.

6. On punitive spectacle, see Michel Foucault, *Discipline and Punish: The Birth of the Prison* (New York: Pantheon Books, 1975).

7. For grounded accounts of state terror, see for example J. Arch Getty, *Origins of the Great Purges: The Soviet Communist Party Reconsidered, 1933–1938* (Cambridge: Cambridge University Press, 1985); Kenneth Hewitt, "Between Pinochet and Kropotkin: State Terror, Human Rights and the Geographers," *Canadian Geographer* 45, no. 3 (2001): 338–55; Richard Lee Turits, *Foundations of Despotism: Peasants, the Trujillo Regime, and Modernity in Dominican History* (Stanford: Stanford University Press, 2003). For a rare exception of punitive and celebratory spectacle being analyzed jointly, see Daniel Goldstein, *The Spectacular City: Violence and Performance in Urban Bolivia* (Durham: Duke University Press, 2004).

8. Clifford Geertz, "Centers, Kings, and Charisma: Reflections on the Symbolics of Power," in *Local Knowledge: Further Essays in Interpretive Anthropology*, ed. Clifford Geertz (New York: Basic Books, 1983), 123.

9. On the methodological imperative of taking autocrats seriously, see chapter 1 of Michael Mann, *Fascists* (New York: Cambridge University Press, 2004). There is a large literature, primarily in political science, that seeks to develop typologies of authoritarian regimes, exemplified in Juan Linz, *Totalitarian and Authoritarian Regimes* (Boulder: Lynne Rienner, 2000). I do not find typological approaches to be especially useful or productive because they tend to analytically reify the state and divert attention from the constantly fluctuating practices of state-*making*.

10. See especially Hannah Arendt, *The Origins of Totalitarianism* (New York: Harcourt, 1951), and *Eichmann in Jerusalem: A Report on the Banality of Evil* (New York: Viking Press, 1963); Zygmunt Bauman, *Modernity and the Holocaust* (Ithaca: Cornell University Press, 1989); Timur Kuran, *Private Truths, Public Lies: The Social Consequences of Preference Falsification* (Cambridge: Harvard University Press, 1995).

11. Clifford Geertz, *Negara: The Theatre State in Nineteenth-Century Bali* (Princeton: Princeton University Press, 1980), 123.

12. For a full discussion of these labels and Western media coverage of Astana, see Natalie Koch, "Urban 'Utopias': The Disney Stigma and Discourses of 'False Modernity,'" *Environment and Planning A* 44, no. 10 (2012): 2445–62.

13. Rowan Moore, "Astana, Kazakhstan: The Space Station in the Steppes," *The Guardian*, August 8, 2010, http://www.guardian.co.uk/world/2010/aug/08/astana-kazakhstan-space-station-steppes (accessed July 9, 2017).

14. Mike Davis, "Fear and Money in Dubai," *New Left Review* 41 (2006): 51.

15. Foucault, *Discipline and Punish*, 16–217. Despite Foucault's constant effort to push away from such a periodization of the governmentalities he considers (sovereignty, discipline, biopolitics), he repeatedly confines spectacle to a temporally distant period in *Discipline and Punish*. In his later lectures at the Collège de France, Foucault emphasizes that "there is not a series of successive elements, the appearance of the new causing the earlier ones to disappear.

There is not the legal age, the disciplinary age, and then the age of security. Mechanisms of security do not replace disciplinary mechanisms, which would have replaced juridico-legal mechanisms. In reality you have a series of complex edifices in which, of course, the techniques themselves change and are perfected, or anyway become more complicated, but in which what above all changes is the dominant characteristic, or more exactly, the system of correlation between juridico-legal mechanisms, disciplinary mechanisms, and mechanisms of security." Michel Foucault, *Security, Territory, Population: Lectures at the Collège de France, 1977–1978* (New York: Picador, 2007), 8.

16. The literature is vast, but on spectacle in nondemocratic settings, see especially Laura Adams, *The Spectacular State: Culture and National Identity in Uzbekistan* (Durham: Duke University Press, 2010); James Duncan, *The City as Text: The Politics of Landscape Interpretation in the Kandyan Kingdom* (New York: Cambridge University Press, 1990); Geertz, *Negara*; Simonetta Falasca-Zamponi, *Fascist Spectacle: The Aesthetics of Power in Mussolini's Italy* (Berkeley: University of California Press, 1997); Joshua Hagen, "Parades, Public Space, and Propaganda: The Nazi Culture Parades in Munich," *Geografiska Annaler: Series B, Human Geography* 90, no. 4 (2008): 349–67; Kong and Yeoh, "The Construction of National Identity"; Karen Petrone, *Life Has Become More Joyous, Comrades: Celebrations in the Time of Stalin* (Bloomington: Indiana University Press, 2000); Malte Rolf, *Soviet Mass Festivals, 1917–1991* (Pittsburgh: University of Pittsburgh Press, 2013); Paul Veyne, *Bread and Circuses: Historical Sociology and Political Pluralism* (London: Penguin Press, 1990); James Von Geldern, *Bolshevik Festivals, 1917–1920* (Berkeley: University of California Press, 1993); Lisa Wedeen, *Ambiguities of Domination: Politics, Rhetoric, and Symbols in Contemporary Syria* (Chicago: University of Chicago Press, 1999); Alexei Yurchak, *Everything Was Forever, until It Was No More: The Last Soviet Generation* (Princeton: Princeton University Press, 2006). On spectacle in democratic states, see especially Debord, *Society of the Spectacle*; David Glassberg, *American Historical Pageantry: The Uses of Tradition in the Early Twentieth Century* (Chapel Hill: University of North Carolina Press, 1990); Eric Hobsbawm, "Mass-Producing Traditions: Europe, 1870–1914," in *The Invention of Tradition*, ed. Eric Hobsbawm and Terence Ranger (Cambridge: Cambridge University Press, 1983), 263–307.

17. Adams, *The Spectacular State*, 5.

18. Geertz, *Negara*, 13.

19. Ibid.

20. Paul Veyne, "Foucault Revolutionizes History," in *Foucault and His Interlocutors*, ed. A.I. Davidson (Chicago: University of Chicago Press, 1997), 155.

21. Foucault defines governmentality in multiple ways, but my interpretation of his meaning is informed by a wide reading of his work and that of key critics. See especially Foucault, *Security, Territory, Population*; Foucault, *The Birth of Biopolitics*; Lemke, *Foucault, Governmentality, and Critique*; Johanna Oksala, *Foucault on Freedom* (Cambridge: Cambridge University Press, 2005); Jeffrey Nealon, *Foucault beyond Foucault: Power and Its Intensifications since 1984* (Stanford: Stanford University Press, 2008); Nikolas S. Rose, *Powers of Freedom: Reframing Political Thought* (Cambridge: Cambridge University Press, 1999); Veyne, *Bread and Circuses*; Paul Veyne, *Foucault, His Thought, His Character* (Malden, Mass.: Polity, 2010).

22. Foucault, *The Birth of Biopolitics*, 297.

23. Veyne, "Foucault Revolutionizes History," 150–51.

24. Peter Kenez, *The Birth of the Propaganda State: Soviet Methods of Mass Mobilization, 1917–1929* (Cambridge: Cambridge University Press, 1985).

25. Foucault, *Security, Territory, Population*, 108.

26. Natalie Koch, "The Shifting Geopolitics of Higher Education: Inter/Nationalizing Elite Universities in Kazakhstan, Saudi Arabia, and Beyond," *Geoforum* 56 (2014): 46–54;

Natalie Koch, "We Entrepreneurial Academics: Governing Globalized Higher Education in 'Illiberal' States," *Territory, Politics, Governance* 4, no. 4 (2016): 438–52; Natalie Koch, "Orientalizing Authoritarianism: Narrating U.S. Exceptionalism in Popular Reactions to the Trump Election and Presidency," *Political Geography* 58 (2017): 145–47.

27. Paul Cloke and Ron Johnston, "Deconstructing Human Geography's Binaries," in *Spaces of Geographical Thought: Deconstructing Human Geography's Binaries*, ed. Paul Cloke and Ron Johnston (Thousand Oaks, Calif.: Sage, 2005), 1–20; Jenna Christian, Lorraine Dowler, and Dana Cuomo, "Fear, Feminist Geopolitics and the Hot and Banal," *Political Geography* 54 (2016): 64–72.

28. Mann, *Fascists*, 2.

29. See Natalie Koch, "Is Nationalism Just for Nationals? Civic Nationalism for Noncitizens and Celebrating National Day in Qatar and the UAE," *Political Geography* 54 (2016): 43–53; Neha Vora and Natalie Koch, "Everyday Inclusions: Rethinking Ethnocracy, *Kafala,* and Belonging in the Arabian Peninsula," *Studies in Ethnicity and Nationalism* 15, no. 3 (2015): 540–52.

30. The rentier state framework originates with Hazem Beblawi and Giacomo Luciani, *The Rentier State* (New York: Croom Helm, 1987). It has stimulated a large body of scholarship, primarily in political science, applying these concepts to a broad range of contexts. On the Arabian Peninsula, see Christopher Davidson, *Abu Dhabi: Oil and Beyond* (New York: Columbia University Press, 2009); Allen Fromherz, *Qatar: A Modern History* (New York: Palgrave Macmillan, 2011); Michael Herb, *The Wages of Oil: Parliaments and Economic Development in Kuwait and the UAE* (Ithaca: Cornell University Press, 2014); Giacomo Luciani, *Nation, State, and Integration in the Arab World* (New York: Croom Helm, 1987); Kristian Ulrichsen, *Insecure Gulf: The End of Certainty and the Transition to the Post-Oil Era* (New York: Columbia University Press, 2011). On Central Asia, see Anja Franke, Andrea Gawrich, and Gurban Alakbarov, "Kazakhstan and Azerbaijan as Post-Soviet Rentier States: Resource Incomes and Autocracy as a Double 'Curse' in Post-Soviet Regimes," *Europe-Asia Studies* 61, no. 1 (2009): 109–40; Yelena Kalyuzhnova, *Economics of the Caspian Oil and Gas Wealth: Companies, Governments, Policies* (New York: Palgrave Macmillan, 2008); Boris Najman, Richard Pomfret, and Gaël Raballand, *The Economics and Politics of Oil in the Caspian Basin: The Redistribution of Oil Revenues in Azerbaijan and Central Asia* (New York: Routledge, 2008); Indra Øverland, Heidi Kjærnet, and Andrea Kendall-Taylor, *Caspian Energy Politics: Azerbaijan, Kazakhstan and Turkmenistan* (New York: Routledge, 2010). On Myanmar, see David Pick and Htwe Htwe Thein, "Development Failure and the Resource Curse: The Case of Myanmar," *International Journal of Sociology and Social Policy* 30, no. 5/6 (2010): 267–79.

31. World Bank, "Oil Rents (% of GDP)," *World Bank Group* (2015), http://data.world bank.org/indicator/NY.GDP.PETR.RT.ZS?locations=KZ (accessed June 29, 2017).

32. Steve LeVine, *The Oil and the Glory: The Pursuit of Empire and Fortune on the Caspian Sea* (New York: Random House, 2007), 261. See also Edward Schatz, "What Capital Cities Say about State and Nation Building," *Nationalism and Ethnic Politics* 9, no. 4 (2004): 111–40; Saulesh Yessenova, "The Political Economy of Oil Privatization in Post-Soviet Kazakhstan," in *Subterranean Estates: Life Worlds of Oil and Gas*, ed. Hannah Appel, Arthur Mason, and Michael Watts (Ithaca: Cornell University Press, 2015), 281–98.

33. Nursultan Nazarbayev, *V Serdtse Evrazii* (In the Heart of Eurasia) (Astana: no publisher, 2005), 355–56. He explicitly names as contributors Agip (Italy), the Saudi government, the Kuwait fund, the Abu Dhabi fund, the Oman government, TengizChevrOil, KazMunaiGas, Eurasian Group, and several other Kazakhstani firms.

It is important to note that texts authored by President Nazarbayev constitute a particular genre within Kazakhstan, which are indicative of the official discourse rather than his own thoughts or ideas per se. As under many personalistic regimes, the president does not actually write these texts, but has a staff of writers, who might be philologists or historians, produce initial drafts. For clarity, I still treat "Nazarbayev" as an individual actor and author: although it is a fiction, it is a necessary one for the narrative thread. Regarding language, if I could find an official English translation, I have cited and quoted that text; if not, the translations are my own. For more on this issue and for a detailed analysis of how Nazarbayev has justified the capital change, see Natalie Koch, "The 'Heart' of Eurasia? Kazakhstan's Centrally Located Capital City," *Central Asian Survey* 32, no. 2 (2013): 134–47.

34. LeVine, *The Oil and the Glory*, 322; Schatz, "What Capital Cities Say," 126.

35. With the 2016 release of leaked documents from the Panamanian law firm Mossack Fonseca, much more will be known in coming years, though they already implicate Nazarbayev's grandson Nurali Aliyev in money laundering. See Vlad Lavrov and Irene Velska, "Kazakhstan: President's Grandson Hid Assets Offshore," Organized Crime and Corruption Reporting Project, April 4, 2016, https://www.occrp.org/en/panamapapers/kazakh-presidents-grandson-offshores/ (accessed January 23, 2017).

36. Quoted in Gulnoza Saidazimova, "Nazarbaev Celebrates 'Day of Astana,' but Critics Scoff at Grandiose Festivities," Radio Free Europe/Radio Liberty, July 5, 2008, http://www.rferl.org/content/Nazarbaev_Celebrates_Day_Of_Astana/1181848.html (accessed June 29, 2017).

37. Stephen Daniels and Denis Cosgrove, "Spectacle and Text: Landscape Metaphors in Cultural Geography," in *Place/Culture/Representation*, ed. James Duncan and David Ley (New York: Routledge, 1993), 59.

38. James Duncan and Nancy Duncan, "Doing Landscape Interpretation," in *The Sage Handbook of Qualitative Methods in Human Geography*, ed. Dydia DeLyser, Steve Herbert, Stuart Aitken, Mike Crang, and Linda McDowell (London: Sage, 2010), 225–47.

39. Timothy Mitchell, *Colonising Egypt* (Berkeley: University of California Press, 1988), 18.

40. Veyne, "Foucault Revolutionizes History," 153.

41. Aihwa Ong, "Introduction: Worlding Cities, or the Art of Being Global," in *Worlding Cities: Asian Experiments and the Art of Being Global*, ed. Ananya Roy and Aihwa Ong (Malden, Mass.: Wiley-Blackwell, 2011), 18.

42. Fredric Jameson, *A Singular Modernity: Essay on the Ontology of the Present* (New York: Verso, 2002); Koch, "Urban 'Utopias'"; John Law, *Organizing Modernity* (Cambridge: Blackwell, 1994); Mitchell, *Colonising Egypt*; Timothy Mitchell, *Questions of Modernity* (Minneapolis: University of Minnesota Press, 2000).

43. Mitchell, *Colonising Egypt*.

44. Clifford Geertz, *The Interpretation of Cultures: Selected Essays* (New York: Basic Books, 1973), 237.

1. Approaching Spectacle Geographically

1. Nursultan Nazarbayev, "Future Vision," *K Magazine* 1 (2010): 53.

2. Natalie Koch, "The Monumental and the Miniature: Imagining 'Modernity' in Astana," *Social & Cultural Geography* 11, no. 8 (2010): 769–87; James C. Scott, *Seeing Like a State: How Certain Schemes to Improve the Human Condition Have Failed* (New Haven: Yale University Press, 1998); Susan Stewart, *On Longing: Narratives of the Miniature, the Gigantic, the Souvenir, the Collection* (Baltimore: Johns Hopkins University Press, 1984).

3. Brian Martin, "Statist Language," *ETC: A Review of General Semantics* 66, no. 4 (2009): 377–81.

4. Paul Veyne, *Bread and Circuses: Historical Sociology and Political Pluralism* (London: Penguin Press, 1990), 56.

5. John Agnew, "Nationalism," in *The Wiley-Blackwell Companion to Cultural Geography*, ed. Nuala Johnson, Richard Schein, and Jamie Winders (Malden, Mass.: Wiley-Blackwell, 2013), 134.

6. Whereas metonymy (Greek for "name change") is a metaphor that replaces the referent with the name of something that is closely associated with it, synecdoche "replaces the name of a referent by the name of another referent which belongs to the same field of meaning and which is either semantically wider or semantically narrower." Ruth Wodak, *The Discursive Construction of National Identity* (Edinburgh: Edinburgh University Press, 2009), 43.

7. For the handful of analyses of synecdoche I have encountered in the social sciences, see Karen Foss and Kathy Domenici, "Haunting Argentina: Synecdoche in the Protests of the Mothers of the Plaza de Mayo," *Quarterly Journal of Speech* 87, no. 3 (2001): 237–58; Roderick Hart, *Political Keywords: Using Language That Uses Us* (New York: Oxford University Press, 2005); John E. Joseph, "Dialect, Language, and 'Synecdoche,'" *Linguistics* 20, no. 7–8 (1982): 473–92; Martin, "Statist Language"; Mark Moore, "Constructing Irreconcilable Conflict: The Function of Synecdoche in the Spotted Owl Controversy," *Communication Monographs* 60, no. 3 (1993): 258–74; Mark Moore, "Making Sense of Salmon: Synecdoche and Irony in a Natural Resource Crisis," *Western Journal of Communication* 67, no. 1 (2003): 74–96; A. J. Prats, *Invisible Natives: Myth and Identity in the American Western* (Ithaca: Cornell University Press, 2002).

8. On metonymy, see, for example, Ash Amin and Stephen Graham, "The Ordinary City," *Transactions of the Institute of British Geographers* 22, no. 4 (1997): 411–29; James Duncan, *The City as Text: The Politics of Landscape Interpretation in the Kandyan Kingdom* (New York: Cambridge University Press, 1990); James Holston, *The Modernist City: An Anthropological Critique of Brasília* (Chicago: University of Chicago Press, 1989); Doreen Massey, *World City* (Malden, Mass.: Polity Press, 2007); Nigel Thrift, "Not a Straight Line but a Curve: Or Cities Are Not Mirrors of Modernity," in *City Visions*, ed. David Bell and Azzedine Haddour (London: Longman, 2000), 233–63.

9. For important exceptions, see Anne Buttimer, "Musing on Helicon: Root Metaphors and Geography," *Geografiska Annaler. Series B, Human Geography* 64, no. 2 (1982): 89–96; Anne Buttimer, *Geography and the Human Spirit* (Baltimore: Johns Hopkins University Press, 1993); Denis Cosgrove, *Geography and Vision: Seeing, Imagining and Representing the World* (New York: Palgrave Macmillan, 2008); Denis Cosgrove and Stephen Daniels, eds., *The Iconography of Landscape: Essays on the Symbolic Representation, Design, and Use of Past Environments* (Cambridge: Cambridge University Press, 1988); Stephen Daniels and Denis Cosgrove, "Spectacle and Text: Landscape Metaphors in Cultural Geography," in *Place/Culture/Representation*, ed. James Duncan and David Ley (New York: Routledge, 1993), 57–77; Duncan, *The City as Text*; Neil Smith and Cindi Katz, "Ground Metaphor: Towards a Spatialized Politics," in *Place and the Politics of Identity*, ed. Michael Keith and Steve Pile (New York: Routledge, 1993), 67–83.

10. Critical geopolitics is an intellectual project to challenge the realist and essentialist traditions that historically prevailed in "classical geopolitics"—whose advocates positioned themselves as neutral observers in their deeply political writings of space. See Gearóid Ó Tuathail, *Critical Geopolitics: The Politics of Writing Global Space* (Minneapolis: University of Minnesota Press, 1996). On power/knowledge, see Michel Foucault, *Power/Knowledge: Selected Interviews and Other Writings, 1972–1977* (New York: Pantheon, 1980).

11. Gearoid Ó Tuathail and John Agnew, "Geopolitics and Discourse: Practical Geopolitical Reasoning in American Foreign Policy," *Political Geography* 11, no. 2 (1992): 190–204.

12. Gearóid Ó Tuathail, "Thinking Critically about Geopolitics," in *The Geopolitics Reader*, ed. Gearóid Ó Tuathail, Simon Dalby, and Paul Routledge (New York: Routledge, 2006), 7.

13. Gearoid Ó Tuathail and John Agnew, "Geopolitics and Discourse: Practical Geopolitical Reasoning in American Foreign Policy," *Political Geography* 11, no. 2 (1992): 195.

14. See especially John Agnew, *Geopolitics: Re-Visioning World Politics* (New York: Routledge, 2003); John Agnew and Stuart Corbridge, *Mastering Space: Hegemony, Territory and International Political Economy* (New York: Routledge, 1995); Simon Dalby, "Threats from the South? Geopolitics, Equity, and Environmental Security," in *Contested Grounds: Security and Conflict in the New Environmental Politics*, ed. Daniel Deudney and Richard Matthew (Albany: State University of New York Press, 1999), 155–85; John Lewis Gaddis, *Strategies of Containment: A Critical Appraisal of Postwar American National Security Policy* (New York: Oxford University Press, 1982); John Lewis Gaddis, *The Cold War: A New History* (New York: Penguin Press, 2005); Ó Tuathail, *Critical Geopolitics*.

15. George Lakoff and Mark Johnson, *Metaphors We Live By* (Chicago: University of Chicago Press, 1980), 3, 156, 8.

16. See George Lakoff, "Metaphor and War: The Metaphor System Used to Justify War in the Gulf," *Peace Research* 23, nos. 2/3 (1991): 25–32; Friedrich Nietzsche, "On Truth and Lies in the Non-Moral Sense," Nietzsche's Features, http://nietzsche.holtof.com/Nietzsche_various/on_truth_and_lies.htm (accessed June 30, 2017); James Underhill, *Creating Worldviews: Metaphor, Ideology and Language* (Edinburgh: Edinburgh University Press, 2011).

17. Agnew, "Nationalism," 136.

18. Agnew, *Geopolitics*, 15. For related arguments, see also Timothy Mitchell, *Colonising Egypt* (Berkeley: University of California Press, 1988), 44; Ó Tuathail, *Critical Geopolitics*, 23–24.

19. Ó Tuathail, *Critical Geopolitics*, 23; Timothy Mitchell, "Everyday Metaphors of Power," *Theory and Society* 19, no. 5 (1990): 545–77.

20. Massey, *World City*, 87; Robert Sack, *Human Territoriality: Its Theory and History* (Cambridge: Cambridge University Press, 1986).

21. Sack, *Human Territoriality*, 33–34. Long considered a seminal work in political geography, Sack's *Human Territoriality* is indeed one of the most significant political geographic contributions to tracing how abstract spatial thinking has come to dominate contemporary geographic thought. Critical work on mapping as a technology of government has consistently shown that the ability to define space as an abstraction marks an important source of power. See, for example, J. B. Harley, "Maps, Knowledge, and Power," in Cosgrove and Daniels, *The Iconography of Landscape*, 277–312; Reuben Rose-Redwood, "With Numbers in Place: Security, Territory, and the Production of Calculable Space," *Annals of the Association of American Geographers* 102, no. 2 (2012): 295–319; Thongchai Winichakul, *Siam Mapped: A History of the Geo-Body of a Nation* (Honolulu: University of Hawaii Press, 1994).

22. The argument that territory can have many different forms and expressions is a recurring theme in political geography. See especially John Agnew, "The Territorial Trap: The Geographical Assumptions of International Relations Theory," *Review of International Political Economy* 1, no. 1 (1994): 53–80; Jean Gottmann, *The Significance of Territory* (Charlottesville: University Press of Virginia, 1973); Jean Gottmann, *Centre and Periphery: Spatial Variation in Politics* (Beverly Hills: Sage Publications, 1980); Henri Lefebvre, *The Production of Space* (Oxford: Blackwell, 1991); Torsten Malmberg, *Human Territoriality: Survey of Behavioural Territories in Man with Preliminary Analysis and Discussion of Meaning* (The Hague: Mouton, 1980); Anssi Paasi, *Territories, Boundaries, and Consciousness: The Changing*

Geographies of the Finnish-Russian Boundary (New York: J. Wiley & Sons, 1996); Claude Raffestin, *Pour une Géographie du Pouvoir* (Paris: Librairies techniques, 1980); Claude Raffestin, "Territoriality: A Reflection of the Discrepancies between the Organization of Space and Individual Liberty," *International Political Science Review* 5, no. 2 (1984): 139–46.

23. Sack, *Human Territoriality*, 63.

24. Colonialism involved the imposition of new territorial borders and the forcible settlement of nomadic groups, which was ultimately about imposing abstract spatial thinking. I elaborate on this argument in Natalie Koch, "'Spatial Socialization': Understanding the State Effect Geographically," *Nordia Geographical Publications* 44, no. 4 (2015): 29–35. See also Benedict Anderson, *Imagined Communities: Reflections on the Origin and Spread of Nationalism* (London: Verso, 1983); Kate Brown, "Gridded Lives: Why Kazakhstan and Montana Are Nearly the Same Place," *American Historical Review* 106, no. 1 (2001): 17–48; Kate Brown, *A Biography of No Place: From Ethnic Borderland to Soviet Heartland* (Cambridge: Harvard University Press, 2004); Sarah Cameron, "The Hungry Steppe: Famine, Violence and the Making of Soviet Kazakhstan" (forthcoming from Cornell University Press); Adrienne Edgar, *Tribal Nation: The Making of Soviet Turkmenistan* (Princeton: Princeton University Press, 2004); Terry Martin, *The Affirmative Action Empire: Nations and Nationalism in the Soviet Union, 1923–1939* (Ithaca: Cornell University Press, 2001); William Miles, *Scars of Partition: Postcolonial Legacies in French and British Borderlands* (Omaha: University of Nebraska Press, 2014); Mitchell, *Colonising Egypt;* Timothy Mitchell, *Rule of Experts: Egypt, Techno-Politics, Modernity* (Berkeley: University of California Press, 2002); Winichakul, *Siam Mapped.*

25. On these examples, see Michel Foucault, *Madness and Civilization: A History of Insanity in the Age of Reason* (New York: Pantheon, 1965); Michel Foucault, *Discipline and Punish: The Birth of the Prison* (New York: Pantheon, 1975); Foucault, *Security, Territory, Population.*

26. The idea that a city should serve as a shop window for the country's political-ideological system was especially strong in the Soviet Union; see R. A. French, *Plans, Pragmatism and People: The Legacy of Soviet Planning for Today's Cities* (Pittsburgh: University of Pittsburgh Press, 1995); Paul Stronski, *Tashkent: Forging a Soviet City, 1930–1966* (Pittsburgh: University of Pittsburgh Press, 2010).

27. Martin, "Statist Language."

28. Nursultan Nazarbayev, *Kazakhstanskii Put'* (The Kazakhstan Way) (Karaganda: no publisher, 2006), 351.

29. Lakoff and Johnson, *Metaphors We Live By*, 157.

30. Anthony D. King, "Planning Perspectives: Worlds in the City: Manhattan Transfer and the Ascendance of Spectacular Space," *Planning Perspectives* 11, no. 2 (1996): 97–114; Leslie Sklair, *The Icon Project: Architecture, Cities, and Capitalist Globalization* (New York: Oxford University Press, 2017).

31. Kenneth Burke, "Four Master Tropes," *Kenyon Review* 3, no. 4 (1941): 427.

32. Anderson, *Imagined Communities.*

33. Anthony Cardoza, "'Making Italians'? Cycling and National Identity in Italy: 1900–1950," *Journal of Modern Italian Studies* 15, no. 3 (2010): 354; Jon Fox, "Consuming the Nation: Holidays, Sports, and the Production of Collective Belonging," *Ethnic and Racial Studies* 29, no. 2 (2006): 217–36; David Ley and Kris Olds, "Landscape as Spectacle: World's Fairs and the Culture of Heroic Consumption," *Environment and Planning D: Society and Space* 6, no. 2 (1988): 191–212; Lisa Wedeen, *Ambiguities of Domination: Politics, Rhetoric, and Symbols in Contemporary Syria* (Chicago: University of Chicago Press, 1999), 21.

34. James Von Geldern, *Bolshevik Festivals, 1917–1920* (Berkeley: University of California Press, 1993), 42.

35. Veyne, *Bread and Circuses*, 20. See also Holston, *The Modernist City;* Natalie Koch, "The 'Heart' of Eurasia? Kazakhstan's Centrally Located Capital City," *Central Asian Survey* 32, no. 2 (2013): 134–47; Stephen Kotkin, *Magnetic Mountain: Stalinism as a Civilization* (Berkeley: University of California Press, 1995); Lawrence Vale, *Architecture, Power, and National Identity* (New Haven: Yale University Press, 1992).

36. Sallie Marston, "The Social Construction of Scale," *Progress in Human Geography* 24, no. 2 (2000): 219–42.

37. See, for example, Robert Bellah, "Civil Religion in America," *Daedalus* 96, no. 1 (1967): 1–21; Eric Hobsbawm, Mass-Producing Traditions: Europe, 1870–1914," in *The Invention of Tradition*, ed. Eric Hobsbawm and Terence Ranger (Cambridge: Cambridge University Press, 1983), 263–307.

38. See Graeme Hayes and John Karamichas, *Olympics Games, Mega-Events, and Civil Societies: Globalization, Environment, Resistance* (New York: Palgrave Macmillan, 2012).

39. Martin Müller, "State Dirigisme in Megaprojects: Governing the 2014 Winter Olympics in Sochi," *Environment and Planning A* 43, no. 9 (2011): 2091–2108; Elena Trubina, "Mega-Events in the Context of Capitalist Modernity: The Case of [the] 2014 Sochi Winter Olympics," *Eurasian Geography and Economics* 55, no. 6 (2014): 610–27.

40. On these cases, see especially Laura Adams, *The Spectacular State: Culture and National Identity in Uzbekistan* (Durham: Duke University Press, 2010); Joshua Hagen, "Parades, Public Space, and Propaganda: The Nazi Culture Parades in Munich," *Geografiska Annaler: Series B, Human Geography* 90, no. 4 (2008): 349–67; Kotkin, *Magnetic Mountain*; Karen Petrone, *Life Has Become More Joyous, Comrades: Celebrations in the Time of Stalin* (Bloomington: Indiana University Press, 2000); Malte Rolf, *Soviet Mass Festivals, 1917–1991* (Pittsburgh University of Pittsburgh Press, 2013).

41. Foucault, *Discipline and Punish*.

42. This argument is laid out in chapter 2 of Foucault, *Discipline and Punish*.

43. Veyne, *Bread and Circuses*.

44. Michel Foucault, *Fearless Speech* (Los Angeles: Semiotext(e), 2001), 74.

45. Mitchell, "Everyday Metaphors of Power"; Jeffrey Nealon, *Foucault beyond Foucault: Power and Its Intensifications since 1984* (Stanford: Stanford University Press, 2008).

46. See, for example, Lily Kong and Brenda S. A. Yeoh, "The Construction of National Identity through the Production of Ritual and Spectacle: An Analysis of National Day Parades in Singapore," *Political Geography* 16, no. 3 (1997): 213–39.

47. Nicholas Dirks, "Ritual and Resistance: Subversion as a Social Fact," in *Contesting Power: Resistance and Everyday Social Relations in South Asia*, ed. Douglas Haynes and Gyan Prakash (Berkeley: University of California Press, 1992), 213–38; Natalie Koch, "Technologising the Opinion: Focus Groups, Performance and Free Speech," *Area* 45, no. 4 (2013): 411–18; Nealon, *Foucault beyond Foucault*; Johanna Oksala, *Foucault on Freedom* (Cambridge: Cambridge University Press, 2005); Wedeen, *Ambiguities of Domination*.

48. Petrone, *Life Has Become More Joyous*, 4. See also Rolf, *Soviet Mass Festivals*.

49. Wedeen, *Ambiguities of Domination*.

50. Michel Foucault, "The Subject and Power," *Critical Inquiry* 8, no. 4 (1982): 789.

51. Adams, *The Spectacular State*; Natalie Koch, "Technologizing Complacency: Spectacle, Structural Violence, and 'Living Normally' in a Resource-Rich State," *Political Geography* 37 (2013): A1–A2; Natalie Koch, "Is Nationalism Just for Nationals? Civic Nationalism for Noncitizens and Celebrating National Day in Qatar and the UAE," *Political Geography* 54 (2016): 43–53; Michael Mann, *Fascists* (New York: Cambridge University Press, 2004); Alexei Yurchak, "The Cynical Reason of Late Socialism: Power, Pretense, and the *Anekdot*," *Public Culture* 9, no. 2 (1997), 161–88.

52. Laura Adams, "Cultural Elites in Uzbekistan: Ideological Production and the State," in *The Transformation of Central Asia: States and Societies from Soviet Rule to Independence*, ed. Pauline Jones Luong (Ithaca: Cornell University Press, 2004), 93–119; Adams, *The Spectacular State*; Laura Adams and Assel Rustemova, "Mass Spectacle and Styles of Governmentality in Kazakhstan and Uzbekistan," *Europe-Asia Studies* 61, no. 7 (2009): 1249–76; Sally Cummings, *Symbolism and Power in Central Asia: Politics of the Spectacular* (London: Routledge, 2010); Adrien Fauve, "A Tale of Two Statues in Astana: The Fuzzy Process of Nationalistic City Making," *Nationalities Papers* 43, no. 3 (2015): 383–98; Natalie Koch, "The Violence of Spectacle: Statist Schemes to Green the Desert and Constructing Astana and Ashgabat as Urban Oases," *Social & Cultural Geography* 16, no. 6 (2015): 675–97; Natalie Koch and Anar Valiyev, "Urban Boosterism in Closed Contexts: Spectacular Urbanization and Second-Tier Mega-Events in Three Caspian Capitals," *Eurasian Geography and Economics* 56, no. 5 (2015): 575–98; Müller, "State Dirigisme in Megaprojects"; Trubina, "Mega-Events"; Veyne, *Bread and Circuses*.

53. Clifford Geertz, *Negara: The Theatre State in Nineteenth-Century Bali* (Princeton: Princeton University Press, 1980), 120. Adams, *The Spectacular State*, 188.

54. Adams, *The Spectacular State*, 87.

55. Peter Eisinger, "The Politics of Bread and Circuses: Building the City for the Visitor Class," *Urban Affairs Review* 35, no. 3 (2000): 316–33; David Harvey, "From Managerialism to Entrepreneurialism: The Transformation in Urban Governance in Late Capitalism," *Geografiska Annaler. Series B, Human Geography* 71, no. 1 (1989): 3–17.

56. Rob Nixon, *Slow Violence and the Environmentalism of the Poor* (Cambridge: Harvard University Press, 2011), 7.

57. Nixon, *Slow Violence*, 7–8.

58. Johan Galtung, "Violence, Peace, and Peace Research," *Journal of Peace Research* 6, no. 3 (1969): 167–91. See also Paul Farmer, "On Suffering and Structural Violence: A View from Below," *Daedalus* 125, no. 1 (1996): 261–83; Paul Farmer, *Pathologies of Power: Health, Human Rights, and the New War on the Poor* (Berkeley: University of California Press, 2003); Johan Galtung, "Cultural Violence," *Journal of Peace Research* 27, no. 3 (1990): 291–305; Joseph Nevins, "Embedded Empire: Structural Violence and the Pursuit of Justice in East Timor," *Annals of the Association of American Geographers* 99, no. 5 (2009): 914–21; Michael Watts, *Silent Violence: Food, Famine, and Peasantry in Northern Nigeria* (Berkeley: University of California Press, 1983).

59. Clifford Geertz, "Centers, Kings, and Charisma: Reflections on the Symbolics of Power," in *Local Knowledge: Further Essays in Interpretive Anthropology*, ed. Clifford Geertz (New York: Basic Books, 1983), 123.

60. Geertz, *Negara*, 135.

61. Nixon, *Slow Violence*, 8.

62. Lakoff and Johnson, *Metaphors We Live By*, 159.

63. Nietzsche, "On Truth and Lies"; Lakoff and Johnson, *Metaphors We Live By*, 159–60.

2. From Almaty to Astana

1. Nursultan Nazarbayev, "Future Vision," *K Magazine* 1 (2010): 53.

2. Nursultan Nazarbayev, *V Serdtse Evrazii* (in the Heart of Eurasia) (Astana: no publisher, 2005). See also Nursultan Nazarbayev, *Epitsentr Mira* (Epicenter of Peace) (Almaty: Atamyra, 2003).

3. On the Foucauldian approach to the state as an effect, see Natalie Koch, "'Spatial Socialization': Understanding the State Effect Geographically," *Nordia Geographical*

Publications 44, no. 4 (2015): 29–35; Merje Kuus and John Agnew, "Theorizing the State Geographically: Sovereignty, Subjectivity, Territoriality," in *The Sage Handbook of Political Geography*, ed. Kevin Cox, Murray Low, and Jennifer Robinson (Los Angeles: Sage, 2008), 95–106; Thomas Lemke, *Foucault, Governmentality, and Critique* (Boulder: Paradigm Publishers, 2011); Timothy Mitchell, "The Limits of the State: Beyond Statist Approaches and Their Critics," *American Political Science Review* 85, no. 1 (1991): 77–96; Timothy Mitchell, "Society, Economy, and the State Effect," in *State/Culture: State-Formation after the Cultural Turn*, ed. George Steinmetz (Ithaca: Cornell University Press, 1999), 76–97.

4. Anthony Giddens, *Central Problems in Social Theory: Action, Structure, and Contradiction in Social Analysis* (Berkeley: University of California Press, 1979). See also John Agnew, *Place and Politics: The Geographical Mediation of State and Society* (Boston: Allen & Unwin, 1987); Peter Berger and Stanley Pullberg, "Reification and the Sociological Critique of Consciousness," *History and Theory* 4, no. 2 (1965): 196–211; Pierre Bourdieu, *Outline of a Theory of Practice* (Cambridge: Cambridge University Press, 1977); Philip Corrigan and Derek Sayer, *The Great Arch: English State Formation as Cultural Revolution* (New York: Blackwell, 1985); John Law, "Notes on the Theory of the Actor-Network: Ordering, Strategy, and Heterogeneity," *Systemic Practice and Action Research* 5, no. 4 (1992): 379–93; Doreen Massey, *Spatial Divisions of Labor: Social Structures and the Geography of Production* (New York: Methuen, 1984); Allan Pred, *Place, Practice, and Structure: Social and Spatial Transformation in Southern Sweden, 1750–1850* (Totowa, N. J.: Barnes & Noble, 1986).

5. Michel Foucault, *The Birth of Biopolitics: Lectures at the Collège de France, 1978–1979* (New York: Picador, 2008), 297.

6. This task is ultimately a historical one. In writing about transactional realities, Foucault stresses the importance of "showing by what conjunctions a whole set of practices—from the moment they become coordinated with a regime of truth—was able to make what does not exist (madness, disease, delinquency, sexuality, etcetera) nonetheless become something, something however that continues not to exist." It is *not* about showing something to be an error or illusion, but rather about showing "how a particular regime of truth, and therefore not an error, makes something that does not exist able to become something. It is not an illusion since it is precisely a set of practices, real practices, which establish it and thus imperiously marks it out in reality. . . . Politics and the economy are not things that exist, or errors, or illusions, or ideologies. They are things that do not exist and yet which are inscribed in reality and fall under a regime of truth dividing the true and the false." Foucault, *The Birth of Biopolitics*, 19–20.

7. Natalie Koch, "The Violence of Spectacle: Statist Schemes to Green the Desert and Constructing Astana and Ashgabat as Urban Oases," *Social & Cultural Geography* 16, no. 6 (2015): 678.

8. Quoted in Michel Foucault, *Security, Territory, Population: Lectures at the Collège de France, 1977–1978* (New York: Picador, 2007), 14.

9. Soviet urban planning, albeit unique in many ways, has much in common with that of other industrial countries and global high-modernist planning traditions. For more on urban planning during Russian colonial and Soviet times, see especially Susan Buck-Morss, *Dreamworld and Catastrophe: The Passing of Mass Utopia in East and West* (Cambridge: MIT Press, 2000); Heather DeHaan, *Stalinist City Planning: Professionals, Performance, and Power* (Toronto: University of Toronto Press, 2013); R. A. French, *Plans, Pragmatism and People: The Legacy of Soviet Planning for Today's Cities* (Pittsburgh: University of Pittsburgh Press, 1995); Stephen Kotkin, *Magnetic Mountain: Stalinism as a Civilization* (Berkeley: University of California Press, 1995); Richard Stites, *Revolutionary Dreams: Utopian Vision and Experimental Life in the Russian Revolution* (New York: Oxford University Press, 1989); Paul Stronski, *Tashkent: Forging a Soviet City, 1930–1966* (Pittsburgh: University of Pittsburgh Press, 2010).

10. Katerina Clark, "Socialist Realism and the Sacralizing of Space," in *The Landscape of Stalinism: The Art and Ideology of Soviet Space*, ed. E. A. Dobrenko and Eric Naiman (Seattle: University of Washington Press, 2003), 3–18.

11. Catherine Alexander and Victor Buchli, introduction to *Urban Life in Post-Soviet Asia*, ed. Catherine Alexander, Victor Buchli, and Caroline Humphrey (London: University College London Press, 2007), 8.

12. Ibid., 2.

13. Kotkin, *Magnetic Mountain*, 35. On state-building as a form of internal colonialism, see also James C. Scott, *Seeing Like a State: How Certain Schemes to Improve the Human Condition Have Failed* (New Haven: Yale University Press, 1998).

14. Robert Crews, "Civilization in the City: Architecture, Urbanism, and the Colonization of Tashkent," in *Architectures of Russian Identity: 1500 to the Present*, ed. James Cracraft and Daniel Rowland (Ithaca: Cornell University Press, 2003), 118. See also Robert Crews, *For Prophet and Tsar: Islam and Empire in Russia and Central Asia* (Cambridge: Harvard University Press, 2006).

15. See especially Kate Brown, "Gridded Lives: Why Kazakhstan and Montana Are Nearly the Same Place," *American Historical Review* 106, no. 1 (2001): 17–48; Sarah Cameron, *The Hungry Steppe: Famine, Violence and the Making of Soviet Kazakhstan* (forthcoming from Cornell University Press); Adrienne Edgar, *Tribal Nation: The Making of Soviet Turkmenistan* (Princeton: Princeton University Press, 2004).

16. Crews, "Civilization in the City," 120. See also Stronski, *Tashkent*.

17. Heather DeHaan, *Stalinist City Planning: Professionals, Performance, and Power* (Toronto: University of Toronto Press, 2013); Olga Gritsai and Herman van der Wusten, "Moscow and St. Petersburg, a Sequence of Capitals, a Tale of Two Cities," *GeoJournal* 51, no. 1–2 (2000): 39.

18. Catherine Alexander, "Almaty: Rethinking the Public Sector," in Alexander, Buchli, and Humphrey, *Urban Life in Post-Soviet Asia* (London: University College London Press, 2007), 76.

19. See Robert Saunders, "In Defence of *Kazakshilik*: Kazakhstan's War on Sacha Baron Cohen," *Identities* 14, no. 3 (2007): 225–55; Robert Saunders, "Buying into Brand Borat: Kazakhstan's Cautious Embrace of Its Unwanted 'Son,'" *Slavic Review* 67, no. 1 (2008): 63–80; Edward Schatz, "Transnational Image Making and Soft Authoritarian Kazakhstan," *Slavic Review* 67, no. 1 (2008): 50–62.

20. According to my interviews, this campaign, which involves "glossy" publications, paid advertising space in several Western newspapers (including the *Washington Times, International Herald Tribune,* and *Telegraph of London*), and a range of other initiatives, was not the result of a presidential request or order but an independent initiative of the Ministry of Foreign Relations. Some speculate that the PR campaign is just an element of Nazarbayev's self-aggrandizement and pursuit of international accolades. One anonymous informant working for a United States–based PR firm hired by the ministry explained that the firm's charge is to promote Kazakhstan's international image abroad—but admits that this is inseparable from promoting Nazarbayev himself. Some analysts suggest that the state's "multilateralism in the extreme" is part of the state- and nation-building process, absent any other viable sources of legitimacy (such as economic performance or a majority ethnic community), while others suggest it is merely a continuation of the Great Power mentality inherited from Soviet times. On these imaging campaigns, see Adrien Fauve, "Global Astana: Nation Branding as a Legitimization Tool for Authoritarian Regimes," *Central Asian Survey* 34, no. 1 (2015): 110–24; Natalie Koch, "Sport and Soft Authoritarian Nation-Building," *Political Geography* 32 (2013): 42–51; Natalie Koch, "Bordering on the Modern: Power, Practice and Exclusion

in Astana," *Transactions of the Institute of British Geographers* 39, no. 3 (2014): 432–43; Schatz, "Transnational Image Making."

21. Edward Schatz, "Access by Accident: Legitimacy Claims and Democracy Promotion in Authoritarian Central Asia," *International Political Science Review* 27, no. 3 (2006): 270.

22. Nazarbayev, *V Serdtse Evrazii*, 338–44; Nazarbayev, "Future Vision," 53.

23. Quoted in Natalia Antelava, "Giant Tent to Be Built in Astana," *BBC News*, December 9, 2006, http://news.bbc.co.uk/2/hi/asia-pacific/6165267.stm (accessed January 23, 2017).

24. Nazarbayev, *V Serdtse Evrazii*, 348.

25. Ibid., 342.

26. Ibid., 338.

27. Schatz, "What Capital Cities Say," 125.

28. Nazarbayev, "Future Vision," 53.

29. Buck-Morss, *Dreamworld and Catastrophe*, 196. For more, see Rico Isaacs, "'Papa'— Nursultan Nazarbayev and the Discourse of Charismatic Leadership and Nation-Building in Post-Soviet Kazakhstan," *Studies in Ethnicity and Nationalism* 10, no. 3 (2010): 435–52; Natalie Koch, "The 'Personality Cult' Problematic: Personalism and Mosques Memorializing the 'Father of the Nation' in Turkmenistan and the UAE," *Central Asian Affairs* 3, no. 4 (2016): 330–59.

30. Schatz, "Access by Accident"; Schatz, "Transnational Image Making."

31. Nazarbayev, *V Serdtse Evrazii*, 32–38.

32. He also describes it as especially appropriate for Kazakhstan given the state's youth, explicitly associating grand capital city projects with young states, such as Atatürk's Ankara project in post-Ottoman Turkey. On the connections between Astana and Ankara, see Natalie Koch, "Why Not a World City? Astana, Ankara, and Geopolitical Scripts in Urban Networks," *Urban Geography* 34, no. 1 (2013): 109–30.

33. Nazarbayev, "Future Vision," 53. The coincidence of these construction metaphors is not chance but common to many nation-building discourses that accompany the many capital city projects. On Astana, see also Mateusz Laszczkowski, "Building the Future: Construction, Temporality, and Politics in Astana," *Focaal: Journal of Global and Historical Anthropology* 60 (2011): 77–92; Mateusz Laszczkowski, "State Building(s): Built Forms, Materiality, and the State in Astana," in *Ethnographies of the State in Central Asia: Performing Politics*, ed. Madeleine Reeves, Johan Rasanayagam, and Judith Beyer (Bloomington: Indiana University Press, 2013), 149–72.

34. Nazarbayev, *V Serdtse Evrazii*.

35. Buck-Morss, *Dreamworld and Catastrophe*, 209.

36. Nazarbayev, *V Serdtse Evrazii*, 336.

37. Ibid., 350, 349.

38. See, for example, Nursultan Nazarbayev, "Kazakhstan's Strategy of Joining the World's 50 Most Competitive Countries," Official Site of the President of the Republic of Kazakhstan (2006), http://www.akorda.kz/en/speeches/addresses_of_the_president_of_kazakhstan/march_2006 (accessed March 1, 2011).

39. Nursultan Nazarbayev, "Presentation of the Book *In the heart of Eurasia*," Official Site of the President of the Republic of Kazakhstan (2006), http://www.akorda.kz/en/speeches/summit_conference_sittings_meetings/presentation_of_the_book_in_the_heart_of_eurasia_ (accessed March 1, 2011).

40. See, for example, James Holston, *The Modernist City: An Anthropological Critique of Brasília* (Chicago: University of Chicago Press, 1989); Duygu Kacar, "Ankara, a Small Town, Transformed to a Nation's Capital," *Journal of Planning History* 9, no. 1 (2010): 43–65.

41. Paul Veyne, *Bread and Circuses: Historical Sociology and Political Pluralism* (London: Penguin Press, 1990), 294.

42. Ibid., 389, 384, 386.

43. Ibid., 383.

44. Ibid., 95.

45. Laszczkowski, "State Building(s)," 164.

46. An occasional opposition voice can, of course, be found in a news source such as Radio Free Europe/Radio Liberty. For example, one reporter quotes a deputy chairman of the opposition Social Democratic Party, Amirzhan Qosanov, as saying that the 2008 Astana Day celebrations "are nothing but gross adulation of Nazarbayev." She also cites an independent journalist, Sergei Duvanov, who criticized the celebrations as "an attempt by some politicians to curry favor with Nazarbayev." This sort of open criticism of politics is rare in Kazakhstan. Most people who disapprove of the arrangement simply say nothing at all, and/or do not attend the events (especially the most blatantly ideological ones). The main exception to the generally low attendance at Astana Day events is the musical concerts by famous Western, Russian, and Kazakh stars. See Gulnoza Saidazimova, "Nazarbayev Celebrates 'Day of Astana,' but Critics Scoff at Grandiose Festivities," Radio Free Europe/Radio Liberty, July 5, 2008, http://www.rferl.org/content/Nazarbaev_Celebrates_Day_Of_Astana/1181848.html (accessed June 30, 2017).

47. For more, see Mateusz Laszczkowski, *"City of the Future": Built Space, Modernity, and Change in Astana* (New York: Berghahn Books, 2016).

48. Alexei Yurchak, "The Cynical Reason of Late Socialism: Power, Pretense, and the *Anekdot,*" *Public Culture* 9, no. 2 (1997): 161–88; Alexei Yurchak, *Everything Was Forever, until It Was No More: The Last Soviet Generation* (Princeton: Princeton University Press, 2006). See also Karen Petrone, *Life Has Become More Joyous, Comrades: Celebrations in the Time of Stalin* (Bloomington: Indiana University Press, 2000); Malte Rolf, *Soviet Mass Festivals, 1917–1991* (Pittsburgh University of Pittsburgh Press, 2013).

49. Yurchak, *Everything Was Forever,* 25.

50. Yurchak, "The Cynical Reason," 171, 174.

51. Laura Adams, *The Spectacular State: Culture and National Identity in Uzbekistan* (Durham: Duke University Press, 2010), 186.

52. See chapter 4 of Petrone, *Life Has Become More Joyous.*

53. Jeffrey T. Nealon, *Foucault beyond Foucault: Power and Its Intensifications since 1984* (Stanford: Stanford University Press, 2008), 102. See also Timothy Mitchell, "Everyday Metaphors of Power," *Theory and Society* 19, no. 5 (1990): 545–77. By "liberalist" notions I mean conceptions of agency and power that are biased toward liberal worldviews. Following the critique of Nealon and Mitchell, my reading of the issue of nonparticipation stands in contrast to the common liberal habit of looking for "alternative" readings of texts or public spaces, or unconventional forms of engaging with these sites as a form of veiled protest. The first problem with this reading is that it is predicated on a one-dimensional, top-down understanding of power, and reaffirms the imagined primary authorship of the spectacle's meaning to the state. This effectively attributes to the state a degree of coherence that it does not deserve—not just because spectacles the world over are typically planned by cultural elites who tend to have their own (opportunistic) motivations for participating in the events, but also because the masses are involved in bringing them to life in far more complicated ways. The second problem with this approach is that it assumes that the spectacle's organizers do not benefit from these "tactical ways" of "appropriating" the parades. On the contrary, these forms of participation or nonparticipation are practices that are *essential* to supporting the system.

54. Mitchell, "Everyday Metaphors of Power."

55. Elmer Schattschneider, *The Semisovereign People: A Realist's View of Democracy in America* (New York: Holt, Rinehart and Winston, 1960), 2.

56. Ibid., 7.

57. Gramsci writes: "One of the most banal commonplaces which get repeated against the elective system of forming State organs is the following: that in it numbers decide everything, and that the opinions of any idiot who knows how to write (or in some countries even of an illiterate) have exactly the same weight in determining the political course of the State as the opinions of somebody who devotes his best energies to the State and the nation, etc. . . . The counting of 'votes' is the final ceremony of a long process, in which it is precisely those who devote their best energies to the State and the nation (when such they are) who carry the greatest weight." Antonio Gramsci, *Selections from the Prison Notebooks of Antonio Gramsci* (New York: International Publishers, 2008), 193.

58. The Semipalatinsk Nuclear Test Site, colloquially referred to as "the Polygon," is where the Soviets tested most of their nuclear weapons above and below ground, and it is still highly contaminated. The Aral Sea disaster is discussed in the following chapter. Semipalatinsk cannot be discussed at length here, but see Stanley Brunn, "Fifty Years of Soviet Nuclear Testing in Semipalatinsk, Kazakhstan: Juxtaposed Worlds of Blasts and Silences, Security and Risks, Denials and Memory," in *Engineering Earth: The Impacts of Megaengineering Projects*, ed. Stanley Brunn (New York: Springer, 2011), 1789–1818; Magdalena Stawkowski, "'I Am a Radioactive Mutant': Emergent Biological Subjectivities at Kazakhstan's Semipalatinsk Nuclear Test Site," *American Ethnologist* 43, no. 1 (2016): 144–57; Cynthia Werner and Kathleen Purvis-Roberts, "Cold War Memories and Post–Cold War Realities: The Politics of Memory and Identity in the Everyday Life of Kazakhstan's Radiation Victims," in *Ethnographies of the State in Central Asia: Performing Politics*, ed. Madeleine Reeves, Johan Rasanayagam, and Judith Beyer (Bloomington: Indiana University Press, 2013), 285–309.

59. Jessica Allina-Pisano, "How to Tell an Axe Murderer: An Essay on Ethnography, Truth, and Lies," in *Political Ethnography: What Immersion Contributes to the Study of Power*, ed. Edward Schatz (Chicago: University of Chicago Press, 2009), 68–69.

60. Schattschneider, *The Semisovereign People*, 106.

61. For a similar argument, see chapter 5 of Zygmunt Bauman, *Modernity and the Holocaust* (Ithaca: Cornell University Press, 1989).

62. Often with great pleasure, as Mateusz Laszczkowski underscores in "State Building(s)" and *City of the Future*.

63. Nazarbayev, "Future Vision," 53.

64. Yurchak, "The Cynical Reason," 183.

65. Paul Veyne, "Foucault Revolutionizes History," in *Foucault and His Interlocutors*, ed. A. I. Davidson (Chicago: University of Chicago Press, 1997), 172.

66. Veyne, *Bread and Circuses,* 95, 398, 403.

67. George Lakoff and Mark Johnson, *Metaphors We Live By* (Chicago: University of Chicago Press, 1980), 236.

3. From Astana to Aral

1. Artur Nigmetov, "Tired, Angry, but Determined, Striking Kazakh Oil Workers Say Fight Will Go On," Radio Free Europe/Radio Liberty, September 14, 2011, http://www.rferl.org/content/striking_kazakh_oil_workers_say_fight_will_go_on/24328725.html (accessed January 23, 2017). For more on the Zhanaozen protests, see David Lewis, "Blogging Zhanaozen: Hegemonic Discourse and Authoritarian Resilience in Kazakhstan," *Central Asian Survey* 35, no. 3 (2016): 421–38.

2. "Sting Cancels Kazakhstan Concert over 'Rights Abuses,'" BBC News, July 4, 2011, http://www.bbc.co.uk/news/entertainment-arts-14011860 (accessed January 23, 2017).

3. Sarah Kendzior, "Inventing Akromiya: The Role of Uzbek Propagandists in the Andijon Massacre," *Demokratizatsiya* 14, no. 4 (2006): 545–62; Natalie Koch, "Security and Gendered National Identity in Uzbekistan," *Gender, Place & Culture* 18, no. 4 (2011): 499–518; Nick Megoran, "Framing Andijon, Narrating the Nation: Islam Karimov's Account of the Events of 13 May 2005," *Central Asian Survey* 27, no. 1 (2008): 15–31.

4. This account is drawn from Natalie Koch, "Technologizing Complacency: Spectacle, Structural Violence, and 'Living Normally' in a Resource-Rich State," *Political Geography* 37 (2013): A1–A2.

5. Anna Matveeva, "Legitimising Central Asian Authoritarianism: Political Manipulation and Symbolic Power," *Europe-Asia Studies* 61, no. 7 (2009): 1107.

6. This problem is classically explored in Raymond Williams, *The Country and the City* (New York: Oxford University Press, 1973).

7. Natalie Koch, "Why No 'Water Wars' in Central Asia? Lessons Learned from the Aral Sea Disaster," *PONARS Eurasia Policy Memo 410* (January 2016), http://www.ponarseurasia.org/memo/why-no-water-wars-central-asia-aral-sea-disaster (accessed January 23, 2017).

8. See, for example, Dianne Rocheleau, Barbara Thomas-Slayter, and Esther Wangari, *Feminist Political Ecology: Global Issues and Local Experiences* (New York: Routledge, 1996); Adriana Petryna, *Life Exposed: Biological Citizens after Chernobyl* (Princeton: Princeton University Press, 2002); Magdalena Stawkowski, "'I Am a Radioactive Mutant': Emergent Biological Subjectivities at Kazakhstan's Semipalatinsk Nuclear Test Site," *American Ethnologist* 43, no. 1 (2016): 144–57; Farhana Sultana, "Producing Contaminated Citizens: Toward a Nature-Society Geography of Health and Well-Being," *Annals of the Association of American Geographers* 102, no. 5 (2012): 1165–72.

9. Carl Death, *Critical Environmental Politics* (New York: Routledge, 2014); Rob Nixon, *Slow Violence and the Environmentalism of the Poor* (Cambridge: Harvard University Press, 2011); Shannon O'Lear and Angela Gray, "Asking the Right Questions: Environmental Conflict in the Case of Azerbaijan," *Area* 38, no. 4 (2006): 390–401.

10. Cynthia Buckley, "Rural/Urban Differentials in Demographic Processes: The Central Asian States," *Population Research and Policy Review* 17, no. 1 (1998): 71–89; Natalie Koch and Kristopher White, "Cowboys, Gangsters, and Rural Bumpkins: Constructing the 'Other' in Kazakhstan's 'Texas,'" in *Kazakhstan in the Making: Legitimacy, Symbols, and Social Changes*, ed. Marlene Laruelle (Lanham, Md.: Lexington, 2016), 181–207; Madeleine Reeves, Johan Rasanayagam, and Judith Beyer, *Ethnographies of the State in Central Asia: Performing Politics* (Bloomington: Indiana University Press, 2013); Halil Sakal, "Natural Resource Policies and Standard of Living in Kazakhstan," *Central Asian Survey* 34, no. 2 (2015): 237–54.

11. Quoted in Alla Bolotova, "Colonization of Nature in the Soviet Union: State Ideology, Public Discourse, and the Experience of Geologists," *Historical Social Research* 29, no. 3 (2004): 110.

12. Bernd Richter, "Nature Mastered by Man: Ideology and Water in the Soviet Union," *Environment and History* 3 (1997): 69–96.

13. Murray Feshbach, *Ecological Disaster: Cleaning up the Hidden Legacy of the Soviet Regime* (New York: Twentieth Century Fund Press, 1995).

14. Clifford Geertz, "Centers, Kings, and Charisma: Reflections on the Symbolics of Power," in *Local Knowledge: Further Essays in Interpretive Anthropology*, ed. Clifford Geertz (New York: Basic Books, 1983), 123.

15. On the Virgin Lands campaign, see especially Michaela Pohl, "The Virgin Lands between Memory and Forgetting: People and Transformation in the Soviet Union, 1954–1960" (Ph.D. diss., Indiana University, 1999).

16. During Soviet times (and still today in parts of Central Asia), irrigation canals were primitive—hastily constructed and unlined. It is estimated that around 60 percent of water withdrawn from the Amu Darya is lost to seepage and evapotranspiration. Max Spoor, "The Aral Sea Basin Crisis: Transition and Environment in Former Soviet Central Asia," *Development & Change* 29, no. 3 (1998): 423. The poor construction has been attributed to the Soviet incentive system that prioritized speedy construction and rewarded gross output, measured in terms of kilometers of canals or tons of earth moved, instead of the number of completed projects and the quality of those projects. Erika Weinthal, *State Making and Environmental Cooperation: Linking Domestic and International Politics in Central Asia* (Cambridge: MIT Press, 2002), 94.

17. In the 1960s, Khrushchev promoted the further expansion of irrigation in Central Asia, which led to a 1.7-fold increase in irrigated areas and a significant increase in river diversions. The central Soviet administration advanced these projects in the name of "economic development," despite the fact that they eventually led to economic and environmental disaster in the region. During the 1950s, when the expansion and mechanization of irrigation was in full swing, the eventual shrinkage of the sea was recognized. Yet this was justified on the basis that economic benefits from diversion were expected to exceed the resulting cost of environmental degradation, which, it was assumed, would be minimal. See Michael Glantz, *Creeping Environmental Problems and Sustainable Development in the Aral Sea Basin* (New York: Cambridge University Press, 1999); Philip Micklin, "The Aral Sea Disaster," *Annual Review of Earth and Planetary Sciences* 35, no. 1 (2007): 47–72; Kai Wegerich, "Water: The Difficult Path to a Sustainable Future for Central Asia," in *Central Asia: Aspects of Transition*, ed. Tom Everett-Heath (New York: RoutledgeCurzon, 2003), 244–63; Weinthal, *State Making and Environmental Cooperation.*

18. I do not provide citations for each interview quoted here, but for full references to the anonymized data, see Natalie Koch, "Geopolitical Discourses and the Aral Sea Desiccation: A Case Study of Kyzylorda *Oblast*'" (B.A. thesis, Dartmouth College, 2006).

19. For my critique of the "water wars" literature on Central Asia, see Koch, "Why No 'Water Wars'?"

20. For the full survey analysis and methods, see Natalie Koch, "The City and the Steppe: Territory, Technologies of Government, and Kazakhstan's New Capital" (Ph.D. diss., University of Colorado, 2012).

21. Natalie Koch, "Introduction—Field Methods in 'Closed Contexts': Undertaking Research in Authoritarian States and Places," *Area* 45, no. 4 (2013): 390–95; Natalie Koch, "Kazakhstan's Changing Geopolitics: The Resource Economy and Popular Attitudes about China's Growing Regional Influence," *Eurasian Geography and Economics* 54, no. 1 (2013): 110–33.

22. Spoor, "The Aral Sea Basin Crisis," 420.

23. Micklin, "The Aral Sea Disaster."

24. The response of most locals included a reference to poor water management policies in Central Asia as the cause of the sea's desiccation. Some laid the blame on neighboring Central Asian states, most often Uzbekistan. One woman even asserted that the sea disappeared because the Uzbeks had taken Kazakhstan's water for themselves: "The people are to blame. Uzbekistan, it turns out, took our water for itself. There . . . they are to blame. Not ecology, but them. At the hands of these people our water disappeared." While Uzbekistan continues to be the largest water user in Central Asia, other countries mentioned were Kyrgyzstan and Tajikistan. Some specifically mentioned Russia or the USSR, but without describing the sea's desiccation as resulting from Soviet agricultural policies. There were also several people who described the sea's disappearance as a result of generally poor water use or improper

regulation. Another common claim was that the ecological problems were connected with the Russian-leased Baikonur Cosmodrome. Not everyone saw the environmental changes as a result of human activity. Among both older villagers and younger respondents, there was sometimes a sense that no one was guilty, but that it was simply God's will. A handful of others indicated that it was not people who were guilty but the "laws of nature."

25. Christopher Pala, "$85 Million Project Begins for Revival of the Aral Sea." *New York Times*, September 27, 2005, http://www.nytimes.com/2003/08/05/science/85-million-project-begins-for-revival-of-the-aral-sea.html (accessed January 23, 2017).

26. "Kazakhstan: Focus on Northern Aral Sea Fishery," Integrated Regional Information Networks (October 8, 2003), http://www.irinnews.org/print.asp?ReportID=37063 (accessed December 20, 2005).

27. V. M. Kemalashev, personal communication, September 7, 2005.

28. World Bank, *Aral Sea Basin Program (Kazakhstan, Kyrgyz Republic, Tajikistan, Turkmenistan and Uzbekistan): Water and Management Program, Project Document* (Washington, D.C.: World Bank, 1998), 5–6.

29. V. M. Kemalashev, personal communication, September 7, 2005.

30. "Dam Splits Aral Sea, New Boost for Northern Part Seen," Embassy of Kazakhstan to the USA and Canada, August 10, 2005, http://www.kazakhembus.com/081005.html (accessed December 13, 2005).

31. For more on Nazarbayev's use of these tropes, see Natalie Koch, "The 'Heart' of Eurasia? Kazakhstan's Centrally Located Capital City," *Central Asian Survey* 32, no. 2 (2013): 134–47.

32. When I returned in 2015, it was clear that the dike had made a significant impact at the local level, as my interlocutors anticipated in 2005. The salinity of the Small Sea had decreased significantly, some freshwater fish had been reintroduced, and commercial fishermen were beginning to return. In fact, the geographer Philip Micklin notes that salinity in the Small Sea was already decreasing by September 2005, when tests indicated levels of 3 g/L by the dam and 11 g/L near the fishing village of Tastubek, putting it at the same level as in the 1960s. Salinity levels increased farther west, but this drop in salinity at least allowed for the return of certain freshwater fish in parts of the sea. In the Big Sea, by contrast, even where there was water, salinity levels were generally at 70–80 g/L on the west side, and the fish were completely gone, though there were some plankton and benthic organisms. Although the Big Sea was continuing to shrink, the rate had slowed over the preceding two years, perhaps because evaporation had lessened. Philip Micklin, personal communication November 18, 2005.

33. Stawkowski, "'I Am a Radioactive Mutant.'"

34. Koch and White, "Cowboys, Gangsters, and Rural Bumpkins." See also Mateusz Laszczkowski, *"City of the Future": Built Space, Modernity, and Change in Astana* (New York: Berghahn Books, 2016); Joma Nazpary, *Post-Soviet Chaos: Violence and Dispossession in Kazakhstan* (London: Pluto Press, 2002).

35. A number of people named the government but did not specify the level, or said that increased financial resources from the government would help. For example, some specifically named the mayor or local government (*Akimat*), while others also pointed to President Nazarbayev as being in a position to solve local problems.

36. Koch, "The 'Heart' of Eurasia?"

37. Timothy Mitchell, *Rule of Experts: Egypt, Techno-Politics, Modernity* (Berkeley: University of California Press, 2002), 153.

38. I explain how and why this is the case in Natalie Koch, "Why Not a World City? Astana, Ankara, and Geopolitical Scripts in Urban Networks," *Urban Geography* 34, no. 1 (2013): 109–30.

39. For a more detailed account of the kitchen as a space of open political discussion in Russia, but applicable to the post-Soviet space more generally, see Dale Pesmen, *Russia and Soul: An Exploration* (Ithaca: Cornell University Press, 2000).

40. All respondent names here and elsewhere are pseudonyms.

41. Geertz, "Centers, Kings, and Charisma," 143–44.

42. Edward Shils, *The Constitution of Society* (Chicago: University of Chicago Press, 1982), 100, 102.

43. Ibid., 93, 105–6.

44. See, for example, Arun Elhance, "Conflict and Cooperation over Water in the Aral Sea Basin," *Studies in Conflict & Terrorism* 20, no. 2 (1997): 207–18; Max Spoor and Anatoly Krutov, "The 'Power of Water' in a Divided Central Asia," *Perspectives on Global Development and Technology* 2, no. 3–4 (2003): 593–614. This scholarship follows the arguments of the broader "resource-conflict" literature that was popularized in the 1990s in such works as Thomas Homer-Dixon and Jessica Blitt, *Ecoviolence: Links among Environment, Population and Security* (Lanham, Md.: Rowman & Littlefield, 1998).

45. Nixon, *Slow Violence*.

46. Malte Rolf, *Soviet Mass Festivals, 1917–1991* (Pittsburgh: University of Pittsburgh Press, 2013), 140.

47. Shils, *The Constitution of Society*, 105. See also Timur Kuran, *Private Truths, Public Lies: The Social Consequences of Preference Falsification* (Cambridge: Harvard University Press, 1995).

48. Elmer Schattschneider, *The Semisovereign People: A Realist's View of Democracy in America* (New York: Holt, Rinehart and Winston, 1960), 106.

49. Johan Galtung, "Cultural Violence," *Journal of Peace Research* 27, no. 3 (1990): 173.

4. From Astana to Asia

1. Natalie Koch, "Why Not a World City? Astana, Ankara, and Geopolitical Scripts in Urban Networks," *Urban Geography* 34, no. 1 (2013): 109–30; Natalie Koch, "Exploring Divergences in Comparative Research: Citizenship Regimes and the Spectacular Cities of Central Asia and the GCC," *Area* 47, no. 4 (2015): 436–42.

2. Jan Nijman, "Place-Particularity and 'Deep Analogies': A Comparative Essay on Miami's Rise as a World City," *Urban Geography* 28, no. 1 (2007): 92–107.

3. I provide a fuller account of these academic politics in Koch, "Exploring Divergences."

4. Garth Myers, "From Expected to Unexpected Comparisons: Changing the Flows of Ideas about Cities in a Postcolonial Urban World," *Singapore Journal of Tropical Geography* 35, no. 1 (2014): 104–18. I develop this argument more fully in Natalie Koch, "Is a 'Critical' Area Studies Possible?" *Environment and Planning D: Society and Space* 34, no. 5 (2016): 807–14.

5. Paul Veyne, *Bread and Circuses: Historical Sociology and Political Pluralism* (London: Penguin, 1990), 379.

6. I cannot detail the recent developments in Baku and Ashgabat here, but see especially Michael Denison, "The Art of the Impossible: Political Symbolism and the Creation of National Identity and Collective Memory in Post-Soviet Turkmenistan," *Europe-Asia Studies* 61, no. 7 (2009): 1167–87; Bruce Grant, "The Edifice Complex: Architecture and the Political Life of Surplus in the New Baku," *Public Culture* 26, no. 3 (2014): 501–28; Natalie Koch, "The Violence of Spectacle: Statist Schemes to Green the Desert and Constructing Astana and Ashgabat as Urban Oases," *Social & Cultural Geography* 16, no. 6 (2015): 675–97; Natalie Koch, "The 'Personality Cult' Problematic: Personalism and Mosques Memorializing the 'Father of the Nation' in Turkmenistan and the UAE," *Central Asian Affairs* 3

no. 4 (2016): 330–59; Natalie Koch and Anar Valiyev, "Urban Boosterism in Closed Contexts: Spectacular Urbanization and Second-Tier Mega-Events in Three Caspian Capitals," *Eurasian Geography and Economics* 56, no. 5 (2015): 575–98; Melanie Krebs, "Maiden Tower Goes International? Representing Baku in a Global World," in *Urban Spaces after Socialism: Ethnographies of Public Places in Eurasian Cities*, ed. Tsypylma Darieva, Wolfgang Kaschuba, and Melanie Krebs (Frankfurt: Campus, 2011), 107–30; Jan Šír, "Cult of Personality in Monumental Art and Architecture: The Case of Post-Soviet Turkmenistan," *Acta Slavica Japonica* 25 (2008): 203–20; Anar Valiyev, "Baku," *Cities* 31 (2013): 625–40; Anar Valiyev, "The Post-Communist Growth Machine: The Case of Baku, Azerbaijan," *Cities* 41, no. S1 (2014): S45–S53.

7. Ilham Aliyev, "Speech at the Opening of the JW Marriott Absheron Hotel in Baku," official website of the president of Azerbaijan, April 1, 2012, http://en.president.az/articles/4587 (accessed January 13, 2017).

8. "About Ashgabat: City's History," *Ak Säher Ashgabat*, 2013, http://ashgabat.gov.tm/en/2013-05-25-02-53-39/2013-05-25-04-25-07 (accessed January 13, 2017).

9. Koch, "The Violence of Spectacle"; Koch and Valiyev, "Urban Boosterism."

10. Andrew March, "The Use and Abuse of History: 'National Ideology' as Transcendental Object in Islam Karimov's 'Ideology of National Independence,'" *Central Asian Survey* 21, no. 4 (2002): 371–84. See also James Ferguson, *The Anti-Politics Machine: "Development," Depoliticization, and Bureaucratic Power in Lesotho* (New York: Cambridge University Press, 1990); Tania Murray Li, *The Will to Improve: Governmentality, Development, and the Practice of Politics* (Durham: Duke University Press, 2007); Kris Olds and Henry Yeung, "Pathways to Global City Formation: A View from the Developmental City-State of Singapore," *Review of International Political Economy* 11, no. 3 (2004): 489–521; Meredith Woo-Cumings, *The Developmental State* (Ithaca: Cornell University Press, 1999).

11. Susan Buck-Morss, *Dreamworld and Catastrophe: The Passing of Mass Utopia in East and West* (Cambridge: MIT Press, 2000).

12. I give a full analysis of this narrative in Koch, "Why Not a World City?"

13. Peter Savodnik, "Azerbaijan Is Rich. Now It Wants to Be Famous," *New York Times Magazine*, February 8, 2013, http://www.nytimes.com/2013/02/10/magazine/azerbaijan-is-rich-now-it-wants-to-be-famous.html (accessed January 13, 2017). On Dubai's artificial island projects, see Mark Jackson and Veronica della Dora, "'Dreams So Big Only the Sea Can Hold Them': Man-Made Islands as Anxious Spaces, Cultural Icons, and Travelling Visions," *Environment and Planning A* 41, no. 9 (2009): 2086–2104.

14. For more, see Koch, "Is a 'Critical' Area Studies Possible?"

15. I provide a more detailed account of the contemporary narratives about the 1990s-era *bardak* in Natalie Koch, "Disorder over the Border: Spinning the Spectre of Instability through Time and Space in Central Asia," *Central Asian Survey* (forthcoming), http://dx.doi.org/10.1080/02634937.2017.1338667.

16. Catherine Alexander, "Almaty: Rethinking the Public Sector," in *Urban Life in Post-Soviet Asia*, ed. Catherine Alexander, Victor Buchli, and Caroline Humphrey (London: University College London Press, 2007), 70–101; Koch, "The Violence of Spectacle."

17. Clifford Geertz, *The Interpretation of Cultures: Selected Essays* (New York: Basic Books, 1973), 237.

18. Nursultan Nazarbayev, "Future Vision," *K Magazine* 1 (2010): 53.

19. I develop this argument more fully in Koch, "Bordering on the Modern."

20. For a brief introduction to some Baku's architecture from this time, see Fuad Akhundov, Shamil Fatullayev, Fakhreddin Miralayev, and Jala Garibova, "Architecture of the Oil

Baron Period," *Architecture and Development* 6, no. 4 (1998), http://www.azer.com/aiweb/categories/magazine/64_folder/64_articles/OilBarons/64.oilbarons.html (accessed January 3, 2017). See also Valiyev, "Baku"; Valiyev, "The Post-Communist Growth Machine."

21. Koch, "Disorder over the Border"; Natalie Koch, "Urban Life in Central Asia," in *Central Asia in Context: A Thematic Introduction to the Region*, ed. David Montgomery (Pittsburgh: University of Pittsburgh Press, forthcoming).

22. Michael Mann, *Fascists* (New York: Cambridge University Press, 2004), 259.

23. For more on spectacular urbanism in the Arabian Peninsula, see especially Yasser Elsheshtawy, *Planning Middle Eastern Cities: An Urban Kaleidoscope in a Globalizing World* (New York: Routledge, 2004); Yasser Elsheshtawy, *The Evolving Arab City: Tradition, Modernity and Urban Development* (London: Routledge, 2008); Yasser Elsheshtawy, *Dubai: Behind an Urban Spectacle* (New York: Routledge, 2010); Mehran Kamrava, *Gateways to the World: Port Cities in the Persian Gulf* (Oxford: Oxford University Press, 2016); Ahmed Kanna, *Dubai: The City as Corporation* (Minneapolis: University of Minnesota Press, 2011); Robina Mohammad and James Sidaway, "Spectacular Urbanization Amidst Variegated Geographies of Globalization: Learning from Abu Dhabi's Trajectory through the Lives of South Asian Men," *International Journal of Urban and Regional Research* 36, no. 3 (2012): 606–27; Steffen Wippel, Katrin Bromber, Christian Steiner, and Birgit Krawietz, *Under Construction: Logics of Urbanism in the Gulf Region* (Farnham, Surrey: Ashgate, 2014).

24. "About Doha," Doha Cycling, http://www.dohacycling2016.com/about-doha/ (accessed July 6, 2017).

25. "Culture and Heritage," Visit Abu Dhabi, https://visitabudhabi.ae/en/explore/culture.and.heritage.aspx (accessed July 6, 2017).

26. "UAE Capital and Surrounds," Visit Abu Dhabi, https://visitabudhabi.ae/en/explore/regions/uae.capital.aspx (accessed July 6, 2017).

27. Natalie Koch, "Is Nationalism Just for Nationals? Civic Nationalism for Noncitizens and Celebrating National Day in Qatar and the UAE," *Political Geography* 54 (2016): 49.

28. Citizenship is a contested concept in the social sciences, but for the purposes of this discussion, I am interested in the most basic application of the term to designate who is legally entitled to full benefits from the state (*citizens*) and who is not (*noncitizens*, including residents of all backgrounds and entitlements). For more on political geographic approaches to citizenship, see especially Patricia Ehrkamp and Malene Jacobsen, "Citizenship," in *The Wiley Blackwell Companion to Political Geography*, ed. John Agnew, Virginie Mamadouh, Anna Secor, and Joanne Sharp (Hoboken, N.J.: Wiley-Blackwell, 2015), 152–64; Lynn Staeheli, "Political Geography: Where's Citizenship?" *Progress in Human Geography* 35, no. 3 (2011): 393–400; Lynn Staeheli, "Citizenship," in *International Encyclopedia of Geography: People, the Earth, Environment and Technology*, ed. Douglas Richardson, Noel Castree, Michael Goodchild, Audrey Lynn Kobayashi, Weidong Liu, and Richard Marston (Hoboken, N.J.: John Wiley & Sons, 2017), 565–74.

29. Under the local *kafala* (sponsorship) system, unskilled workers must have a local sponsor, who is responsible for their visa and legal status. On this system, see Abdulhadi Khalaf, Omar AlShehabi, and Adam Hanieh, *Transit States: Labour, Migration and Citizenship in the Gulf* (London: Pluto Press, 2014).

30. On the problematic implications of the citizen/noncitizen binary in Gulf studies, see Neha Vora and Natalie Koch, "Everyday Inclusions: Rethinking Ethnocracy, *Kafala*, and Belonging in the Arabian Peninsula," *Studies in Ethnicity and Nationalism* 15, no. 3 (2015): 540–52.

31. This argument is further detailed in Koch, "Exploring Divergences."

32. On the noncitizen populations in Qatar and the UAE, see especially Allen Fromherz, *Qatar: A Modern History* (New York: Palgrave Macmillan, 2011); Mehran Kamrava

and Zahra Babar, *Migrant Labor in the Persian Gulf* (New York: Columbia University Press, 2012); Khalaf, AlShehabi, and Hanieh, *Transit States*; Koch, "Is Nationalism Just for Nationals?"; Mohammad and Sidaway, "Spectacular Urbanization"; Neha Vora, *Impossible Citizens: Dubai's Indian Diaspora* (Durham: Duke University Press, 2013). Most academic research tends to focus on the most marginalized expat populations in the Gulf, but as Neha Vora and I have argued, this narrow view underplays the significance of middle- and upper-middle-class migrants of many different national backgrounds; see Vora and Koch, "Everyday Inclusions."

33. In around 2014, the Qatar and UAE National Days began to be characterized by a thematic focus on what are effectively civic nationalist discourses. These include the Qatari "One Love" theme, as well as a range of other inclusivist frames in the UAE, in which expats are narrated as having sincere love for their "home away from home," as well as endless gratitude and loyalty to the governments for being welcoming "hosts" and providing them with the stability and economic opportunity they cannot find in their homelands. For a full analysis of these holidays, see Koch, "Is Nationalism Just for Nationals?"

34. Part of this scheme involves state funds being used to overpay the companies for the services rendered, which contractors seek to further maximize by developing the project at the lowest cost possible, cutting corners on materials and pay to laborers, and oftentimes not even completing projects once the façade is deemed acceptable. See John Heathershaw and Alexander Cooley, "Offshore Central Asia: An Introduction," *Central Asian Survey* 34, no. 1 (2015): 1–10; Koch, "The Violence of Spectacle"; Koch and Valiyev, "Urban Boosterism."

35. Lawrence Vale, *Architecture, Power, and National Identity* (New Haven: Yale University Press, 1992), 15.

36. Claude Lévi-Strauss, *Introduction to the Work of Marcel Mauss* (London: Routledge, 1987).

37. Timothy Mitchell, *Colonizing Egypt* (Berkeley: University of California Press, 1988), 33.

38. On these cases, see especially Tim Bunnell, *Malaysia, Modernity and the Multimedia Super Corridor: A Critical Geography of Intelligent Landscapes* (New York: Routledge-Curzon, 2004); Kris Olds, *Globalization and Urban Change: Capital, Culture, and Pacific Rim Mega-Projects* (Oxford: Oxford University Press, 2001); Ananya Roy and Aihwa Ong, *Worlding Cities: Asian Experiments and the Art of Being Global* (Malden, Mass.: Wiley-Blackwell, 2011); Jun Wang and Tim Oakes, *Making Cultural Cities in Asia: Mobility, Assemblage, and the Politics of Aspirational Urbanism* (New York: Routledge, 2016).

39. The 2016 estimate of Brunei's GDP per capita of $79,700 is surpassed only by the similarly diminutive countries of Qatar, Luxembourg, Macau, Liechtenstein, Singapore, Bermuda, and the Isle of Man. *CIA World Factbook,* https://www.cia.gov/library/publications/the-world-factbook/rankorder/2004rank.html (accessed January 13, 2017).

40. Upon independence, Sultan Hassanal Bolkiah created a number of additional posts that he holds in addition to being the sultan, including prime minister, minister of defense and commander in chief of Royal Brunei Armed Forces, minister of finance, minister of foreign affairs and trade, and the chancellor of the country's three major universities. There is relatively little English-language academic writing on Brunei, but for discussions of the country's historical and contemporary politics, see B. A. Hussainmiya, *Sultan Omar Ali Saifuddin III and Britain: The Making of Brunei Darussalam* (Oxford: Oxford University Press, 1995); Damien Kingsbury, *Politics in Contemporary Southeast Asia: Authority, Democracy and Political Change* (New York: Routledge, 2017); Harun Abdul Majid, *Rebellion in Brunei: The 1962 Revolt, Imperialism, Confrontation and Oil* (New York: I. B. Tauris, 2007); Keat Gin Ooi and Stephen Druce, *Brunei: History, Islam, Society and Contemporary Issues* (London: Routledge, 2016); Pushpa Thambipillai, "Brunei: Making Progress Slowly," *Southeast*

Asian Affairs 2012, no. 1 (2012): 89–100; Marie-Sybille de Vienne and Aemilia Lanyer, *Brunei: From the Age of Commerce to the 21st Century* (Singapore: NUS Press, 2015).

41. Kingsbury, *Politics in Contemporary Southeast Asia*, 88–89.

42. Ibid.; Erik Paul, *Obstacles to Democratization in Southeast Asia: A Study of the Nation State, Regional and Global Order* (New York: Palgrave Macmillan, 2010); Robert Rangel and Steve Hui, *The Organ Grinder's Monkey* (Bloomington: Xlibris, 2013); Julie Zeveloff, "The Royals of Brunei Lead Lives of Almost Incomprehensible Wealth," *Business Insider,* May 8, 2014, http://www.businessinsider.com/royal-family-of-brunei-wealth-2014-5 (accessed January 13, 2017).

43. On urban change in Brunei, see Khairul Hazmi Zaini, *Urban Brunei,* http://urban brunei.com/ (accessed July 8, 2017).

44. Veyne, *Bread and Circuses,* 384.

45. David Steinberg, *Burma/Myanmar: What Everyone Needs to Know* (Oxford: Oxford University Press, 2010), 128.

46. Mary Callahan, "The Generals Loosen Their Grip," *Journal of Democracy* 23, no. 4 (2012): 120–31; Moe Thuzar, "Myanmar: No Turning Back," *Southeast Asian Affairs* 2012, no. 1 (2012): 203–19; Min Zin, "You Can't Go Home Again," *Foreign Policy* 200 (2013): 32–34, 39.

47. Or seventy-eight times the size of Manhattan. See Katie Amey, "Inside Myanmar's Haunting Capital City, Naypyidaw," *Daily Mail Online,* April 18, 2015, http://www.daily mail.co.uk/travel/travel_news/article-3043503/Inside-Myanmar-s-haunting-capital-city.html (accessed January 8, 2017); Veronica Pedrosa, "Myanmar's 'Seat of Kings,'" *Al Jazeera,* November 20, 2006, http://english.aljazeera.net/news/asia-pacific/2006/11/2008525184150 766713.html (accessed January 8, 2017).

48. Roee Ruttenberg, "Myanmar's Capital Nay Pyi Taw Open to Foreigners," CCTV English, July 18, 2013, http://english.cntv.cn/program/asiatoday/20130718/106068.shtml (accessed January 9, 2017).

49. Steinberg, *Burma/Myanmar,* 150. For additional images and journalistic accounts of Naypyidaw, see Amey, "Inside Myanmar's Haunting Capital"; Matt Kennard and Claire Provost, "Burma's Bizarre Capital: A Super-Sized Slice of Post-Apocalypse Suburbia," *The Guardian,* March 19, 2015, http://www.theguardian.com/cities/2015/mar/19/burmas-capital-naypyidaw-post-apocalypse-suburbia-highways-wifi (accessed October 31, 2015); Matt Kennard and Claire Provost, "The Lights Are On but No One's Home in Myanmar's Capital Naypyidaw," *South China Morning Post Magazine,* 2015, http://www.scmp.com/magazines/post-magazine/article/1755128/lights-are-no-ones-home-myanmars-new-capital-naypyidaw (accessed January 8, 2017); Pedrosa, "Myanmar's 'Seat of Kings'"; Ruttenberg, "Myanmar's Capital." See also Benedict Rogers, *Than Shwe: Unmasking Burma's Tyrant* (Chiang Mai: Silkworm Books, 2010); Steinberg, *Burma/Myanmar.*

50. "Built to Order: Myanmar's New Capital Isolates and Insulates Junta," *New York Times,* June 24, 2008, http://www.nytimes.com/2008/06/24/world/asia/24myanmar-sub.html (accessed January 8, 2017); Ruttenberg, "Myanmar's Capital." On the country's resource politics, see David Allan and Rainer Einzenberger, "Myanmar's Natural Resources: Blessing or Curse?" *Heinrich Böll Stiftung, Perspectives Asia,* December 11, 2013, https://www. boell.de/en/2013/12/11/myanmars-natural-resources-blessing-or-curse (accessed July 8, 2017); Laur Kiik, "Nationalism and Anti-Ethno-Politics: Why 'Chinese Development' Failed at Myanmar's Myitsone Dam," *Eurasian Geography and Economics* 57, no. 3 (2016): 374–402; Sudha Ramachandran, "China Secures Myanmar Energy Route," *Asia Times Online,* April 3, 2009, http://www.atimes.com/atimes/South_Asia/KD03Df03.html (accessed January 9, 2017); David Pick and Htwe Htwe Thein, "Development Failure and the Resource

Curse: The Case of Myanmar," *International Journal of Sociology and Social Policy* 30, no. 5/6 (2010): 267–79; Sean Turnell, "Myanmar's Fifty-Year Authoritarian Trap," *Journal of International Affairs* 65, no. 1 (2011): 79–92; John Walsh and Fuengfa Amponstira, "Infrastructure Development and the Repositioning of Power in Three Mekong Region Capital Cities," *International Journal of Urban and Regional Research* 37, no. 3 (2013): 879–93.

51. Pedrosa, "Myanmar's 'Seat of Kings.'" Speculation otherwise abounds as to why the capital was moved, but most commentators cite Than Shwe's megalomania, his belief in numerology and astrology, his paranoid fear of an invasion by sea in the old capital, as well as a fear of domestic uprising among Yangon's dense urban population.

52. Allan and Einzenberger, "Myanmar's Natural Resources."

53. Myanmar's complicated history and its deplorable human rights record cannot be detailed here, but see especially Priscilla Clapp, "Burma: Poster Child for Entrenched Repression," in *Worst of the Worst: Dealing with Repressive and Rogue Nations*, ed. Robert Rotberg (Washington, D.C.: Brookings Institution Press, 2007), 135–65; Matthew Mullen, *Pathways That Changed Myanmar* (New York: Zed Books, 2016); Peter Perry, *Myanmar (Burma) since 1962: The Failure of Development* (Farnham, Surrey: Ashgate, 2007); Steinberg, *Burma/Myanmar*, 128–30; David Steinberg, *Myanmar: The Dynamics of an Evolving Polity* (Boulder: Lynne Rienner, 2015); Turnell, "Myanmar's Fifty-Year Authoritarian Trap"; Maung Zarni and Alice Cowley, "The Slow-Burning Genocide of Myanmar's Rohingya," *Pacific Rim Law & Policy Journal* 23, no. 3 (2014): 681–752. In 2017, over 300,000 ethnic Rohingya fled to Bangladesh as persecution reached new heights, which led to renewed international outrage and accusations of genocide; Michael Safi, "Myanmar Treatment of Rohingya Looks Like 'Textbook Ethnic Cleansing,' Says UN," *The Guardian*, September 11, 2017, https://www.theguardian.com/world/2017/sep/11/un-myanmars-treatment-of-rohingya-textbook-example-of-ethnic-cleansing (accessed October 26, 2017).

54. "Built to Order." For a detailed account of Cyclone Nargis and the government's tragic response to it, see Emma Larkin, *Everything Is Broken: A Tale of Catastrophe in Burma* (New York: Penguin Press, 2010).

55. Paul, *Obstacles to Democratization*, 77; Pedrosa, "Myanmar's 'Seat of Kings'"; Rogers, *Than Shwe*, 168.

56. Steinberg, *Burma/Myanmar*, 135.

57. Timur Kuran, *Private Truths, Public Lies: The Social Consequences of Preference Falsification* (Cambridge: Harvard University Press, 1995).

58. Lisa Wedeen, *Ambiguities of Domination: Politics, Rhetoric, and Symbols in Contemporary Syria* (Chicago: University of Chicago Press, 1999), 19.

59. Clifford Geertz, *Negara: The Theatre State in Nineteenth-Century Bali* (Princeton: Princeton University Press, 1980).

Conclusion

1. Edward Shils, *The Constitution of Society* (Chicago: University of Chicago Press, 1982), 105.

2. Alexei Yurchak, *Everything Was Forever, Until It Was No More: The Last Soviet Generation* (Princeton: Princeton University Press, 2006). See also Karen Petrone, *Life Has Become More Joyous, Comrades: Celebrations in the Time of Stalin* (Bloomington: Indiana University Press, 2000); Malte Rolf, *Soviet Mass Festivals, 1917–1991* (Pittsburgh: University of Pittsburgh Press, 2013).

3. It is important to note that the language of "exclusion" may be somewhat misleading, so an alternative framing would suggest that non-elites are not exactly necessarily *excluded*, but are differently *included* in the benefits offered by the state. See Rogers Brubaker, *Ethnicity*

without Groups (Cambridge: Harvard University Press, 2004); Neha Vora and Natalie Koch, "Everyday Inclusions: Rethinking Ethnocracy, *Kafala,* and Belonging in the Arabian Peninsula," *Studies in Ethnicity and Nationalism* 15, no. 3 (2015): 540–52.

4. Clifford Geertz, "Centers, Kings, and Charisma: Reflections on the Symbolics of Power," in *Local Knowledge: Further Essays in Interpretive Anthropology,* ed. Clifford Geertz (New York: Basic Books, 1983), 123.

5. As scholars have pointed out, there is a sliding scale between "soft" and "hard" authoritarian regimes, with some using more punitive tactics than others, but typically tracking back and forth between periods of harder and softer rule. See Edward Schatz, "Transnational Image Making and Soft Authoritarian Kazakhstan," *Slavic Review* 67, no. 1 (2008): 50–62.

6. Yi-Fu Tuan, *Dominance and Affection: The Making of Pets* (New Haven: Yale University Press, 1984), 5.

7. Edward W. Said, *Culture and Imperialism* (New York: Knopf, 1993), 22.

8. Mitchell Dean, *Governmentality: Power and Rule in Modern Society* (London: Sage, 1999), 133. See also James C. Scott, *Seeing Like a State: How Certain Schemes to Improve the Human Condition Have Failed* (New Haven: Yale University Press, 1998).

9. Paul Veyne, *Bread and Circuses: Historical Sociology and Political Pluralism* (London: Penguin, 1990), 380.

10. Ibid., 379.

11. Fernando Coronil, *The Magical State: Nature, Money, and Modernity in Venezuela* (Chicago: University of Chicago Press, 1997), 2.

12. Ibid., 178.

13. On recent developments in Central Asia, see Natalie Koch and Anar Valiyev, "Restructuring Extractive Economies in the Caspian Basin: Too Little, Too Late?" PONARS Eurasia Policy Memo 441, September 2016, http://www.ponarseurasia.org/memo/restructur ing-extractive-economies-caspian-basin-too-little-too-late (accessed January 24, 2017). On recent developments in the Arabian Peninsula, see Samuel Osborne, "Six Gulf States Will Start Taxing People for the First Time," *The Independent,* December 10, 2015, http://www. independent.co.uk/news/world/middle-east/six-gulf-states-will-start-taxing-people-for-the-first-time-a6768206.html (accessed July 7, 2017).

14. Rob Nixon, *Slow Violence and the Environmentalism of the Poor* (Cambridge: Harvard University Press, 2011), 7, 8.

15. George Lakoff and Mark Johnson, *Metaphors We Live By* (Chicago: University of Chicago Press, 1980), 10.

16. Clifford Geertz, *The Interpretation of Cultures: Selected Essays* (New York: Basic Books, 1973), 210–11.

17. Lakoff and Johnson, *Metaphors We Live By,* 3.

18. Harold D. Lasswell, *Politics: Who Gets What, When, How* (New York: McGraw-Hill, 1936).

19. James D. Sidaway, "Geography, Globalization, and the Problematic of Area Studies," *Annals of the Association of American Geographers* 103, no. 4 (2013): 993.

20. Michel Foucault, *Discipline and Punish: The Birth of the Prison* (New York: Pantheon Books, 1975), 154; Antonio Gramsci, *Selections from the Prison Notebooks of Antonio Gramsci* (New York: International Publishers, 2008), 247.

21. John Agnew, "The Territorial Trap: The Geographical Assumptions of International Relations Theory," *Review of International Political Economy* 1, no. 1 (1994): 53–80.

Index